Microsoft

Step by Step

Microsoft®
PowerPoint®
Version 2002 Microsoft® Office XP Application

Perspection, Inc.

PUBLISHED BY
Microsoft Press
A Division of Microsoft Corporation
One Microsoft Way
Redmond, Washington 98052-6399

Library of Congress Cataloging-in-Publication Data
Microsoft PowerPoint Version 2002 Step by Step / Perspection.
     p. cm.
   ISBN 0-7356-1297-8
   1. Computer graphics.   2. Microsoft PowerPoint (Computer file).   I. Perspection, Inc..

   T385 .M5235   2001
   006.6'869--dc21   2001030473

Printed and bound in the United States of America.

9   QWT   6 5 4 3

Distributed in Canada by H.B. Fenn and Company Ltd.

A CIP catalogue record for this book is available from the British Library.

Microsoft Press books are available through booksellers and distributors worldwide. For further information about international editions, contact your local Microsoft Corporation office or contact Microsoft Press International directly at fax (425) 936-7329. Visit our Web site at www.microsoft.com/mspress. Send comments to *mspinput@microsoft.com*.

FrontPage, Microsoft, MS-DOS, NetMeeting, Outlook, PowerPoint, SharePoint, Visual Basic, Windows, and Windows NT are either registered trademarks of trademarks of Microsoft Corporation in the United States and/or other countries. Other product and company names mentioned herein may be the trademarks of their respective owners.

The example companies, organizations, products, domain names, e-mail addresses, logos, people, places, and events depicted herein are fictitious. No association with any real company, organization, product, domain name, e-mail address, logo, person, place, or event is intended or should be inferred.

For Perspection, Inc.
Managing Editors: Steve Johnson
Authors: Melinda Lankford and Steve Johnson
Developmental Editor: Elise Bishop
Production Editors: Tracy Teyler, Beth Teyler, and
   Virginia Felix-Simmons
Copy Editor: Elise Bishop
Technical Editors: Kristy Thielen and Nicholas Chu
Indexer: Michael Brackney of Savage Indexing

For Microsoft Press
Acquisitions Editor: Kong Cheung
Project Editors: Jean Cockburn and Wendy Zucker

Body Part No. X08-06209

Contents

1 Creating a Presentation 1

2 Working with a Presentation 24

3 Printing a Presentation 44

Contents

4 Outlining Your Ideas 62

5 Adding and Modifying Slide Text 80

6 Applying and Modifying Design Templates 100

7 Viewing and Changing Presentation Colors 118

Contents

What's New in Microsoft PowerPoint 2002

You'll notice some changes as soon as you start Microsoft PowerPoint 2002. The toolbars and menu bar have a new look, and there's a new task pane on the right side of your screen. But the features that are new or greatly improved in this version of PowerPoint go beyond just changes in appearance. Some changes won't be apparent to you until you start using the program.

new for OfficeXP

To help you quickly identify features that are new or greatly enhanced with this version, this book uses the icon in the margin whenever those features are discussed or shown. If you want to learn about only the new features of the program, you can skim through the book, completing only those topics that show this icon.

The following table lists the new features that you might be interested in, as well as the chapters in which those features are discussed.

To learn how to	Using this new feature	See
Quickly view a presentation outline or slide miniatures	Outline/Slides pane	Chapter 1, page 3
Quickly access commonly grouped commands	Task pane	Chapter 1, page 3
Quickly access Help by asking a question	Ask A Question	Chapter 1, page 20
Search for presentations	Search task pane	Chapter 3, page 47
Print a presentation using unusual paper sizes	Additional paper sizes	Chapter 3, page 50
Preview presentation material before you print	Print Preview	Chapter 3, page 53
Find a printer on a network	Find Printer	Chapter 3, page 61
Change AutoCorrect settings	AutoCorrect Options	Chapter 5, page 92
Change AutoFit settings	AutoFit Options	Chapter 5, page 92
Add more than one master to a presentation	Multiple masters	Chapter 6, page 104
Quickly access design templates	Slide Design task pane	Chapter 7, page 120

(continued)

To learn how to	Using this new feature	See
Quickly access the Office Clipboard	Office Clipboard task pane	Chapter 8, page 137
Display a grid to align objects	Visible grid	Chapter 8, page 147
Rotate pictures	Picture rotation	Chapter 8, page 155
Select an object in a group without having to ungroup	Single selection in a group	Chapter 8, page 160
Quickly access clip art	Insert Clip Art task pane	Chapter 9, page 166
Insert an organization chart	Organization Chart	Chapter 9, page 185
Insert a diagram	Insert diagrams	Chapter 9, page 188
Create a presentation photo album	Photo album	Chapter 9, page 190
Insert more than one picture at a time	Insert multiple pictures	Chapter 9, page 190
Compress the size of pictures	Compress pictures	Chapter 9, page 192
Quickly apply a set of animations to an object or slide	Animation Schemes	Chapter 10, page 200
Add an electronic secure stamp of authentication to a presentation	Digital signature	Chapter 12, page 245
Review and respond to comments and changes in a presentation	Track changes	Chapter 13, page 258
Quickly review changes in a document	Revisions Pane	Chapter 13, page 260
Protect a presentation using passwords	Password protection	Chapter 13, page 253

For more information about the PowerPoint product, see *http://www.microsoft.com /office/xp.*

Getting Help

Every effort has been made to ensure the accuracy of this book and the contents of its CD-ROM. If you do run into problems, please contact the appropriate source for help and assistance.

Getting Help with This Book and Its CD-ROM

If your question or issue concerns the content of this book or its companion CD-ROM, please first search the online Microsoft Knowledge Base, which provides support information for known errors in or corrections to this book, at the following Web site:

http://mspress.microsoft.com/support/search.htm

If you do not find your answer at the online Knowledge Base, send your comments or questions to Microsoft Press Technical Support at:

mspinput@microsoft.com

Getting Help with Microsoft PowerPoint 2002

If your question is about a Microsoft software product, including PowerPoint, and not about the content of this Microsoft Press book, please search the Microsoft Knowledge Base at:

http://support.microsoft.com/directory

In the United States, Microsoft software product support issues not covered by the Microsoft Knowledge Base are addressed by Microsoft Product Support Services. The Microsoft software support options available from Microsoft Product Support Services are listed at:

http://support.microsoft.com/directory

Outside the United States, for support information specific to your location, please refer to the Worldwide Support menu on the Microsoft Product Support Services Web site for the site specific to your country:

http://support.microsoft.com/directory

Using the Book's CD-ROM

The CD-ROM inside the back cover of this book contains all the practice files you'll use as you work through the exercises in this book. By using practice files, you won't waste time creating samples and typing presentation information—instead, you can jump right in and concentrate on learning how to use Microsoft PowerPoint 2002.

Important

This book does not contain the PowerPoint 2002 software. You should purchase and install that program before using this book.

System Requirements

To use this book, you will need:

- **Computer/Processor**

  Computer with a Pentium 133-megahertz (MHz) or higher processor

- **Memory**

  RAM requirements depend on the operating system used:

  - **Windows 98, or Windows 98 Second Edition**

    24 MB of RAM plus an additional 8 MB of RAM for each Office program (such as Microsoft Word) running simultaneously

  - **Windows Me, or Microsoft Windows NT**

    32 MB of RAM plus an additional 8 MB of RAM for each Office program (such as Microsoft Word) running simultaneously

  - **Windows 2000 Professional**

    64 MB of RAM plus an additional 8 MB of RAM for each Office program (such as Microsoft Word) running simultaneously

- **Hard Disk**

  Hard disk space requirements will vary depending on configuration; custom installation choices may require more or less hard disk space.

  - 245 MB of available hard disk space with 115 MB on the hard disk where the operating system is installed. (Users without Windows 2000, Windows Me, or Office 2000 Service Release 1 [SR-1] require an extra 50 MB of hard disk space for System Files Update.)

■ An additional 20 MB of hard drive space is required for installing the practice files.

■ **Operating System**

Windows 98, Windows 98 Second Edition, Windows Millennium Edition (Windows Me), Windows NT 4.0 with Service Pack 6 (SP6) or later, or Windows 2000 or later. (On systems running Windows NT 4.0 with SP6, Microsoft Internet Explorer must be upgraded to at least version 4.01 with SP1.)

■ **Drive**

CD-ROM drive

■ **Display**

Super VGA (800 × 600) or higher-resolution monitor with 256 colors

■ **Peripherals**

Microsoft Mouse, Microsoft IntelliMouse® or compatible pointing device

■ **Software**

Microsoft PowerPoint 2002, Microsoft Word 2002, Microsoft Excel 2002, Microsoft Outlook 2002, and Microsoft Internet Explorer 5 or later

Installing the Practice Files

You need to install the practice files on your hard disk before you use them in the chapters' exercises. Follow these steps to prepare the CD's files for your use:

1 Insert the CD-ROM into the CD-ROM drive of your computer.

A menu screen appears.

Important

If the menu screen does not appear, start Windows Explorer. In the left pane, locate the icon for your CD-ROM and click this icon. In the right pane, double-click the **StartCD** file.

2 Click **Install Practice Files**.

3 Click **OK** in the initial message box.

4 If you want to install the practice files to a location other than the default folder (C:\SBS\PowerPoint), click the **Change Folder** button, select the new drive and path, and then click **OK**.

5 Click the **Continue** button to install the selected practice files.

6 After the practice files have been installed, click **OK**.

Within the installation folder are subfolders for each chapter in the book.

7 Remove the CD-ROM from the CD-ROM drive, and return it to the envelope at the back of the book.

Using the Practice Files

Each chapter's introduction lists the files that are needed for that chapter and explains any file preparation that you need to take care of before you start working through the chapter.

Each topic in the chapter explains how and when to use any practice files. The file or files that you'll need are indicated in the margin at the beginning of the procedure above the CD icon:

EditText

The following table lists each chapter's practice files.

Chapter	Folder	Files
1	Creating	BrowsePres, EditText, and ViewPres
2	Working	EnterText, NewSlide, InsertSlide, SlideInsert, OrderSlides, EnterNotes, and StorePres
3	Printing	FilePrint, HeaderFooter, PrintSetting, PrintPreview, and PrintFile
4	Outlining	TextOutline, InsertOutline, Outline, ArrangeText, FormatText, and SendOutline
5	AddingText	AddText, AlignText, ReplaceText, CorrectText, and SpellCheck
6	Applying	AddTemplate, ChangeMaster, FormatMaster, and SaveTemplate
7	Coloring	ColorScheme, CreateScheme, AddColor, and AddBackgrnd
8	Drawing	DrawShape, CopyMove, ChangeShape, AlignShape, ConnectShape, 3DShape, StackShape, RotateFlip, DrawArc, and GroupShape
9	Inserting	ChangeLayout, InsertArt, Logo, SizeImage, ColorImage, InsertTable, InsertExcel, Budget, InsertGraph, Sales, InsertOrg, InsertDiagrm, InsertPic, InsertPhoto, Picture1, Picture2, Picture3, Picture4, ModifyPic, and InsertWrdArt

(continued)

Chapter	Folder	Files
10	ShowingSlides	AnimateSlide, AddTrans, CustomShow, DeliverShow, and TakeNotes
11	InsertingMedia	InsertMedia, InsertMovie, PlayMedia, AddTimings, RecNarration, and CreateShow
12	CreatingWeb	CreateAgenda, CreateLink, GardenBudget, CreateWeb, and AddSignature
13	Reviewing	AddComments, AddPassword, EmailPres, TrackChanges, Merge, Broadcast, NetMeet, and RoadPres
14	No folder	No files

Uninstalling the Practice Files

After you finish working through this book, you should uninstall the practice files to free up hard disk space.

1 On the Windows taskbar, click the **Start** button, point to **Settings**, and then click **Control Panel**.

2 Double-click the **Add/Remove Programs** icon.

3 In the list of installed programs, click **Microsoft PowerPoint 2002 SBS Files**, and then click **Add/Remove**. (If you're using Windows 2000 Professional, click the **Remove** or **Change/Remove** button.)

4 Click **Yes** when the confirmation dialog box appears.

Important

If you need additional help installing or uninstalling the practice files, please see the section "Getting Help" earlier in this book. Microsoft's product support does not provide support for this book or its CD-ROM.

Conventions and Features

You can save time when you use this book by understanding how the Step by Step series shows special instructions, keys to press, buttons to click, and so on.

Convention	Meaning
1 **2**	Numbered steps guide you through hands-on exercises in each topic.
●	A round bullet indicates an exercise that has only one step.
(CD icon)	This icon at the beginning of a chapter lists the files that the lesson will use and explains any file preparation that needs to take place before starting the lesson.
FileName (CD icon)	Practice files that you'll need to use in a topic's procedure are shown above the CD icon.
PP2002-3-5 (MICROSOFT OFFICE SPECIALIST logo) Approved Courseware	This icon indicates a section that covers a MOS exam objective. The numbers above the icon refer to the specific MOS objective.
new for **Office**XP	This icon indicates a new or greatly improved feature in this version of Microsoft PowerPoint.
Tip	This section provides a helpful hint or shortcut that makes working through a task easier.
Important	This section points out information that you need to know to complete the procedure.
Troubleshooting	This section shows you how to fix a common problem.
Save (button icon)	When a button is referenced in a topic, a picture of the button appears in the margin area with a label.
Alt + Tab	A plus sign (+) between two key names means that you must hold down the first key while you press the other key. For example, "Press Alt + Tab" means that you hold down the Alt key while you press Tab.

(continued)

Convention	Meaning
Black Boldface type	Program features that you click or press are shown in black boldface type.
Blue Boldface type	Terms that are explained in the glossary at the end of the book are shown in blue boldface type within the chapter.
Red Boldface type	Text that you are supposed to type appears in red boldface type in the procedures.

MOS Objectives

Each Microsoft Office Specialist (MOS) certification level has a set of objectives, which are organized into broader skill sets. To prepare for the MOS certification exam, you should confirm that you can meet its respective objectives.

This book will prepare you fully for the PowerPoint 2002 comprehensive MOS exam. Throughout this book, content that pertains to a MOS objective is identified with the MOS logo and objective number in the margin:

PP2002-3-2

Approved Courseware

Comprehensive MOS Objectives

Objective	Skill	Page
PP2002-1	**Creating Presentations**	
PP2002-1-1	Create presentations	6–9, 26–29, 64–65
PP2002-1-2	Add slides to and delete slides from presentation	31-34, 71-74
PP2002-1-3	Modify headers and footers in the Slide Master	49–50
PP2002-2	**Inserting and Modifying Text**	
PP2002-2-1	Import text from Word	69–70
PP2002-2-2	Insert, format, and modify text	12–16, 29–30, 75–76, 81–86, 86–90, 92–95
PP2002-3	**Inserting and Modifying Visual Elements**	
PP2002-3-1	Add tables, charts, clip art, and bitmap images to slides	166–171, 174–177, 179–184, 185–188, 188–189, 190–192
PP2002-3-2	Customize slide backgrounds	128–131
PP2002-3-3	Add OfficeArt elements to slides	185–188, 188–189, 195–197
PP2002-3-4	Apply custom format to tables	174–177
PP2002-4	**Modifying Presentation Formats**	

(continued)

Objective	Skill	Page
PP2002-4-1	Apply formats to presentations	102–103
PP2002-4-2	Apply animation schemes	200–206
PP2002-4-3	Apply slide transitions	206–208
PP2002-4-4	Customize slide formats	104–109, 109–115
PP2002-4-5	Customize slide templates	104–109, 115–116
PP2002-4-6	Manage a Slide Master	104–109
PP2002-4-7	Rehearse timing	225–227
PP2002-4-8	Rearrange slides	36–37, 71–74
PP2002-4-9	Modify slide layout	164–165
PP2002-4-10	Add links to a presentation	235–240
PP2002-5	**Printing Presentations**	
PP2002-5-1	Preview and print slides, outlines, handouts, and speaker notes	53–56
PP2002-6	**Working with Data from Other Sources**	
PP2002-6-1	Import Excel charts to slides	177–179
PP2002-6-2	Add sound and video to slides	217–221
PP2002-6-3	Insert Word tables on slides	177
PP2002-6-4	Export a presentation as an outline	77–79
PP2002-7	**Managing and Delivering Presentations**	
PP2002-7-1	Set up slide shows	210–213
PP2002-7-2	Deliver presentations	210–213
PP2002-7-3	Manage files and folders for presentations	40–42
PP2002-7-4	Work with embedded fonts	274–277
PP2002-7-5	Publish presentations to the Web	241–245
PP2002-7-6	Use Pack and Go	274–277
PP2002-8	**Workgroup Collaboration**	
PP2002-8-1	Set up a review cycle	256–258
PP2002-8-2	Review presentation comments	250–253, 258–264
PP2002-8-3	Schedule and deliver presentation broadcasts	264–269
PP2002-8-4	Publish presentations to the Web	241–245

Taking a MOS Exam

As desktop computing technology advances, more employers rely on the objectivity and consistency of technology certification when screening, hiring, and training employees to ensure the competence of these professionals. As an employee, you can use technology certification to prove that you meet the standards set by your current or potential employer. The Microsoft Office Specialist (MOS) program is the only Microsoft-approved certification program designed to assist employees in validating their competence using Microsoft Office applications.

About the MOS program

A Microsoft Office Specialist is an individual who has certified his or her skills in one or more of the Microsoft Office desktop applications of Microsoft Word, Microsoft Excel, Microsoft PowerPoint, Microsoft Outlook, Microsoft Access, Microsoft FrontPage, or Microsoft Project. The MOS program typically offers certification exams at the "core" and "expert" skill levels. (The availability of Microsoft Office Specialist certification exams varies by application, application version, and language. Visit *http://www.microsoft.com/officespecialist* for exam availability.) The Microsoft Office Specialist Program is the only Microsoft-approved program in the world for certifying proficiency in Microsoft Office desktop applications and Microsoft Project. This certification can be a valuable asset in any job search or career advancement.

What Does This Logo Mean?

It means this courseware has been approved by the Microsoft Office Specialist Program to be among the finest available for learning PowerPoint 2002. It also means that upon completion of this courseware, you may be prepared to become a Microsoft Office Specialist.

Selecting a MOS Certification Level

In selecting the MOS certification(s) level that you would like to pursue, you should assess the following:

- The Office application and version(s) of the application with which you are familiar
- The length of time you have used the application
- Whether you have had formal or informal training

Candidates for the core-level MOS certification exams are expected to successfully complete a wide range of standard business tasks, such as formatting a document. Successful candidates generally have six or more months of experience with the application, including either formal instructor-led training with a MOS Authorized Instructor or self-study using MOS-approved books, guides, or interactive computer-based materials.

Candidates for expert-level certification, by comparison, are expected to complete more complex business-oriented assignments utilizing the application's advanced functionality, such as importing data and recording macros. Successful candidates generally have two or more years of experience with the application, again including formal instructor-led training with a MOS Authorized Instructor or self-study using MOS-approved materials.

MOS Exam Objectives

Every MOS certification exam is developed from a list of exam objectives, which are derived from studies of how the Office application is actually used in the workplace. Because these objectives dictate the scope of each exam, they provide you with critical information on how to prepare for MOS certification.

MOS Approved Courseware, including the Microsoft Press' Step by Step series, is reviewed and approved on the basis of its coverage of the MOS exam objectives.

The Exam Experience

The MOS certification exams are unique in that they are performance-based examinations that allow you to interact with a "live" version of the Office application as you complete a series of assigned tasks. All the standard menus, toolbars, and keyboard shortcuts are available—even the Help menu. MOS exams for Office XP applications consist of 25 to 35 questions, each of which requires you to complete one or more tasks using the Office application for which you are seeking certification. For example:

Prepare the document for publication as a Web page by completing the following three tasks:

1 Convert the memo to a Web page.

2 Title the page **Revised Company Policy**.

3 Name the memo **Policy Memo.htm**.

The duration of MOS exams ranges from 45 to 60 minutes, depending on the application. Passing percentages range from 70 to 80 percent correct.

The Exam Interface and Controls

After you fill out a series of information screens, the testing software starts the exam and the respective Office application. You will see the exam interface and controls, including the test question, in the dialog box in the lower right corner of the screen.

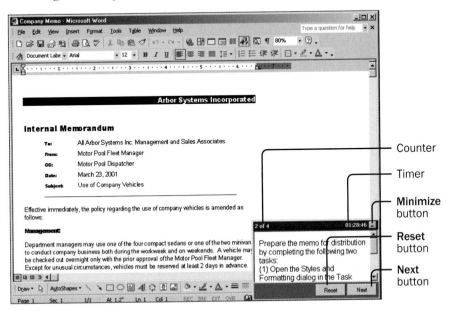

Counter

Timer

Minimize button

Reset button

Next button

■ If the exam dialog box gets in the way of your work, you can hide it by clicking the **Minimize** button in the upper right corner, or you can drag it to another position on the screen.

■ The timer starts when the first question appears on your screen and displays the remaining exam time. The timer will not count the time required for the exam to be loaded between questions. It keeps track of only the time you spend answering questions. If the timer and the counter are distracting, click the timer to remove the display.

■ The counter tracks how many questions you have completed and how many remain.

■ The **Reset** button allows you to restart work on a question if you think you have made an error. The **Reset** button will *not* restart the entire exam or extend the exam time limit.

■ When you complete a question, click the **Next** button to move to the next question.

Important

It is not possible to move back to a previous question on the exam.

Test-Taking Tips

- Follow all instructions provided in each question completely and accurately.

- Enter requested information as it appears in the instructions but without duplicating the formatting. For example, all text and values that you will be asked to enter will appear in the instructions as **bold** and **underlined**; however, you should enter the information without applying this formatting unless you are specifically instructed to do otherwise.

- Close all dialog boxes before proceeding to the next exam question unless you are specifically instructed otherwise.

- There is no need to save your work before moving on to the next question unless you are specifically instructed otherwise.

- Do not cut and paste information from the exam interface into the application.

- For questions that ask you to print a document, spreadsheet, chart, report, slide, and so forth, nothing will actually be printed.

- Responses are scored based on the result of your work, not the method you use to achieve that result (unless a specific method is explicitly required), and not the time you take to complete the question. Extra keystrokes or mouse clicks do not count against your score.

- If your computer becomes unstable during the exam (for example, if the application's toolbars or the mouse no longer functions) or if a power outage occurs, contact a testing center administrator immediately. The administrator will then restart the computer, and the exam will return to the point before the interruption occurred.

Certification

At the conclusion of the exam, you will receive a score report, which you can print with the assistance of the testing center administrator. If your score meets or exceeds the minimum required score, you will also be mailed a printed certificate within approximately 14 days.

For More Information

To learn more about becoming a Microsoft Office Specialist, visit *http://www.microsoft.com/officespecialist.net*

To purchase a Microsoft Office Specialist certification exam, visit *http://www.microsoft.com/traincert/mcp/officespecialist_locator.asp*

To learn about other Microsoft Office Specialist approved courseware from Microsoft Press, visit *http://microsoft.com/mspress/certification/officespecialist/default.asp/*

Perspection

Microsoft PowerPoint 2002 Step by Step has been created by the professional trainers and writers at Perspection, Inc. to the exacting standards you've come to expect from Microsoft Press. Together, we are pleased to present this training book.

Perspection, Inc. is a software training company committed to providing information and training to help people use software more effectively in order to communicate, make decisions, and solve problems. Perspection writes and produces software training books, and develops multimedia and Web-based training. This book incorporates Perspection's training expertise to ensure that you'll receive the maximum return on your time. With this straightforward, easy-to-read training tool, you'll get the information and training you need to get the job done. You'll focus on the skills that increase productivity while working at your own pace and convenience.

We invite you to visit the Perspection Web site at:

www.perspection.com

Microsoft Press, the book publishing division of Microsoft Corporation, is the leading publisher of information about Microsoft products and services. Microsoft Press is dedicated to providing the highest quality computer books and multimedia training and reference tools that make using Microsoft software easier, more enjoyable, and more productive.

Acknowledgments

The task of creating any book requires the talents of many hard-working people pulling together to meet impossible deadlines and untold stresses. We'd like to thank the outstanding team responsible for making this book possible: the writers, Melinda Lankford and Steve Johnson; the editor, Elise Bishop; the technical editors, Kristy Thielen and Nicholas Chu; the production team, Tracy Teyler, Beth Teyler, and Virginia Felix-Simmons; and the indexer, Michael Brackney.

At Microsoft Press, we'd like to thank Kong Cheung for the opportunity to undertake this project, Jenny Benson and Jean Cockburn for their editorial expertise and support during the writing and production of the book, and Barbara Norfleet and Paula Gorelick for their FrameMaker training and "tricks of the trade."

Perspection

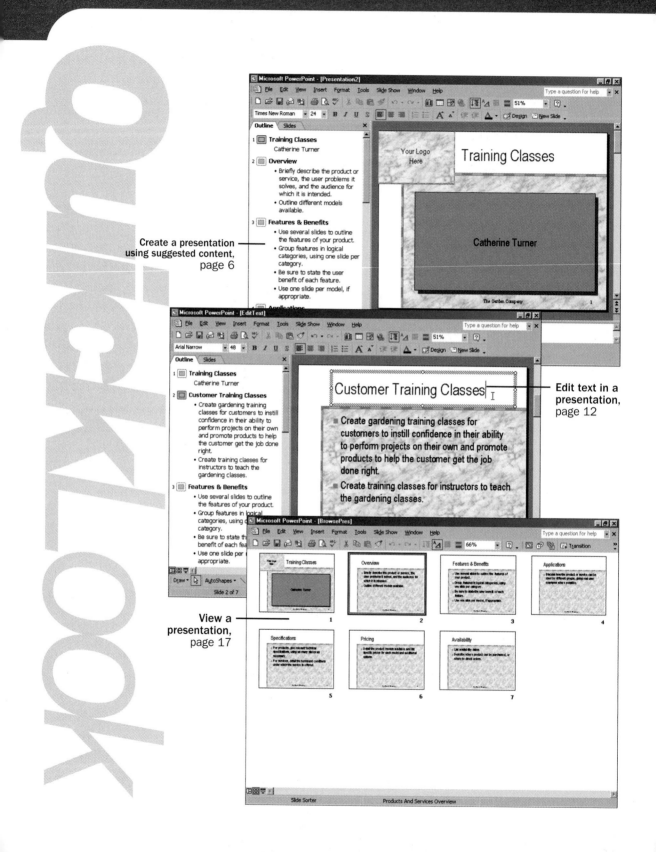

Create a presentation
using suggested content,
page 6

Edit text in a
presentation,
page 12

View a
presentation,
page 17

Chapter 1
Creating a Presentation

After completing this chapter, you will be able to:

✔ Get started with PowerPoint.
✔ Choose the best method to start a presentation.
✔ Create a presentation using suggested content.
✔ Browse through a presentation.
✔ Edit text in a presentation.
✔ View a presentation.
✔ Get help using PowerPoint.

Microsoft PowerPoint is a presentation program that allows you to create overhead slides, speaker notes, audience handouts, and outlines—all in a single presentation file. For example, you can create presentations for training, brainstorming, business planning, progress reports, project management, and marketing. PowerPoint offers powerful tools to help you create and organize a presentation step by step.

Catherine Turner is the owner of The Garden Company, a fictional business used in the Step by Step series. She wants to increase the name recognition of the company and promote its products. As part of her promotional efforts, she wants to provide gardening classes to increase product awareness and customer skills.

In this chapter, you'll create a presentation that promotes gardening classes provided by The Garden Company. During the process, you'll create the presentation using suggested content from PowerPoint, browse through the presentation slides, edit the suggested text, look at content in different views, and get help if you have a question.

 This chapter uses the practice files BrowsePres, EditText, and ViewPres that you installed from this book's CD-ROM. For details about installing the practice files, see "Using the Book's CD-ROM" at the beginning of this book.

Important

If you haven't done so yet, you should install the book's practice files so that you can work through the exercises in this chapter. You can find instructions for installing the practice files in the "Using the CD-ROM" section at the beginning of the book.

Getting Started with PowerPoint

The most common way to start PowerPoint is to use the **Start** button on the Windows taskbar. When you start PowerPoint, the program window displays a blank presentation and a task pane on the right side of the screen. The **program window** is an area of the screen that is used to display the PowerPoint program and the presentation window. The **presentation window** is the electronic canvas on which you type text, draw shapes, create graphs, add color, and insert objects. The program window contains many components common to every Microsoft Office XP program—such as the title bar, menu bar, Standard and Formatting toolbars, Ask A Question box, and status bar—and other components unique to PowerPoint—such as the view buttons, Slide pane, Notes pane, and several other task panes. As with any Windows program, you can adjust the size of the PowerPoint window with the **Minimize** and **Restore/Maximize** buttons, and you can close PowerPoint with the **Close** button on the title bar or close the presentation with the **Close Window** button on the menu bar.

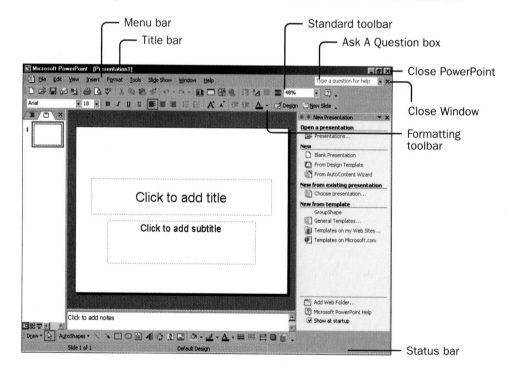

Tip

PowerPoint uses personalized menus and toolbars to reduce the number of menu commands and toolbar buttons that you see on the screen and to display the ones that you use most often. When you click a menu name, a short menu appears, containing the commands that you use most. To make the complete long menu appear, you can leave the pointer over the menu name for several seconds, you can double-click the menu name, or you can click the menu name and then click the small double arrow at the bottom of the short menu. When the long menu is displayed, the commands that did not appear on the short menu are light gray.

Important

When the Standard and Formatting toolbars share one row, which is the default setting, you can't see all the available buttons, but you can access other buttons by clicking the **Toolbar Options** down arrow at the end of the toolbar. If a button mentioned in this book doesn't appear on a toolbar, click the **Toolbar Options** down arrow on that toolbar to display the rest of the buttons available on that toolbar. To make it easier for you to find buttons, the Standard and Formatting toolbars in this book appear on two rows. To change your settings to match the screens in this book, click **Customize** on the **Tools** menu, select the **Show Standard and Formatting toolbars on two rows** check box on the **Options** tab, and then click **Close**.

Outline/Slides pane
new for
OfficeXP

At the bottom of the presentation window are view buttons that allow you to look at a presentation in different ways. **Normal view** is the main editing view, which you use to write and design your presentation. The view is made up of three panes: Outline/Slides, Slide, and Notes. The Outline/Slides pane shows tabs that let you alternate between seeing an outline of your slide text (**Outline** tab) and seeing the slides displayed as thumbnails (**Slides** tab). The Slide pane shows slides as they will appear in the presentation. The Notes pane is where you enter speaker notes. You can resize any of the panes by dragging the gray bar that separates them.

Task pane
new for
OfficeXP

On the right side of the PowerPoint window is a **task pane**, which displays commonly used commands that you'll need as you work on your presentation. A task pane allows you to quickly access commands related to a specific task without having to use menus and toolbars. PowerPoint displays a task pane when you need it. For example, when you start PowerPoint, you'll see the **New Presentation** task pane with commands that you can use to create a presentation. When you add a new slide to your presentation, you'll see the **Slide Layout** task pane with common slide designs from which you can choose. If you want to use a task pane and the one that you want does not appear, you can manually show the task pane and then select the specific task pane that you want from the **Other Task Panes** menu on the task pane. If you no longer need the task pane, you can hide it to free up valuable screen space in the program window. On the **View** menu, click **Task Pane**; clicking the command hides the task pane if it's currently displayed or shows it if it's currently hidden.

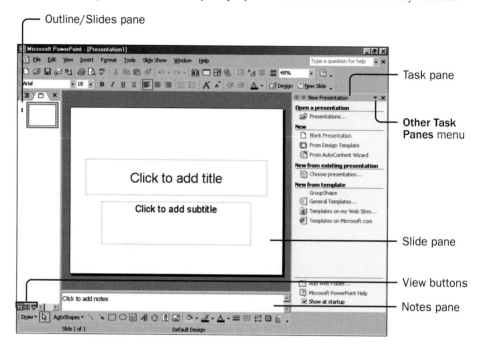

Outline/Slides pane — Task pane — Other Task Panes menu — Slide pane — View buttons — Notes pane

In this exercise, you start PowerPoint and close and open a task pane.

1   On the taskbar, click **Start**, point to **Programs**, and then click **Microsoft PowerPoint**.

The PowerPoint program window opens.

Tip

You can also start PowerPoint by creating a shortcut icon on the Windows desktop. Simply double-click a shortcut icon to start its associated program. To create a shortcut, click the **Start** button, point to **Programs**, right-click **Microsoft PowerPoint**, point to **Send To**, and then click **Desktop** (**create shortcut**).

2   In the title bar of the **New Presentation** task pane, click the **Other Task Panes** down arrow.

The **Other Task Panes** menu appears.

3   Press the [Esc] key, or click an empty place in the slide.

PowerPoint deselects the **Other Task Panes** menu and doesn't perform any commands on the menu.

Close

4   On the title bar of the **New Presentation** task pane, click the **Close** button to close the **New Presentation** task pane.

5   On the **View** menu, click **Task Pane**.

The **New Presentation** task pane appears.

Choosing the Best Method to Start a Presentation

To begin working with PowerPoint, you can create a new presentation or you can open one that you've already worked on. You can use the **New Presentation** task pane as your starting point. The option that you choose on the task pane depends on how you want to start a presentation. If you need help with content and a presentation look, choose the **From AutoContent Wizard** option. If you have content ready but need help with a presentation look, choose the **From Design Template** option. If you have content ready and have a design in mind, choose the **Blank Presentation** option. The following table describes the methods available to you when you start or open a presentation from the **New Presentation** task pane.

Click	To
From AutoContent Wizard under **New**	Create a new presentation using the **AutoContent Wizard**, which prompts you for a presentation title and information about the presentation. After you choose a presentation style and type, PowerPoint provides a basic outline to help you organize the content into a professional presentation.
From Design Template under **New**	Create a new presentation based on a design template, which is a presentation with predefined slide colors and text styles. After you click this option, the **Slide Design** task pane appears, in which you can choose a template.
Blank Presentation under **New**	Create a new, blank presentation. After you click this option, the **Slide Layout** task pane appears with 27 predesigned slide layouts from which you can choose to create a new slide.
Presentations or **More presentations** under **Open a presentation**	Open an existing PowerPoint presentation. A list of recently opened files appears above the option. If the file that you want is not in the list, click **Presentations** or **More presentations**. The **Open** dialog box appears, from which you can browse to find the presentation that you want to open.

Creating a Presentation Using Suggested Content

PP2002-1-1

Approved Courseware

The **AutoContent Wizard** can save you time by helping you organize and write the text for a new presentation. The wizard takes you through a step-by-step process, prompting you for presentation information, starting with the type of presentation that you want to give and output that you will use, and ending with the **title slide**, which is the first slide in the presentation. When you finish, the wizard provides you with suggested content on your slides, which you can modify to meet your specific needs.

When you create a presentation, the work that you complete is stored only in your computer's temporary memory until you save it. To save your work for further use, you must give the presentation a name and store it on your computer's hard disk. The first time that you save a new presentation, the **Save As** dialog box opens, where you name the presentation and choose where to save it. After you've saved the presentation once using the **Save As** dialog box, you can save new changes that you make by clicking the **Save** button on the Standard toolbar. In other words, the newer version overwrites the original version. If you want to keep both the original file and the version with your recent changes, you click the **Save As** command on the **File** menu to save the new version with a new name.

In this exercise, you use the **AutoContent Wizard** to create a presentation promoting The Garden Company's gardening classes, and then you save the results.

1   In the **New Presentation** task pane, click **From AutoContent Wizard** under **New**.

The **New Presentation** task pane closes, and the **AutoContent Wizard** appears, displaying the **Start** page. On the left side of the wizard is a list of the pages in the wizard.

Troubleshooting

If the Office Assistant appears, click **No, don't provide help now** in the help screen. For more information about the Office Assistant, see the "Getting Help" section later in this chapter.

2   Read the introduction, and then click **Next**.

The second page in the **AutoContent Wizard** appears, and the square next to *Presentation type* on the left side of the wizard turns green to indicate that this is the current page. The wizard prompts you to select a presentation type. To help you identify presentation types quickly, the wizard organizes presentations by category.

3   Click the **Sales / Marketing** button.

Presentations in the sales and marketing category appear in the list on the right side of the page.

4   In the list, click **Product/Services Overview**.

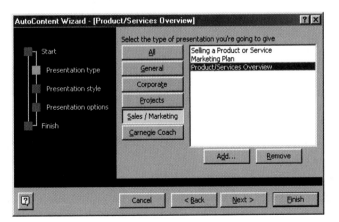

5   Click **Next**.

The wizard prompts you to select a media type for the presentation.

6 Click the **On-screen presentation** option, if necessary, to select that presentation type, and then click **Next**.

The wizard prompts you to enter information for the title slide and for footer information to be included on each slide.

7 Click in the **Presentation title** box, type **Training Classes**, and then press the [Tab] key to move the insertion point to the **Footer** box.

8 In the **Footer** box, type **The Garden Company**.

9 Clear the **Date last updated** check box so the date will not be included on each slide.

10 Verify that the **Slide number** check box is selected to include the slide number on each slide.

11 Click **Next**, and then click **Finish**.

The PowerPoint presentation window appears with content provided by the wizard in outline form on the left and the title slide on the right. The name on the title slide is the name of the registered PowerPoint user.

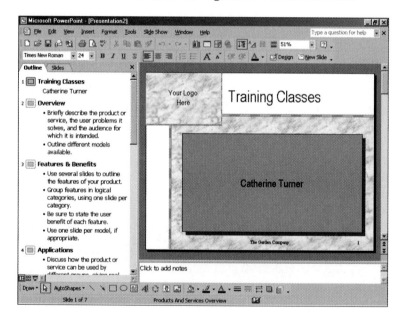

Save

12 On the Standard toolbar, click the **Save** button.

PowerPoint displays the **Save As** dialog box. The text in the **File name** box is selected.

13 In the **File name** box, type **AutoContent**.

14 Click the **Save in** down arrow, and then click your hard disk, typically drive C.

15 In the list of file and folder names, double-click the **SBS** folder, double-click the **PowerPoint** folder, and then double-click the **Creating** folder.

The files and folders in the **Creating** folder appear.

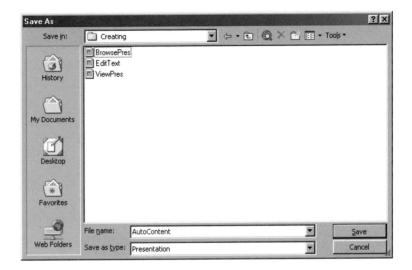

Tip

Depending on your Windows setup, file names might appear with an extension, a dot followed by a three-letter program identifier. For PowerPoint, the extension is .ppt.

16 Click **Save,** or press the [Enter] key to save the presentation.

The title bar name changes from *Presentation2* to *AutoContent*.

Tip

PowerPoint saves presentations for recovery in case the program stops responding or you lose power. PowerPoint saves the changes in a recovery file based on the amount of time indicated in the AutoRecover option. To turn on the AutoRecover option and specify a time interval in which to save, on the **Tools** menu, click **Options**, click the **Save** tab, select the **Save AutoRecover info** check box, specify the period of time, and then click **OK**.

Close Window
❌

17 Click the **Close Window** button in the presentation window.

The AutoContent presentation closes.

Browsing Through a Presentation

You might want to browse through a completed presentation to view the contents and design of each slide and to evaluate the types of changes that you want to make. In PowerPoint, you can browse through the slides in a presentation in several ways. You can click the scroll arrows to scroll line by line, click above or below the scroll box to scroll window by window, or drag the scroll box to move immediately to a specific slide. In the Slide pane, you can click the **Next Slide** and **Previous Slide** buttons, which are located at the bottom of the vertical scroll bar, to switch between slides in the presentation. You can also press the [Page Up] or [Page Down] key to scroll window by window. If you use these keys, the slides in the Slide pane will change also.

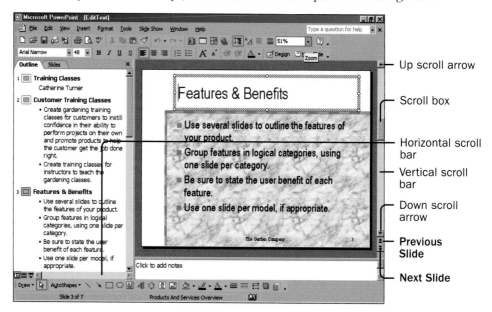

BrowsePres

In this exercise, you use scroll bars and the **Next Slide** and **Previous Slide** buttons to move around in the Outline/Slides pane and to move from slide to slide in the Slide pane to browse through the presentation.

1 On the Standard toolbar, click the **Open** button.

Open

The **Open** dialog box appears.

2 Navigate to the **SBS** folder on your hard disk, double-click the **PowerPoint** folder, double-click the **Creating** folder, and then double-click the **BrowsePres** file.

The BrowsePres presentation opens, displaying Slide 1 in Normal view.

3 In the Outline/Slides pane, click the down scroll arrow a few times to see the text below the current window.

4   In the Outline/Slides pane, click below the scroll box in the scroll bar.

The next window of information in the outline appears.

5   In the Outline/Slides pane, drag the scroll box to the end of the scroll bar.

The end of the outline appears.

6   In the Slide pane, click below the scroll box in the vertical scroll bar.

Slide 2 appears in the Slide pane.

Previous Slide

7   In the Slide pane, click the **Previous Slide** button.

Slide 1 appears in the Slide pane.

Next Slide

8   In the Slide pane, click the **Next Slide** button repeatedly until you reach the end of the presentation.

9   In the Slide pane, drag the scroll box in the vertical scroll bar until you see *Slide 3 of 7* in the slide indicator box, but don't release the mouse button.

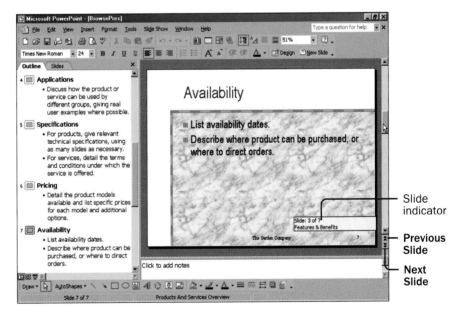

A slide indicator box appears, telling you the slide number and title of the slide to which the scroll box is pointing. In the scroll bar, the scroll box indicates the relative position of the slide in the presentation.

10   Release the mouse button.

The status bar changes from *Slide 7 of 7* to *Slide 3 of 7*.

11   On the Standard toolbar, click the **Save** button to save the presentation.

Close Window

12   Click the **Close Window** button in the presentation window.

The BrowsePres presentation closes.

Editing Text in a Presentation

PP2002-2-2

Approved Courseware

As you create a presentation, you'll often need to delete, modify, and add text to fine-tune your message. You can edit text in the Slide pane or the **Outline** tab of the Outline/Slides pane. In the Slide pane, you edit text one slide at a time, while on the **Outline** tab, you can edit text in all of the slides. A typical slide contains a title, called **title text**, and the major points below the title, called a **paragraph** or **bullet text**. In the Slide pane, slide text appears in boxes called **text objects**, while on the **Outline** tab, slide text appears in bulleted outline form.

I-beam pointer

As you move the pointer over text in PowerPoint, it changes to the I-beam. When you click text in the **Outline** tab or in a text object on the slide, a blinking line, called an insertion point, appears. The **insertion point** indicates where text will be entered or edited as you type. To delete text, you first select the text or place the insertion point next to the text that you want to delete and then press the ⌦ key or the ⌫ key. To modify text in a presentation, you select the text that you want to change and type the revised text. To add an additional bullet point, you place the insertion point at the end of a line of text, press ⏎, and then add another line of text. When you place the insertion point in a text object, the text is surrounded by a rectangle of gray slanted lines, called a **selection box**, with the blinking insertion point placed in the text. The selection box identifies what object you want to change on the slide.

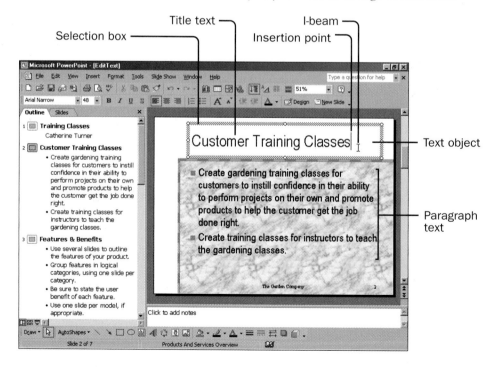

Whenever you perform an action that is not what you intended, you can reverse the action by clicking the **Undo** button. The **Undo** command can reverse up to the last 20 actions, one at a time, unless you change the maximum number of undos in the **Options** dialog box. For example, if you deleted some text by mistake, you can click the **Undo** button to restore the text that you just deleted. If you decide that the undo action is not what you wanted, you can click the **Redo** button to restore the undone action. You must undo or redo actions in the order in which you performed them. That is, you cannot undo your fourth previous action without first reversing the three actions that precede it. To undo a number of actions at the same time, you can click the down arrow next to the **Undo** button and then choose from among the actions that you can undo on the menu.

EditText

In this exercise, you change text on the **Outline** tab of the Outline/Slides pane, undo and redo actions that you recently performed, and change and add text in the Slide pane.

1   On the Standard toolbar, click the **Open** button.

Open

The **Open** dialog box appears.

2   Navigate to the **SBS** folder on your hard disk, double-click the **PowerPoint** folder, double-click the **Creating** folder, and then double-click the **EditText** file.

The EditText presentation opens, displaying Slide 1 in Normal view.

I-beam pointer

3   In the **Outline** tab on the Outline/Slides pane, position the pointer (which changes to an I-beam) to the right of the text *Overview* in Slide 2, and then double-click the blank area to select the title text.

The text is selected, and the subsequent text that you type—regardless of its length—will replace the selection.

4   Type **Customer Training Classes**.

If you make a typing mistake, press Backspace to delete it. Note that the text changes in the Slide pane also.

Tip

You might notice red wavy lines under some of your text. These lines indicate possible spelling errors. You can right-click a word with a red wavy line to display a menu with a list of possible spellings, and then click the correct spelling.

Four-headed arrow pointer

5   Position the I-beam pointer (which changes to the four-headed arrow) over the bullet next to the text *Briefly describe the product …* in Slide 2 in the **Outline** tab, and then click once to select the bulleted text.

6 Type **Create gardening classes for customers to instill confidence in their ability to perform projects on their own and promote products to help the customer get the job done right.**

7 In Slide 2, click the bullet next to the text *Outline different models available* to select the text.

8 Type **Create training classes for instructors to teach the gardening classes.**

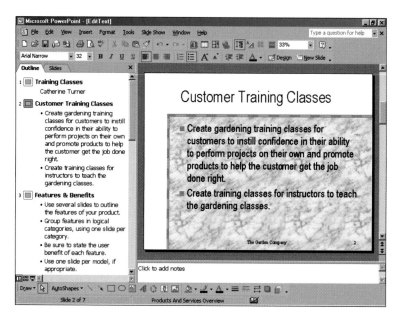

Undo

9 On the Standard toolbar, click the **Undo** button to reverse your last action, the text typing.

10 On the Standard toolbar, click the down arrow next to the **Undo** button.

The **Undo** list appears, displaying the first two items as *Typing*.

11 Click the second item in the list, **Typing**.

The first bullet and title in Slide 2 reverts to the AutoContent Wizard's text.

Tip

You can change the number of actions that the **Undo** command will undo by adjusting the number of actions that appear on the **Undo** list. To do this, click **Options** on the **Tools** menu, click the **Edit** tab, and then change the maximum number of undos at the bottom of the dialog box.

Redo

12 On the Standard toolbar, click the **Redo** button to restore the title text in Slide 2.

13 On the Standard toolbar, click the **Redo** down arrow, and then click the second item in the list, *Typing*, to restore both bulleted text items that you just undid.

Next Slide

14 Click the **Next Slide** button in the Slide pane to display Slide 3.

15 In the Slide pane, position the pointer (which changes to the I-beam) over the title text object before the text *Features*, and then click the title text.

I-beam pointer

A selection box surrounds the text with the blinking insertion point placed in the text.

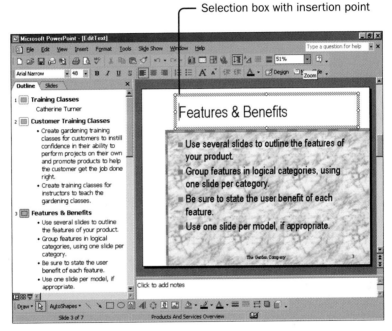

Selection box with insertion point

16 Type **Class**, and then press ⌷Space⌷.

As you change text in the Slide pane, the text in the **Outline** tab changes, too.

17 In the Slide pane, position the pointer (which changes to the I-beam) over any of the bulleted text in Slide 3, and then click the bulleted text to select the text object and place the insertion point.

Four-headed arrow pointer

18 Position the I-beam pointer (which changes to the four-headed arrow) over the bullet next to the text in the first bullet *Use several slides to outline ...*, click the bullet, and then type **Hands-on training**.

19 Position the pointer (which changes to the four-headed arrow) over the bullet next to the text *Group features in logical ...* in Slide 3, and then click the bullet.

20 Type **Step-by-step instruction**, and then press ⌷Enter⌷.

A new bullet appears in the slide. The new bullet appears gray until you add text.

21 Type **Full color handouts**.

22 Click the bulleted text *Be sure to state the user ...* in Slide 3, and then press ⌷Del⌷ to delete the bullet.

23 Click the bulleted text *Use one slide per model ...* in Slide 3, and then press ⌷Del⌷ to delete the bullet.

24 Click outside of the selection box to deselect the text object.

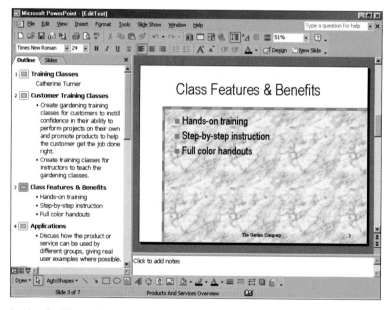

25 In the **Outline** tab on the Outline/Slides pane, click the slide icon in Slide 4, and then press ⌷Del⌷ to delete the slide entitled *Applications*.

26 On the **Edit** menu, click **Delete Slide** to delete the slide entitled *Specifications*.

27 On the Standard toolbar, click the **Save** button to save the presentation.

Close Window

⌷X⌷

28 Click the **Close Window** button in the presentation window.

The EditText presentation closes.

Viewing a Presentation

PowerPoint has four views to help you create, organize, and display presentations: Normal, Slide Sorter, Notes Page, and Slide Show. You can click the view buttons at the bottom of the presentation window to switch among the different views. You can also access all of these view commands on the **View** menu. There is no view button to switch to Notes Page view; instead, you must click **Notes Page** on the **View** menu.

In **Normal view**, you can work with your presentation in three different ways: as an outline or slide miniature in Outline/Slides pane, as a slide in Slide pane, and as speaker notes in Notes pane.

In **Slide Sorter view**, you can preview an entire presentation as slide miniatures—as if you were looking at photographic slides on a light board—and easily reorder the slides in a presentation. When PowerPoint displays slides formatted in Slide Sorter view, titles might be hard to read. You can hide the slide formatting to read the slide titles.

Notes Page view differs slightly from the Notes pane. While you can add speaker notes in the Notes pane, you must be in Notes Page view if you want to add graphics as notes.

Slide Show view displays slides as an electronic presentation, with the slides filling the entire screen. At any time during the development of a presentation, you can quickly and easily review the slides for accuracy and flow in Slide Show view.

Normal view

Slide Sorter view

Notes Page view

Slide Show view

ViewPres

In this exercise, you switch to different PowerPoint views and then display slides in a slide show.

1 On the Standard toolbar, click the **Open** button.

Open

The **Open** dialog box appears.

2 Navigate to the **SBS** folder on your hard disk, double-click the **PowerPoint** folder, double-click the **Creating** folder, and then double-click the **ViewPres** file.

The ViewPres presentation opens, displaying Slide 1 in Normal view.

3 In the Outline/Slides pane, click the **Slides** tab.

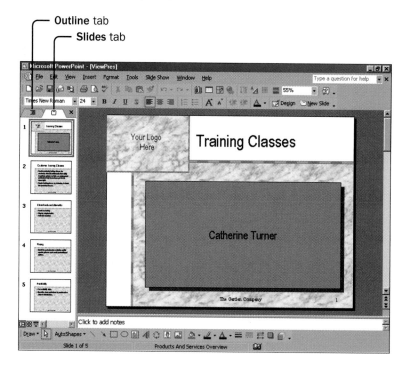

Slide Sorter
View

4 Click the **Slide Sorter View** button.

All the slides now appear in miniature on the screen. Slide 1 is surrounded by a dark box, indicating that the slide is selected.

5 Hold down the `Alt` key, and then click an individual slide.

The formatting for the slide disappears, and the title appears clearly. When you release the mouse button, the display format reappears.

6 Double-click Slide 1 to switch to Normal view.

The presentation view changes back to Normal view, showing Slide 1.

Slide Show

7 Click the **Slide Show** button.

PowerPoint displays the first slide in the presentation.

8 Click the screen to advance to the next slide.

Tip

To end a slide show before you reach the last slide, press Esc.

9 Click one slide at a time to advance through the presentation.

After the last slide in the presentation, PowerPoint displays a black screen.

Troubleshooting

The black screen appears by default when you run a slide show unless you clear the **End with black screen** check box in the **Options** dialog box. To check the setting, on the **Tools** menu, click **Options**, and then click the **View** tab.

10 Click the black screen to return to the current view.

Normal view appears.

11 On the Standard toolbar, click the **Save** button to save the presentation.

Close Window

12 Click the **Close Window** button in the presentation window.

The ViewPres presentation closes.

Getting Help Using PowerPoint

Ask A Question
new for
OfficeXP

When you have a question about using PowerPoint, you can save time by using the Ask A Question box rather than searching through the table of contents or index in the online Help system. After you type a question or keyword and press [Enter], PowerPoint displays a list of Help topics from which you can select the one that most closely relates to your question.

Another way to get help is to use the Office Assistant. With the Office Assistant, PowerPoint provides help as you work before you even ask a question. If you are entering text on a slide or using an advanced feature or doing something else that you might need help with, the Office Assistant appears on its own as an animated character (such as a paper clip, a cat, or a dog) to signal that it has helpful information or a tip. If the Office Assistant is hidden when a tip is available, a light bulb appears on the slide. You can click the light bulb to display the tip and then choose from several options, or you can skip this type of tip and close the Office Assistant. If you prefer to get help using a table of contents or index, you can click **Microsoft PowerPoint Help** on the **Help** menu.

ScreenTip

Bold

To find out about different items on the screen, you can display a **ScreenTip**. Click **What's This?** on the **Help** menu, and then click the item about which you want information. A yellow box appears, telling you more about the item. To display a ScreenTip for a toolbar button, for example, you simply place the pointer over the button without clicking it, and a ScreenTip appears, telling you the name of the button, as shown in the margin.

In this exercise, you get help using the Ask A Question box, display the Office Assistant, use it to get help, and then close the Office Assistant.

1 On the right side of the menu bar, click in the Ask A Question box.

2 Type **How do I use help?**, and then press [Enter].

A drop-down list appears with help topics that relate to the question that you entered in the Ask A Question box.

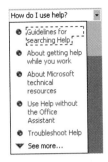

3 Click **About getting help while you work**.

The **Microsoft PowerPoint Help** window opens. You can click any of the help topics to get more information or instructions.

4 Click the Ask A Question box.

The PowerPoint Help displays more information about the topic.

Click to display the table of contents.

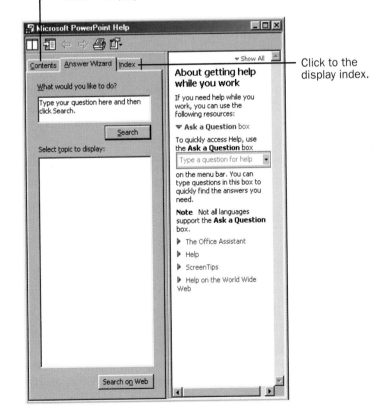

Click to the display index.

Close

5 Click the **Close** button in the **Microsoft PowerPoint Help** window to close the help topic.

6 On the **Help** menu, click **Show the Office Assistant** to display the Office Assistant.

7 Click the **Office Assistant**.

A yellow help box appears, as shown below. You can type a question in the box and click **Search** or click a help topic provided.

8 Right-click the **Office Assistant**, and then click **Hide** on the shortcut menu that appears.

Tip

You can open the **Microsoft PowerPoint Help** window instead of using the Ask A Question box or the Office Assistant. Right-click the **Office Assistant**, click **Options**, clear the **Use the Office Assistant** check box, and then click **OK**. On the **Help** menu, click **Microsoft PowerPoint Help**. To turn on the Office Assistant again, click **Show the Office Assistant** on the **Help** menu.

Chapter Wrap-Up

To finish the chapter:

Close

● On the **File** menu, click **Exit**, or click the **Close** button in the PowerPoint window.

PowerPoint closes.

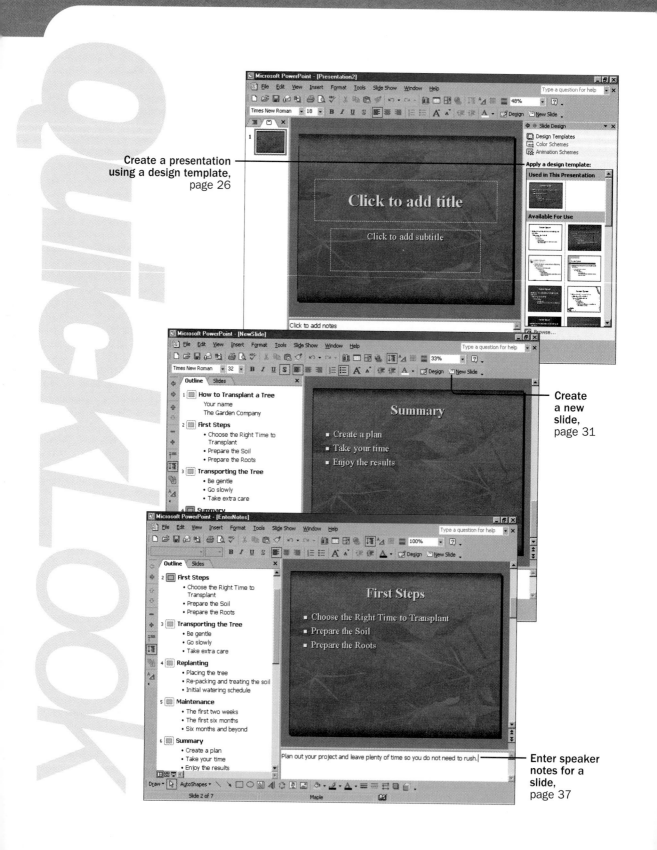

Create a presentation using a design template, page 26

Create a new slide, page 31

Enter speaker notes for a slide, page 37

Chapter 2
Working with a Presentation

After completing this chapter, you will be able to:

✔ Create a presentation using a design template.

✔ Enter text in a slide.

✔ Create a new slide.

✔ Insert slides from other presentations.

✔ Rearrange slides in a presentation.

✔ Enter speaker notes.

✔ Create a folder to store a presentation.

To work efficiently with Microsoft PowerPoint, you need to become familiar with the important capabilities of the product, such as creating a presentation using a design template, creating a new slide and entering text, inserting slides from other presentations and rearranging them in the presentation, and adding speaker notes.

The owner of The Garden Company has decided to use PowerPoint to develop the presentation content for a gardening class to offer customers. The first step is to start a new presentation and develop the content for the first gardening class, "How to Transplant a Tree." The assistant manager has developed several slides to include in the presentation.

In this chapter, you'll start a new presentation using a design template for the first gardening class, enter slide text, create new slides, insert slides from other presentations, rearrange slides, enter speaker notes, and create a folder in which to store a presentation.

 This chapter uses the practice files EnterText, NewSlide, InsertSlide, SlideInsert, OrderSlides, EnterNotes, and StorePres that you installed from this book's CD-ROM. For details about installing the practice files, see "Using the Book's CD-ROM" at the beginning of this book.

Creating a Presentation Using a Design Template

PP2002-1-1

Approved Courseware

Instead of starting a presentation with suggested text from the AutoContent Wizard, you can start a new presentation without any sample text. You can choose a design template or a blank presentation. A **design template** is a presentation with a professionally designed format and color scheme to which you need only add text. You can use one of the design templates that comes with PowerPoint, or you can create your own. After you select a design template, you can choose a different layout for each slide to create a specific design look, such as a slide with a graph. You select a layout by clicking it in the **Slide Layout** task pane in the right margin of your screen. The layout title for the selected slide layout appears as you roll the mouse over each choice.

In this exercise, you start a new presentation for the gardening class with a design template.

1 On the taskbar, click **Start**, point to **Programs**, and then click **Microsoft PowerPoint**.

The PowerPoint program window opens.

2 On the **View** menu, click **Task Pane**, if necessary, to display the **New Presentation** task pane.

3 In the **New Presentation** task pane, click **From Design Template**.

The **Slide Design** task pane appears with a variety of design templates in alphabetical order.

Tip

To create a blank presentation or a presentation using the AutoContent Wizard, open the **New Presentation** task pane, and then click **Blank Presentation** or **AutoContent Wizard**. The templates listed in the **Slide Design** task pane are the same ones that the AutoContent Wizard uses.

4 In the **Slide Design** task pane, point to a **design template**.

The name of the design template appears as a ScreenTip, and a down arrow appears on the right side of the design.

5 In the **Slide Design** task pane, click the down arrow on the right side of the design template.

A menu appears with commands that let you apply the design template to the entire presentation or to selected slides or change the size of the preview design templates in the **Slide Design** task pane.

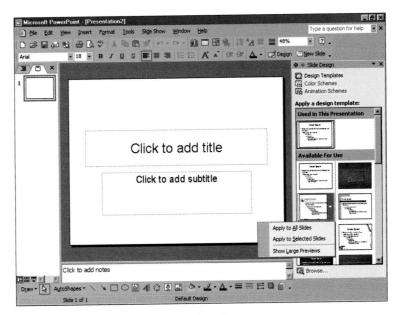

6 On the menu, click **Show Large Previews**.

The size of the preview design templates increases to make it easier to find the design that you want to use.

7 In the **Slide Design** task pane, drag the scroll box down until the Maple slide design appears in the task pane, and then click the **Maple** slide design.

A title slide with the Maple design appears in the slide pane.

8 Click the down arrow on the right side of the design template, click **Show Large Previews** to display the design templates in a smaller size, and then drag the scroll box to the top of the **Slide Design** task pane.

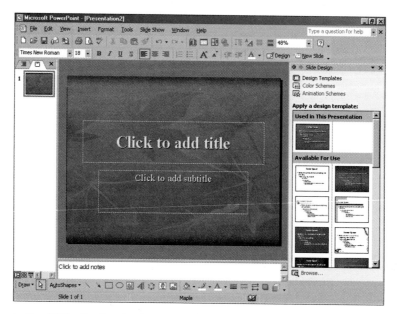

9   In the **Slide Design** task pane, click the **Other Task Panes** down arrow to
     display a list of the task panes, and then click **Slide Layout**.

     The **Slide Layout** task pane appears with slide layouts that you can apply to
     selected slides. The default Title Slide is currently applied to the selected
     slide in the Slide pane.

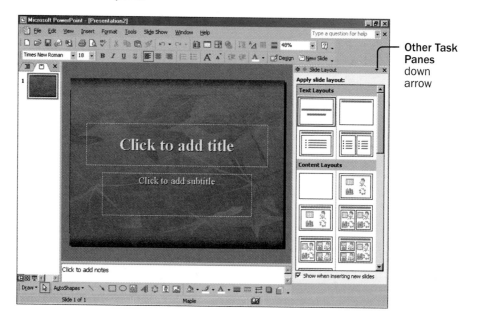

Other Task
Panes
down
arrow

10 In the **Slide Layout** task pane, click the **Title Only** slide layout under **Text Layouts**.

PowerPoint applies the Title Only slide layout to the selected slide.

11 In the **Slide Layout** task pane, click the **Title Slide** slide layout under **Text Layouts**.

PowerPoint applies the **Title Slide** slide layout to the selected slide.

12 In the **Slide Layout** task pane, point to several slide layout choices to read the description of each one.

13 In the **Slide Layout** task pane, click the **Close** button to close the task pane.

Save

14 On the Standard toolbar, click the **Save** button.

The **Save As** dialog box appears.

15 In the **File name** box, type **DesignTemp**.

16 Navigate to the **SBS** folder on your hard disk, double-click the **PowerPoint** folder, and then double-click the **Working** folder.

17 Click **Save**.

PowerPoint saves the DesignTemp presentation.

Close Window

18 Click the **Close Window** button in the presentation window.

The DesignTemp presentation closes.

Entering Text in a Slide

PP2002-2-2

To add text to a presentation, including titles and subtitles, you can enter text into either the Slide pane or the Outline tab in Normal view. The Slide pane allows you to enter text on a slide using a visual method, while the Outline tab allows you to enter text using a content method. The Slide pane displaying the Title Slide slide layout includes two text boxes called **text placeholders**. The upper box is a placeholder for the slide's title text. The lower box is a placeholder for the slide's subtitle text. After you enter text into a placeholder, the placeholder becomes a text object, a box that contains text in a slide.

EnterText

Open

In this exercise, you enter text in the first slide of the gardening presentation.

1 On the Standard toolbar, click the **Open** button.

The **Open** dialog box appears.

2 Navigate to the **SBS** folder on your hard disk, double-click the **PowerPoint** folder, double-click the **Working** folder, and then double-click the **EnterText** file.

The EnterText presentation opens, displaying Slide 1 in Normal view.

3 In the Slides pane, click the text placeholder **Click to add title**.

A selection box surrounds the placeholder, indicating that the placeholder is ready for you to enter or edit text. The placeholder text disappears, and a blinking insertion point appears.

4 Type **How to Transplant a Tree**.

Notice that the text appears in the Outline pane at the same time. If the Thumbnail view is showing instead of the Outline view, click the **Outline** tab.

Tip

If you make a typing error, press [Backspace] to delete the mistake, and then type the correct text.

5 Click the text placeholder **Click to add subtitle**.

The title object is deselected, and the subtitle object is selected.

6 Type **Catherine Turner**, and then press the [Enter] key.

7 Type **The Garden Company**.

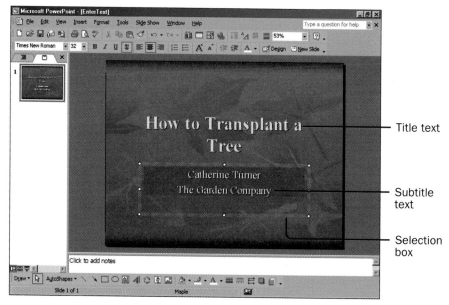

8 On the Standard toolbar, click the **Save** button to save the presentation.

Close Window

9 Click the **Close Window** button in the presentation window.

The EnterText presentation closes.

Creating a New Slide

PP2002-1-2

You can quickly and easily add more slides to a presentation in two ways: by clicking the **New Slide** button on the Formatting toolbar directly above the task pane, or by clicking the **New Slide** command on the **Insert** menu. When you use either of these methods, PowerPoint inserts the new slide into the presentation immediately after the current slide, and the **Slide Layout** task pane appears with 27 pre-designed slide layouts, one of which you can apply to your new slide. You select a layout by clicking it in the **Slide Layout** task pane. The layout title for the selected slide layout appears as you roll your mouse across each scheme. To apply a slide layout to your new slide, simply click on one of the 27 choices.

Once you have created a new slide, you can enter and organize slide title and paragraph text in the Slide pane or Outline tab in the Outline/Slides pane. In the Outline tab, the slide title text appears to the right of each slide icon, and the paragraph text underneath each title appears, indented one level. To enter text in the Outline pane, you click where you want the text to start, and then you begin typing. In the Outline tab, you can also create a new slide and add title and paragraph text by using the **New Slide** command or the Enter key.

NewSlide

In this exercise, you create a new slide and then enter text in the Slide pane. You then switch to the Outline tab in the Outline/Slides pane, enter paragraph text in the existing slide, create a new slide, and add text to that slide in the Outline tab.

1 On the Standard toolbar, click the **Open** button.

Open

The **Open** dialog box appears.

2 Navigate to the **SBS** folder on your hard disk, double-click the **PowerPoint** folder, double-click the **Working** folder, and then double-click the **NewSlide** file.

The NewSlide presentation opens, displaying Slide 1 in Normal view.

New Slide

3 On the Formatting toolbar, click the **New Slide** button.

If it was not already showing, the **Slide Layout** task pane appears, and PowerPoint adds a new, empty slide after the current slide in the Slide pane and creates a new slide icon in the Outline pane. PowerPoint applies the default Title and Text slide layout (a title and bulleted list) to the new slide. The status bar displays *Slide 2 of 2*.

4 Type **First Steps**.

Notice that the new slide and the new title appear in the Outline pane when you create them in the Slide pane. PowerPoint lets you work directly in the Slide and Outline panes and in Slide and Outline views to enter your ideas.

Tip

If you start typing on an empty slide without first having selected a placeholder, PowerPoint enters the text into the title object.

Close

[x]

5 In the **Slide Layout** task pane, click the **Close** button, and then click the **Outline** tab in the Outline/Slides pane, if necessary.

6 Position the pointer (which changes to the I-beam pointer) to the right of the title in Slide 2 in the **Outline** tab, and then click the blank area to place the insertion point.

A blinking insertion point appears.

7 Press [Enter].

PowerPoint adds a new slide in the Slide pane and a new slide icon in the **Outline** tab, with the blinking insertion point next to it.

8 Press the [Tab] key.

The text indents to the right one level. The slide icon changes to a small gray bullet on Slide 2 in the **Outline** tab.

9 Type **Choose the Right Time to Transplant**, and then press [Enter].

PowerPoint adds a new bullet at the same indent level. Notice that once you press [Enter] after typing bulleted text, the bullet becomes black. Also note that the text wraps to the next line in the **Outline** tab without having to press [Enter].

10 Type **Prepare the Soil**, and then press [Enter] to insert a new bullet.

11 Type **Prepare the Roots**, and then press [Enter] to insert a new bullet.

Promote

[←]

12 On the Outlining toolbar, click the **Promote** button.

Important

If the Outlining toolbar is not visible on your screen, click the **View** menu, point to **Toolbars**, and then click **Outlining**.

PowerPoint creates a new slide with the insertion point to the right of the slide icon.

Outlining toolbar

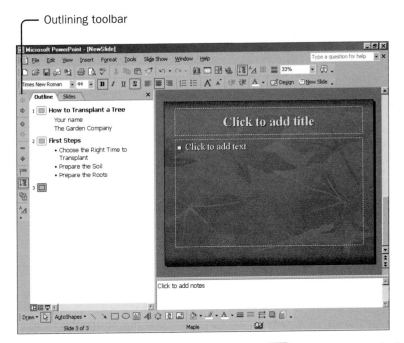

13 Type **Transporting the Tree**, and then press [Enter] to insert a new bullet.

14 Press [Tab].

PowerPoint creates a new indent level for Slide 3.

15 Type **Be gentle**, and then press [Enter].

A new bullet appears.

16 Type **Go slowly**, press [Enter], and then type **Take extra care**.

17 Hold down the [Ctrl] key, and then press [Enter].

A new slide appears.

18 Type **Summary**, press [Enter], and then press [Tab].

PowerPoint creates a new indent level for Slide 4.

19 Type **Create a plan**, and then press [Enter].

A new bullet appears.

20 Type **Take your time**, and then press [Enter].

A new bullet appears.

21 Type **Enjoy the results**.

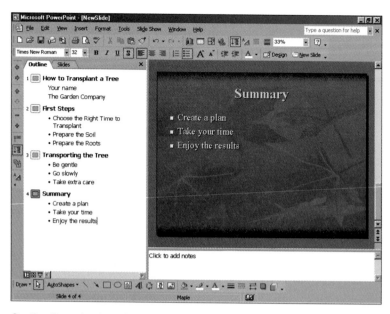

22 On the Standard toolbar, click the **Save** button to save the presentation.

Close Window

23 Click the **Close Window** button in the presentation window.

The NewSlide presentation closes.

Inserting Slides from Other Presentations

You can save time while creating a presentation by using slides that you or someone else has already made. When you insert slides from one presentation into another, the slides conform to the color and design of the current presentation, so you don't have to make many changes.

InsertSlide
SlideInsert

Open

In this exercise, you insert slides from one presentation into another.

1 On the Standard toolbar, click the **Open** button.

The **Open** dialog box appears.

2 Navigate to the **SBS** folder on your hard disk, double-click the **PowerPoint** folder, double-click the **Working** folder, and then double-click the **InsertSlide** file.

The InsertSlide presentation opens, displaying Slide 1 in Normal view.

3 Position the pointer (which changes to the I-beam pointer) to the right of the last bullet in Slide 4 in the **Outline** tab, and then click the blank area to place the insertion point.

4   On the **Insert** menu, click **Slides from Files**.

The **Slide Finder** dialog box appears.

5   Click the **Find Presentation** tab, if necessary, and then click **Browse**.

The **Browse** dialog box appears.

6   Navigate to the **SBS** folder on your hard disk, double-click the **PowerPoint** folder, and then double-click the **Working** folder.

7   In the list of file names, click the **SlideInsert** file, and then click **Open**.

The **Slide Finder** dialog box reappears.

8   Click **Display**, if necessary, to display the slides in the preview boxes.

9   Click Slide 2, click Slide 3, click the right scroll arrow, and then click Slide 4 to select the slides that you want to insert.

The **Slide Finder** dialog box appears.

A dark outline appears around selected slides.

Tip

If you use one or more slides in several presentations, you can click **Add to Favorites** to save the selected slides in the **List of Favorites** tab in the **Slide Finder** dialog box.

10   Click **Insert**.

PowerPoint inserts the slides into the new presentation after the current slide.

11 Click **Close**.

The inserted slide text appears in the **Outline** tab and the last slide appears in the Slide pane.

12 On the Standard toolbar, click the **Save** button to save the presentation.

Close Window

13 Click the **Close Window** button in the presentation window.

The InsertSlide presentation closes.

Rearranging Slides in a Presentation

PP2002-4-8

Approved Courseware

After you insert slides from another presentation into the current one, you may need to rearrange the slides into the order that most effectively communicates your message. This is best done in Slide Sorter view, where you can drag one or more slides from one location to another.

OrderSlides

In this exercise, you rearrange slides in Slide Sorter view.

1 On the Standard toolbar, click the **Open** button.

The **Open** dialog box appears.

Open
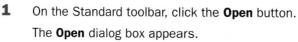

2 Navigate to the **SBS** folder on your hard disk, double-click the **PowerPoint** folder, double-click the **Working** folder, and then double-click the **OrderSlides** file.

The OrderSlides presentation opens, displaying Slide 1 in Normal view.

Slide Sorter View

3 Click the **Slide Sorter View** button.

Notice that the Slide Sorter toolbar appears above the presentation window.

4 Drag Slide 4 ("Summary") to the empty space after Slide 7 ("Maintenance").

Drag pointer

Notice that the pointer changes to the drag pointer when you begin to drag. When you release the mouse button, Slide 4 moves to its new position, and PowerPoint repositions and renumbers the other slides in the presentation.

Tip

In Slide Sorter view, you can also move slides between two or more open presentations. Open each presentation, switch to Slide Sorter view, and then click **Arrange All** on the **Window** menu. Drag the slides from one presentation window to another.

5   Drag Slide 5 ("Resources for Help") between Slides 6 and 7.

6   Double-click Slide 2 to return to the previous view, Normal view.

7   On the Standard toolbar, click the **Save** button to save the presentation.

Close Window

8   Click the **Close Window** button in the presentation window.

The OrderSlides presentation closes.

Entering Speaker Notes

As you create each slide in a presentation, you can also enter speaker notes that relate to the content on the slide and that you can use while you give the presentation. In the Notes pane, you can create speaker notes that appear on separate notes pages. Each slide in a presentation has a corresponding notes page. To enter speaker notes in the Notes pane, you click the **Notes** pane, and then you begin typing. Entering text and changing text in the Notes pane work the same way they do in the Slide and Outline panes. You can also enter speaker notes in Notes Page view by clicking **Notes Page** on the **View** menu. If you want to read all of the speaker notes, it might be easier if you switch to Notes Page view, in which you can move from notes page to notes page the same way as in Slide view.

EnterNotes

In this exercise, you enter text in the Notes pane, switch to Notes Page view, and move from notes page to notes page in Notes Page view.

1 On the Standard toolbar, click the **Open** button.

Open

The **Open** dialog box appears.

2 Navigate to the **SBS** folder on your hard disk, double-click the **PowerPoint** folder, double-click the **Working** folder, and then double-click the **EnterNotes** file.

The EnterNotes presentation opens, displaying Slide 1 in Normal view.

Next Slide

3 In the Slide pane, click the **Next Slide** button, and then click the text place-holder **Click to add notes** in the Notes pane in Slide 2.

The notes placeholder text disappears, and a blinking insertion point appears.

4 Type **Plan out your project and leave plenty of time so you do not need to rush.**

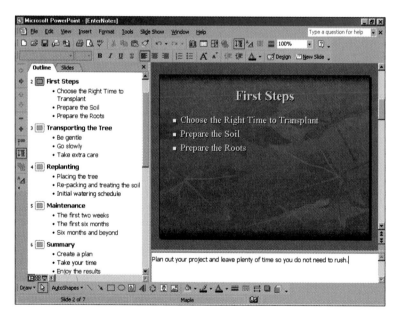

Tip

If you make a mistake, press Backspace to delete the mistake, and then type the correct text.

5 On the **View** menu, click **Notes Page**.

Notes Page view appears at approximately 40% view on most screens to display the entire page. Your view percentage might be different.

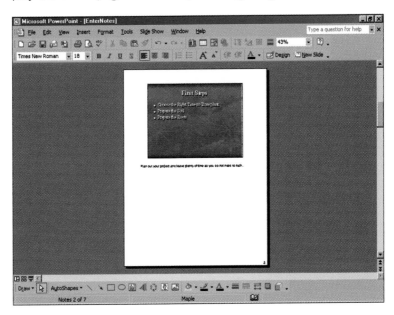

Tip

Your view scale might be different, depending on the size of your monitor.

Zoom
75%

6 On the Standard toolbar, click the **Zoom** down arrow, and then click **75%**. If necessary, click the **Toolbar Options** down arrow on the Standard toolbar to display the option.

The view scale increases to 75%.

Next Slide

7 Click the **Next Slide** button.

The status bar displays *Notes 3 of 7.*

8 Click the text placeholder **Click to add text** in the **Notes** placeholder in Slide 3.

The selection box surrounds the area that contains the Notes text.

9 Type **It is important to have a large enough vehicle to transport the tree, dirt, and supplies that you will need.**

10 On the Standard toolbar, click the **Zoom** down arrow, and then click **Fit**.

The entire notes pages appears in the window.

Normal View

11 Click the **Normal View** button.

The notes that you entered in Notes Page view appear in Notes pane in Normal view.

12 On the Standard toolbar, click the **Save** button to save the presentation.

Close Window

13 Click the **Close Window** button in the presentation window.

The EnterNotes presentation closes.

Creating a Folder to Store a Presentation

PP2002-7-3

Approved Courseware

To keep your presentations organized and easily accessible, you can store them in separate folders that you create and name. For example, the marketing department at The Garden Company might create a folder named New Catalog in which to store all presentations relating to the catalog. If, after a time, there are too many files in the New Catalog folder, the marketing department can create a **subfolder** within the New Catalog folder and name it Products. In the Products folder, they can store files that describe each product included in the catalog.

Create New Folder

My Documents is the default folder displayed in the **Save As** dialog box. If you want to create another folder, you can click the **Create New Folder** button provided in the **Save As** dialog box.

Up One Level

Before clicking the **Create New Folder** button, you might need to click the **Save in** down arrow to locate the drive on which you want to store the new folder. You can also click the **Up One Level** button provided in the dialog box to move up a level in the hierarchy of folders, or use the Places Bar to move to another location in your computer. The **Places Bar** on the left side of the Save As and Open dialog boxes provides quick access to commonly used locations in which to store and open files.

You might sometimes need to save a presentation with another name, which creates a copy of the original. For example, if you update a presentation for a gardening class, you can save the most recent version with a new name. You can then make changes to the copy saved with another name and then compare the differences between it and the original.

You can save the presentation with the new name in the same folder as the original or in a new folder. You cannot store two presentations in the same folder if the presentations have the same name.

StorePres

In this exercise, you create a folder and save an existing presentation with a new name.

1   On the Standard toolbar, click the **Open** button.

Open

The **Open** dialog box appears.

2   Navigate to the **SBS** folder on your hard disk, double-click the **PowerPoint** folder, double-click the **Working** folder, and then double-click the **StorePres** file.

The StorePres presentation opens, displaying Slide 1 in Normal view.

3   On the **File** menu, click **Save As**.

The **Save As** dialog box appears and displays the **Working** folder as the current folder.

Troubleshooting

If the **Working** folder is not displayed in the **Save in** box, click the **Save in** down arrow to locate the folder.

Create New Folder

4   Click the **Create New Folder** button.

The **New Folder** dialog box appears. Note that the folder that you are creating is a subfolder.

Important

Without the **Create New Folder** button provided in the **Open** and **Save As** dialog boxes, you would have to open Windows Explorer or My Computer to create a new folder.

New Folder	? X
	OK
Name:	Cancel

5   Type **NewFolder**, and then click **OK**.

NewFolder becomes the current folder.

6   In the **File name** box, type **StoreFolder** to rename the file.

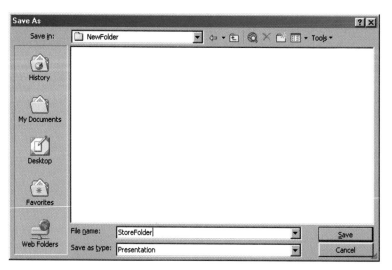

7   Click **Save**.

The file name in the title bar changes to *StoreFolder*. The original StorePres presentation on which this is based is stored in the **Working** folder, and the StoreFolder presentation is stored in the **NewFolder** subfolder.

Close Window

8   Click the **Close Window** button in the presentation window.

The StorePres presentation closes.

Chapter Wrap-Up

To finish the chapter:

Close

● On the **File** menu, click **Exit**, or click the **Close** button in the PowerPoint window.

PowerPoint closes.

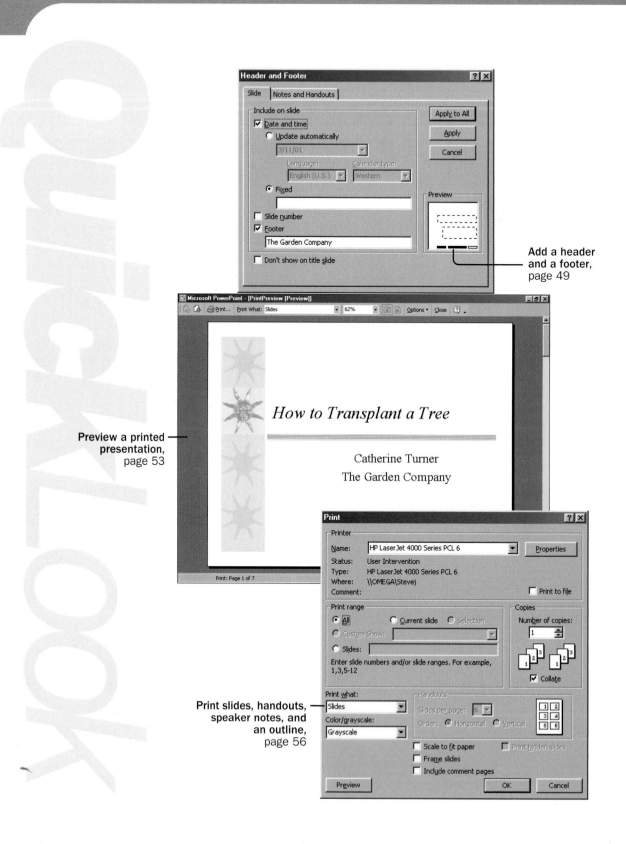

Add a header and a footer, page 49

Preview a printed presentation, page 53

Print slides, handouts, speaker notes, and an outline, page 56

Chapter 3
Printing a Presentation

After completing this chapter, you will be able to:
✔ **Work with an existing presentation.**
✔ **Add a header and a footer.**
✔ **Choose the right print settings.**
✔ **Preview a presentation.**
✔ **Print a presentation.**

Microsoft PowerPoint gives you flexibility when you are preparing to print slides, handouts, and speaker notes. Before you print your presentation, you can add a header and a footer to display the date and time, page number, or other important information. You can easily customize your printouts by selecting the paper size, page orientation, print range, and printer type that meet your needs. When you are ready to print, you can preview your presentation on the screen to make sure it appears the way you want. If you are working on a color presentation, you can preview your presentation in black and white to see how color slides will look after they are printed on a grayscale printer.

The owner of The Garden Company has completed the initial content development on a presentation for a gardening class. The next step is to preview and print the presentation to see how it looks.

In this chapter, you'll open an existing presentation, preview slides, add a header and a footer, choose the right printer settings, and print slides, audience handouts, outlines, and accompanying speaker notes.

 This chapter uses the practice files FilePrint, HeaderFooter, PrintSetting, PrintPreview, and PrintFile that you installed from this book's CD-ROM. For details about installing the practice files, see "Using the Book's CD-ROM" at the beginning of this book.

Working with an Existing Presentation

You can open an existing presentation—for example, one that you or a coworker has already created—and work on it in the same way that you would a new presentation. To open an existing presentation, you must first identify the presentation and its location.

FilePrint

In this exercise, you open an existing presentation.

1 Start PowerPoint, if necessary.

2 On the **View** menu, click **Task Pane**, if necessary, to display the **New Presentation** task pane.

Open

3 In the **New Presentation** task pane, under **Open a presentation**, click **Presentations**, or on the Standard toolbar, click the **Open** button to display the **Open** dialog box.

PowerPoint displays the **Open** dialog box, which is where you specify the name and location of the presentation that you want to open.

Open		? X
Look in:	🗁 My Documents　　　　▾　⇐ ▾ 🔁 　@ ✕ 📑 ▦ ▾ Tools ▾	
History	Name　　　　　　　　　S	
	📁 My Music	
My Documents	📁 My Pictures	
	🌐 My Webs	
Desktop		
Favorites		
	◄ ▶	
Web Folders	File name:　[ ]　▾	Open ▾
	Files of type:　[All PowerPoint Presentations]　▾	Cancel

4 Click the **Look in** down arrow, and then click your hard disk, typically drive C.

5 In the list of file and folder names, double-click the **SBS** folder, double-click the **PowerPoint** folder, and then double-click the **Printing** folder.

6 In the list of file and folder names, click the **FilePrint** file, and then click **Open**.

PowerPoint displays the FilePrint presentation in Normal view.

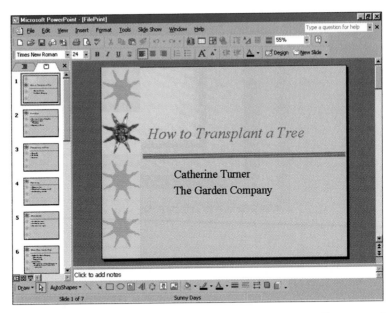

7   On the Standard toolbar, click the **Save** button to save the presentation.

Close Window
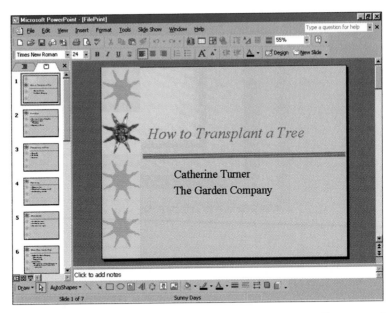

8   Click the **Close Window** button in the presentation window.

The FilePrint presentation closes.

Searching for a Presentation

If you can't remember the exact name or location of a presentation file, but you know part of the name or some of its contents, you can search for a presentation that contains part of the file name or specific words in the file by using the **Basic Search** task pane. For more advanced searches, you can use properties, conditions, and values in the **Advanced Search** task pane to make the search criteria more specific. The Advanced Search pane contains a set of properties—such as file name, text, creation date, last modified, and number of slides—and associated conditions—such as equal to, on or before, more than, or yes/no—to help you find a specific file or set of files. For example, you can type the search criteria "file name includes garden," where *file name* is the property, *includes* is the condition, and *garden* is the value, to find all files that contain the word *garden*. If the fast searching option is installed on your computer, PowerPoint can search through files and organize information for faster retrieval. If fast searching is not installed, you can click **Install** in the **Basic Search** task pane to install it.

Search task pane
new for
OfficeXP

At any time, you can enter presentation property values in the **Presentation Properties** dialog box. These presentation property values can assist you or others later when using the Search functions.

(continued)

To enter presentation property values and search for a file:

1 On the **File** menu, click **Properties**.

The **Presentation Properties** dialog box appears.

2 Click the **Summary** tab.

3 In the **Summary** tab, type presentation information into the specified boxes.

4 Click **OK** to add the presentation properties to the presentation.

Search

5 On the Standard toolbar, click the **Search** button.

The **Basic Search** task pane appears. If the Advanced Search task pane appears, click **Basic Search** at the bottom of the task pane.

6 In the **Search text** box, type the text to search for the files that you want to find.

7 Click the **Search in** down arrow, and then select the check box locations to look for presentation files. Or, select the **Everywhere** check box to search all files on your computer.

8 Click the **Results should be** down arrow, and then select the check box for the types of items to find, or select the **Anything** check box to find all types of files.

9 Click **Advanced Search** at the bottom of the **Basic Search** task pane to display the **Advanced Search** task pane.

10 Click the **Property** down arrow.

The **Property** box displays the properties in the currently open presentation.

11 Choose a property from the list, or type the property name that you are searching for.

12 In the **Condition** box, choose a condition from the list, or type in a condition.

13 In the **Value** box, type the value to associate with the condition.

14 If previous search criteria exists, click **And** to add criteria that must be true in addition to previous criteria, or click **Or** to add a criteria that is sufficient regardless of previous criteria.

15 Click **Add** to add the search criterion.

16 Click **Search**.

PowerPoint searches through the selected files in the indicated folders. When the search is complete, PowerPoint displays the files that meet the search criteria in the **Search Results** task pane. You can double-click files in the **Search Results** task pane to open them.

Adding a Header and a Footer

PP2002-1-3

Approved Courseware

Before you print your presentation, you can add a header and a footer, which will appear on every slide, handout, or notes page. Headers and footers contain useful information about the presentation, such as the author or company name, the date and time, and the page number. Because PowerPoint lets you add more than one header and footer to a presentation, you can have different headers and footers for slides and for notes and handouts. You can quickly and easily add a header and a footer to your slides, audience handouts, outlines, and speaker notes with the **Header and Footer** command on the **View** menu. Header and footer information appear on the master slide.

HeaderFooter

In this exercise, you add a header and a footer to a presentation.

1 On the Standard toolbar, click the **Open** button.

The **Open** dialog box appears.

Open

2 Navigate to the **SBS** folder on your hard disk, double-click the **PowerPoint** folder, double-click the **Printing** folder, and then double-click the **Header-Footer** file.

The HeaderFooter presentation opens, displaying Slide 1 in Normal view.

3 On the **View** menu, click **Header and Footer**.

The **Header and Footer** dialog box appears, displaying the **Slide** tab.

4 Select the **Footer** check box, and then type **The Garden Company**.

In the **Preview** box, a black rectangle highlights the placement of the footer on the slides. Your dialog box should look like the following illustration:

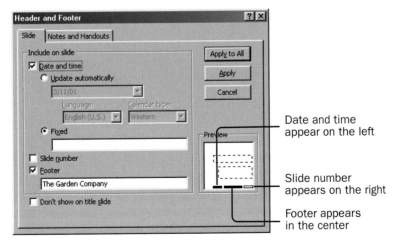

Date and time appear on the left

Slide number appears on the right

Footer appears in the center

5 Select the **Don't show on title slide** check box, if necessary, so that the footer won't appear on the title slide.

6 Click the **Notes and Handouts** tab.

The header and footer settings for the notes and handout pages appear. All four check boxes are selected.

7 Click in the **Header** box, and then type Transplanting a Tree.

8 Click in the **Footer** box, and then type The Garden Company.

9 Clear the **Date and time** check box so that the date and time won't appear on each slide.

PowerPoint includes the header, footer, and page number on each notes or handout page that you print.

10 Click **Apply to All**.

PowerPoint applies the header and footer information to the slides, notes pages, outlines, and handouts pages.

11 On the Standard toolbar, click the **Save** button to save the presentation.

Close Window

×

12 Click the **Close Window** button in the presentation window.

The HeaderFooter presentation closes.

Choosing the Right Print Settings

Additional paper sizes new for **Office**XP

Before you print a presentation, you should review the settings in the **Page Setup** dialog box and the **Print** dialog box. You can use the **Page Setup** dialog box to set the proportions and orientation of your slides, notes pages, handouts, and outlines on the printed page. For a new presentation, PowerPoint opens with default slide page settings: on-screen slide show, **landscape** orientation (10 x 7.5 inches), and slides starting at number one. Notes, handouts, and outlines are printed in **portrait** orientation (7.5 x 10 inches). You can change these options at any time.

There are eleven slide sizes that you can select from in the **Page Setup** dialog box:

- **On-screen Show** Use this setting when you are designing an on-screen slide show. The slide size for the screen is smaller than the Letter Paper size.

- **Letter Paper (8.5 x 11 in)** Use this setting when you are printing a presentation on U.S. letter paper.

- **Ledger Paper (11 x 17 in)** Use this setting when you are printing a presentation on legal size paper.

- **A3 Paper (297 X 420 mm), A4 Paper (210 x 297 mm), B4 (ISO) Paper (250 X 353 mm), B5 (ISO) Paper (176 X 250 mm)** Use one of these settings when you are printing on international paper.

- **35mm Slides** Use this setting when you are designing a presentation for 35mm slides. The slide size is slightly reduced to produce the slides.

- **Overhead** Use this setting when you are printing transparencies for an overhead projector (8.5 x 11 in).

- **Banner** Use this setting when you are designing a banner (8 x 1 in) for a Web page.

- **Custom** Use this setting to design slides with a special size.

Tip

PowerPoint prints presentations on your default Windows printer unless you select a different printer. Your default printer is set up in the Windows print settings in the Control Panel. To change the default printer, click **Start** on the taskbar, point to **Settings**, click **Printers**, right-click the printer that you want to set as default, and then click **Set as Default**. You can select another printer in PowerPoint's **Print** dialog box.

PrintSetting

In this exercise, you change the slide size setting from On-screen Show to Letter Paper and select a printer for a presentation.

1   On the Standard toolbar, click the **Open** button.

Open

The **Open** dialog box appears.

2   Navigate to the **SBS** folder on your hard disk, double-click the **PowerPoint** folder, double-click the **Printing** folder, and then double-click the **PrintSetting** file.

The PrintSetting presentation opens, displaying Slide 1 in Normal view.

3   On the **File** menu, click **Page Setup**.

The **Page Setup** dialog box appears.

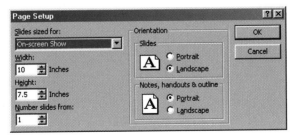

4   Click the **Slides sized for** down arrow, and then click **Letter Paper (8.5 x 11 in)**.

5   Click **OK**.

The slide size changes to Letter Paper.

Troubleshooting

Before you print, it is important to verify that your printer is turned on, connected to your computer, and loaded with paper.

6 On the **File** menu, click **Print**.

The **Print** dialog box appears.

Click to choose printer-specific settings.

Click to choose a printer.

7 In the **Printer** area, click the **Name** down arrow.

A drop-down list appears with the installed printers on your computer.

8 Click one of the printers in the list.

After choosing a printer, you can customize your printer settings.

9 Click **Properties**.

The **Properties** dialog box appears, showing the current printer settings. The **Properties** dialog settings differ, depending on the specific printer that you selected.

10 In the **Properties** dialog box, click **OK**.

The **Properties** dialog box closes to display the **Print** dialog box. The print setup is complete.

11 In the **Print** dialog box, click **OK** to print the presentation with the selected print settings.

12 On the Standard toolbar, click the **Save** button to save the presentation.

Close Window

13 Click the **Close Window** button in the presentation window.

The PrintSetting presentation closes.

Previewing a Presentation

PP2002-5-1

Approved Courseware

Print preview allows you to see how your presentation will look before you print it. While in print preview, you have the option of switching between various views, such as notes, slides, outlines, and handouts, or even landscape and portrait. If you are using a black and white printer to print a color presentation, you need to verify that the printed presentation will be legible. For example, red text against a shaded background shows up well in color, but when seen in black and white or shades of gray, the text tends to be indistinguishable from the background. To prevent this problem, you can preview your color slides in pure black and white or grayscale in print preview to see how they will look when you print them.

Print Preview
new for
OfficeXP

Pure black and white displays colors in black and white, while grayscale displays colors in shades of gray. If you want to make changes to your slides while viewing them in black and white, you can change the color setting to black and white in Normal view.

PrintPreview

In this exercise, you preview your presentation handouts, switch to Pure Black and White view, and then change the way the slide looks in black and white.

1 On the Standard toolbar, click the **Open** button.

Open

The **Open** dialog box appears.

2 Navigate to the **SBS** folder on your hard disk, double-click the **PowerPoint** folder, double-click the **Printing** folder, and then double-click the **PrintPreview** file.

The PrintPreview presentation opens, displaying Slide 1 in Normal view.

Print Preview

3 On the Standard toolbar, click the **Print Preview** button.

The screen switches to print preview and shows your presentation in the currently selected settings.

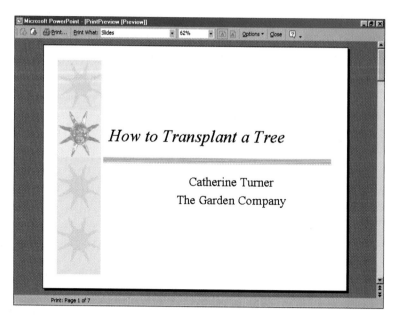

If you are printing to a grayscale printer, your slides are shown in grayscale using print preview.

4 On the Print Preview toolbar, click the **Print What** down arrow, and then click **Handouts (2 slides per page)**.

The preview screen displays your presentation in handout format with two slides per page.

5 On the Print Preview toolbar, click the **Options** down arrow, point to **Color/ Grayscale**, and then click **Color (On Black and White Printer)**.

The preview screen displays your presentation in a shaded grayscale.

If you are printing to a color printer, your options will be different; on the **Color/Gray-scale** menu, click **Color**.

Next Page

6 On the Print Preview toolbar, click the **Next Page** button.

The preview screen displays the next handout page.

Magnifying glass (+)

7 Position the pointer (which changes to a magnifying glass with a plus sign) in the preview area, and then click the center of the top slide.

The preview screen increases to display a magnified view of the slide.

Magnifying glass (-)

8 Position the pointer (which changes to a magnifying glass with a minus sign) in the preview area, and then click the center of the slide.

The preview screen is reduced to display the original view of the slide.

9 On the Print Preview toolbar, click the **Previous Page** button.

The preview screen displays the previous handout page.

Close Preview

10 On the Print Preview toolbar, click the **Close Preview** button.

The preview screen closes, and your slide appears in the previous view.

11 Click the **Normal View** button, if necessary, and then click the **Slides** tab, if necessary, to display slide miniatures in the Outline/Slides pane.

Color/Gray-scale

12 On the Standard toolbar, click the **Color/Grayscale** button, and then click **Grayscale**.

The slide switches from color to grayscale and the Grayscale View toolbar opens. You can still view the slide miniatures in color on the **Slides** tab, making it easier to compare the color slides with the black and white slides.

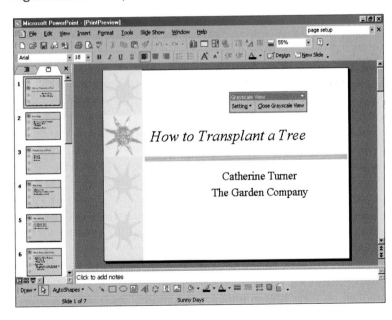

Next Slide

13 Click the **Next Slide** button.

The next slide appears, also in black and white with the slide miniature in color.

55

Slide Sorter
View

14 Click the **Slide Sorter View** button.

All of the slides in the Slide Sorter view appear in black and white.

15 Double-click **Slide 1** to display Slide 1 in Normal view.

16 On the Grayscale View toolbar, click the **Setting** button, and then click **Black with Grayscale Fill**.

The slide background changes from white to gray.

17 On the Grayscale View toolbar, click the **Setting** button, and then click **White**.

The slide background is white again.

18 On the Grayscale View toolbar, click the **Close Grayscale View** button.

The slide switches back to color.

19 On the Standard toolbar, click the **Save** button to save the presentation.

Close Window

20 Click the **Close Window** button in the presentation window.

The PrintPreview presentation closes.

Printing a Presentation

PP2002-5-1

Approved Courseware

You can print your PowerPoint presentation in several ways: as slides, speaker notes, audience handouts, or an outline. PowerPoint makes it easy to print your presentation; it detects the type of printer that you chose—either color or black and white—and prints the appropriate version of the presentation. For example, if you select a black and white printer, your presentation will be set to print in shades of gray (grayscale).

PowerPoint prints slides and supplements based on settings in the **Print** dialog box. In the **Print** dialog box, you can select a printer and set the print range, which defines which slides to print. You can also choose to print multiple copies of a presentation, and if you do print more than one copy of each slide, you can choose to collate the presentation as you print. When you collate the presentation, PowerPoint prints a complete copy before printing the next copy. The **Print** dialog box also contains a **Preview** button that takes you to the **Print Preview** window, allowing you to preview any changes that you may have made.

Tip

If you are working with a professional printer to print your slides, you will need to print your slides to a file instead of a printer. To print your slides to a file, select the **Print to file** check box in the **Print** dialog box.

By clicking the **Print what** down arrow in the **Print** dialog box, you can choose to print a presentation as one of four output types:

- **Slides** Prints slides as they appear on the screen, one per page. You can print a slide as an overhead transparency in the same way that you print any other slide, except you put transparency film in the printer instead of paper.
- **Handouts** Prints one, two, three, four, six, or nine slides per page.
- **Notes Pages** Prints each slide with the speaker notes under it. The notes pages appear with a reduced image of the slide at the top of the page.
- **Outline View** Prints an outline with formatting according to the current view setting. What you see in Outline pane is what you get on the printout.

An example of each printing type is shown in the following illustrations:

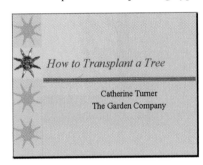

Slide (landscape)

Notes page

Handout page

Outline page

By clicking the **Color/grayscale** down arrow in the **Print** dialog box, you can choose to print a presentation as one of three color options:

■ **Color** Use this option to print a presentation in color on a color printer. If you select a black and white printer with this option, the presentation prints in grayscale.

■ **Grayscale** Use this option to print a presentation in grayscale on a color or black and white printer.

■ **Pure Black and White** Use this option to print a presentation in only black and white with no gray on a color or black and white printer.

Finally, at the bottom of the **Print** dialog box, you can select from the following print options to enhance a printout:

■ **Scale to fit paper** Use this option to scale slides to fit the paper size in the printer if the paper in the printer does not correspond to the slide size and orientation settings.

■ **Frame slides** Use this option to add a frame around the presentation slides when you print.

■ **Include comment pages** Use this option to print any comments that you have inserted throughout the presentation.

■ **Print hidden slides** Use this option to print all hidden slides.

Print

If you are satisfied with the current **Print** dialog box settings, you can click the **Print** button on the Standard toolbar to print directly without first viewing the settings. Otherwise, click the **Print** command on the **File** menu to print with new settings.

PrintFile

In this exercise, you review print output types and options. You then print presentation slides, audience handouts, and speaker notes.

1 On the Standard toolbar, click the **Open** button.

Open

The **Open** dialog box appears.

2 Navigate to the **SBS** folder on your hard disk, double-click the **PowerPoint** folder, double-click the **Printing** folder, and then double-click the **PrintFile** file.

The PrintFile presentation opens, displaying Slide 1 in Normal view.

3 On the **File** menu, click **Print**.

The **Print** dialog box appears.

Click to choose an output type.

Set the print range

Click to choose the number of slides per page when printing handouts.

Click to adjust the presentation for grayscale printing.

4   In the **Print range** area, click the **Current slide** option.

5   Click the **Print what** down arrow, and then click **Slides**.

6   Click the **Color/grayscale** down arrow, click **Grayscale**, and then click **OK**.

PowerPoint prints the current slide in the presentation. A small print icon appears on the status bar located at the bottom of your screen, showing the printing status.

Tip

Every printer prints text and graphics slightly differently. PowerPoint sizes presentation slides to the printer that you choose. Using scalable fonts, such as TrueType fonts, PowerPoint allows you to print a presentation on different printers with the same results. When you print a presentation with scalable fonts, PowerPoint reduces or enlarges the size of the text in the presentation for each printer to get consistent results.

7   On the **File** menu, click **Print**.

The **Print** dialog box appears.

Tip

You can print audience handouts in six formats: one, two, three, four, six, or nine slides per page.

8 Click the **Print what** down arrow, and then click **Handouts**.

9 Click the **Slides per page** down arrow, and then click **2**.

PowerPoint selects the **Frame slides** check box when you select handouts.

10 Click **OK**.

PowerPoint prints the presentation slides as handout pages.

11 On the **File** menu, click **Print**.

The **Print** dialog box appears.

12 Click the **Print what** down arrow, and then click **Notes Pages**.

13 In the **Print range** area, click the **Slides** option.

The insertion point appears in the box next to the **Slides** option.

14 Type **1-2,4**.

Tip

You can print slides or notes pages in any order by entering slide numbers and ranges separated by commas. For example, if you enter 1,3,5-12 in the **Slides** box in the **Print** dialog box, PowerPoint prints slides 1, 3, and 5 through 12.

15 Click **OK**.

PowerPoint prints notes pages 1, 2, and 4.

Tip

When you send a document to a printer with background printing turned on, Windows can work in the background to print the job and let you continue to work. Background printing uses additional system memory. If printing is slow, you can turn off background printing to speed up the process. On the **Tools** menu, click **Options**, click the **Print** tab, and then clear the **Background printing** check box.

16 On the Standard toolbar, click the **Save** button to save the presentation.

Close Window
☒

17 Click the **Close Window** button in the presentation window.

The PrintFile presentation closes.

Printing a Presentation to a Printer on the Web

If your organization uses Microsoft Windows 2000 and the Active Directory directory service, you can search for and use printers across your network, intranet, or Web. **Active Directory** is a network service that stores information about resources, such as computers and printers.

Find Printer
new for
OfficeXP

To search for printers on your network, you use the **Find Printer** button in the **Print** dialog box. If Active Directory is not used at your site or if your operating system does not support it, the **Find Printer** button will not be available.

To find a printer on the Web and print a presentation using the **Print** dialog box:

1   On the **File** menu, click **Print**.

The **Print** dialog box appears.

2   Click **Find Printer**.

The **Find Printer** dialog box appears.

3   Click **Find Now** to find all printers at your network, intranet, or Web site.

4   In the **Find Printer** dialog box, select the printer that you want.

5   Click **OK**.

The **Printer** dialog box appears, and the selected printer appears in the **Name** box.

6   Specify the print settings that you want, and then click **OK** to print the presentation.

Chapter Wrap-Up

To finish the chapter:

Close

●   On the **File** menu, click **Exit**, or click the **Close** button in the PowerPoint window.

PowerPoint closes.

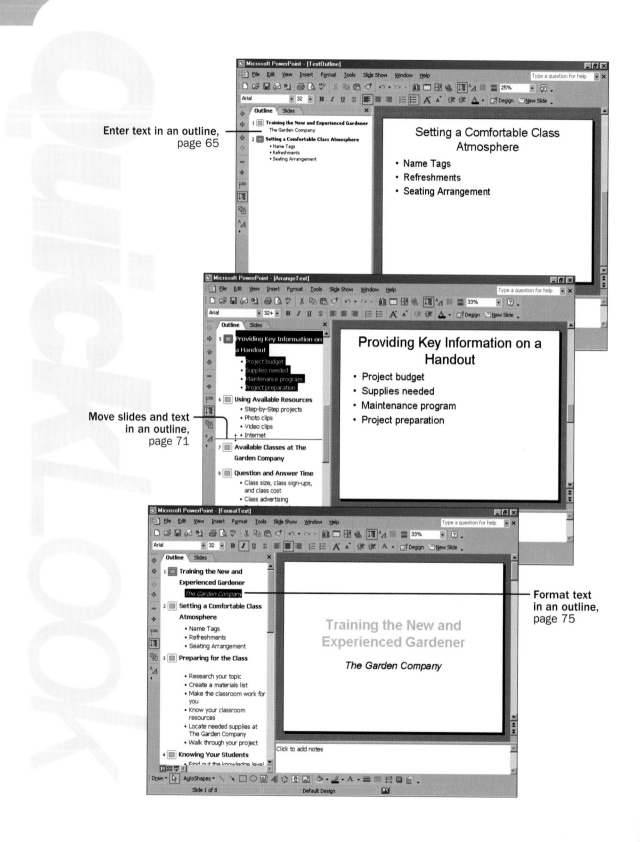

Enter text in an outline, page 65

Move slides and text in an outline, page 71

Format text in an outline, page 75

Chapter 4
Outlining
Your Ideas

After completing this chapter, you will be able to:

✔ **Create a blank presentation.**
✔ **Enter text in an outline.**
✔ **Insert an outline from Microsoft Word.**
✔ **Delete and rearrange slides, paragraphs, and text.**
✔ **Format text in an outline.**
✔ **Send an outline or notes to Word.**

Outlining your thoughts and ideas makes it easier to organize a presentation. In Microsoft PowerPoint, you can organize your thoughts and ideas in the **Outline** tab on the Outline/Slides pane to see the slide title text and paragraph text for each slide in the presentation. You can also edit and rearrange both title and paragraph text in the **Outline** tab, import outlines created in other programs into a PowerPoint outline, and export the results when you are done.

For example, now that The Garden Company has decided to offer gardening classes, the company needs trained teachers to lead the classes. The owner has decided to develop a teachers' training presentation for new class teachers and will conduct the first teacher training class at the end of the month.

In this chapter, you'll create a blank presentation for the teacher training class, enter text into the outline, insert additional information into the outline from a Microsoft Word document, delete and rearrange slides, paragraphs, and text, and then format text. When you finish changing the outline, you'll export the outline into Word for later use and then save a presentation as an outline.

This chapter uses the practice files TextOutline, InsertOutline, Outline, ArrangeText, FormatText, and SendOutline that you installed from this book's CD-ROM. For details about installing the practice files, see "Using the Book's CD-ROM" at the beginning of this book.

Creating a Blank Presentation

PP2002-1-1

Approved Courseware

If you are not sure how you want your presentation to look, you can start a new presentation from scratch. You can create a blank presentation when you first start PowerPoint or after you have already started PowerPoint. Either way, a blank presentation appears, ready for you to use.

In this exercise, you create a blank presentation and then save the presentation.

1   Start PowerPoint, if necessary.

2   On the **View** menu, click **Task Pane**, if necessary, to display the **New Presentation** task pane.

New

3   In the **New Presentation** task pane, click **Blank Presentation** under **New** or click the **New** button on the Standard toolbar.

PowerPoint displays a blank presentation with the default Title Slide layout, and the **Slide Layout** task pane appears, displaying various slide layouts.

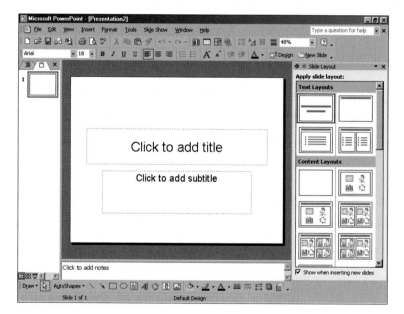

Close

4   On the title bar of the **Slide Layout** task pane, click the **Close** button to close the task pane.

5   On the **File** menu, click **Save As**.

The **Save As** dialog box appears.

6   In the **File name** box, type **BlankPres**.

7   Navigate to the **SBS** folder, double-click the **PowerPoint** folder, and then double-click the **Outlining** folder.

8   Click **Save**.

PowerPoint saves the presentation with the name BlankPres.

Close Window

9   Click the **Close Window** button in the presentation window.

The BlankPres presentation closes.

Entering Text in an Outline

PP2002-2-2

Working with text in the PowerPoint outline makes it easier to see all of the main points in your presentation all in one place. The presentation outline appears in the **Outline** tab on the Outline/Slides pane in Normal view. The **Outline** tab displays the title and bullet points for each slide. In the **Outline** tab, you can edit your presentation's content, and you can move slides or bullet points around by increasing or decreasing text indents. When you increase the text indent, slide titles become bullet points, and bullet points become subpoints. When you decrease the text indent, bullet points become slide titles.

To make it easier to work with the main points in your outline, PowerPoint allows you to collapse and expand slide content to view entire slides or only slide titles. When you format text in the **Outline** tab, sometimes the text can be hard to read, so PowerPoint allows you to show or hide text formatting in the outline. The formatting information is not deleted or cleared; it is just turned off so that you can see the content more easily. When you print an outline, the outline will always appear with formatting on. When you work in the **Outline** tab, you can use the Outlining toolbar to perform many of these tasks.

The outline that you are working on might contain more text than you can see on the screen at one time. To view more of the text in an outline, you can reduce the view scale of the presentation window by using the **Zoom** button on the Standard toolbar or the **Zoom** command on the **View** menu. When you change the view scale, the view of the presentation increases or decreases in size, but the presentation itself does not change size.

Tip

The standard view scales available in the **Outline** tab are 25%, 33%, 50%, 66%, 75%, and 100%. Other views use the following additional view scales: **Fit**, which means the view of the presentation is sized to fit your monitor; or 150%, 200%, 300%, and 400%, which are helpful for working on detailed items, such as graphics or objects. The **Zoom** command allows you to decrease the view size to see more of the presentation outline or increase the view size to see small text that is hard to read. If you need to set a nonstandard view scale, you can also enter any view scale in the **Zoom** box on the Standard toolbar.

TextOutline

In this exercise, you enter paragraph text in the outline, change a paragraph indent to complete a slide, change the view scale, and then collapse and expand the outline.

1 On the Standard toolbar, click the **Open** button.

Open

The **Open** dialog box appears.

2 Navigate to the **SBS** folder on your hard disk, double-click the **PowerPoint** folder, double-click the **Outlining** folder, and then double-click the **TextOutline** file.

The TextOutline presentation opens, displaying Slide 1 in Normal view.

3 In the Outline/Slides pane, click the **Outline** tab, if necessary, and then click to the right of Slide 1 to place the insertion point.

The slide icon for Slide 1 is selected in the outline.

4 On the **View** menu, point to **Toolbars**, and then click **Outlining**, if necessary, to display the Outlining toolbar.

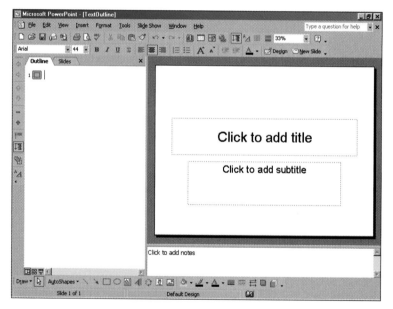

5 Type **Training the New and Experienced Gardener**, and then press ⏎ Enter.

PowerPoint adds a new slide.

Tip

If the **Outline** tab is not wide enough to display the outline text, you can drag the right edge of the pane to the right to expand the Outline/Slides pane. When you change the size of the Outline/Slides pane, the size of the Slide pane and Notes pane changes, too.

Demote

6 On the Outlining toolbar, click the **Demote** button, or press the ⎯Tab⎯ key.

The insertion point shifts to the right to start a new paragraph for the title text above it.

7 Type **The Garden Company**, and then press ⎯Enter⎯.

A new paragraph appears without a bullet next to the subtitle text on the title slide.

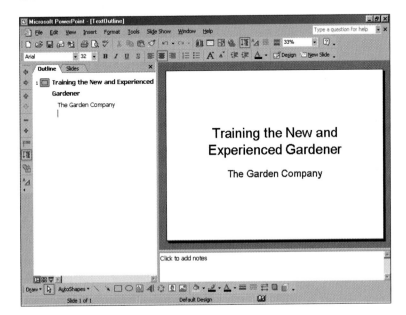

8 Type **Setting a Comfortable Class Atmosphere**.

Promote

9 On the Outlining toolbar, click the **Promote** button.

The paragraph text shifts to the left to create title text for a new slide. A slide icon appears next to the text.

10 Press ⎯Enter⎯, and then type **Name Tags**.

Demote

11 On the Outlining toolbar, click the **Demote** button.

The title text shifts to the right to create paragraph text with a bullet for the title text above it.

12 Press ⎯Enter⎯, and then type **Refreshments**.

13 Press ⎯Enter⎯, and then type **Seating Arrangement**.

Zoom
| 25% | ▾ |

14 On the Standard toolbar, click the **Zoom** down arrow, and then click **25%**.

The view scale for the Outline tab decreases from 33% to 25%.

Tip

Your view scale might be different, depending on the size of your monitor.

15 On the Standard toolbar, click in the **Zoom** box to select the current view scale percentage.

16 Type **33**, and then press `Enter`.

The view scale changes to 33%.

17 Click the blank area to the right of the Slide 2 title to place the insertion point in the title line.

Collapse

18 On the Outlining toolbar, click the **Collapse** button.

Slide 2 collapses to show only the title. The rest of the outline remains fully expanded.

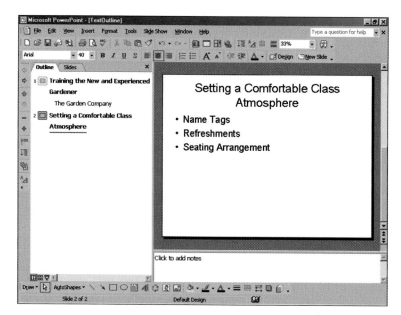

Collapse All

19 On the Outlining toolbar, click the **Collapse All** button.

The view switches from titles and paragraphs to only titles.

20 Click the blank area to the right of the Slide 1 title to place the insertion point in the title line.

Expand

21 On the Outlining toolbar, click the **Expand** button.

Slide 1 expands to include the paragraph text again.

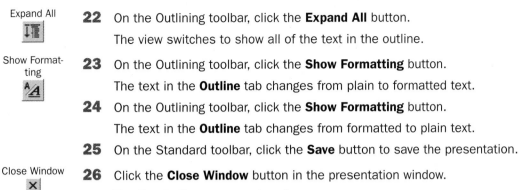

Expand All

22 On the Outlining toolbar, click the **Expand All** button.

The view switches to show all of the text in the outline.

**Show Format-
ting**

23 On the Outlining toolbar, click the **Show Formatting** button.

The text in the **Outline** tab changes from plain to formatted text.

24 On the Outlining toolbar, click the **Show Formatting** button.

The text in the **Outline** tab changes from formatted to plain text.

25 On the Standard toolbar, click the **Save** button to save the presentation.

Close Window

26 Click the **Close Window** button in the presentation window.

The TextOutline presentation closes.

Inserting an Outline from Microsoft Word

PP2002-2-1

Approved Courseware

If you already have text in other programs, such as Microsoft Word, you can insert the text into the **Outline** tab as titles and body text. PowerPoint allows you to insert text in several formats, including Microsoft Word (.doc) format, Rich Text Format (.rtf), and plain text (.txt). When you insert a Word or Rich Text Format document, Power-Point creates an outline of slide titles and paragraphs based on heading styles in the document. When you insert text from a plain text document, paragraphs without tabs at the beginning become a slide title, while paragraphs with tabs at the beginning become paragraph text. You can also insert a Web document in HTML format into your presentation. When you insert the text in the HTML file, it appears within a text box on the slide.

**InsertOutline
Outline**

In this exercise, you insert an outline developed in another program into a presentation.

Open

1 On the Standard toolbar, click the **Open** button.

The **Open** dialog box appears.

2 Navigate to the **SBS** folder on your hard disk, double-click the **PowerPoint** folder, double-click the **Outlining** folder, and then double-click the **InsertOut-line** file.

The InsertOutline presentation opens, displaying Slide 1 in Normal view.

3 In the **Outline** tab under the title in Slide 2, click the blank area to the right of the indented text *Seating Arrangement* to place the insertion point.

4 On the **Insert** menu, click **Slides from Outline**.

The **Insert Outline** dialog box appears.

5 Navigate to the **SBS** folder, double-click the **PowerPoint** folder, and then dou-ble-click the **Outlining** folder.

6   In the list of file and folder names, click **Outline**.

7   Click **Insert**.

PowerPoint inserts the Word outline into the PowerPoint outline.

Tip

If you receive a message telling you that you need to install a converter, insert the CD-ROM that you used to install PowerPoint, and then click **OK** to install it.

8   In the **Outline** tab, click a blank area to deselect the text.

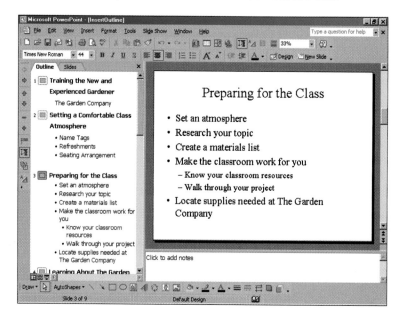

Tip

You can start a new presentation from a Word outline using the **Open** command. On the Standard toolbar, click the **Open** button, click the **Files of type** down arrow, click **All Files**, and then double-click the outline file that you want to use to start the presentation.

9   On the Standard toolbar, click the **Save** button to save the presentation.

Close Window

☒

10   Click the **Close Window** button in the presentation window.

The InsertOutline presentation closes.

Deleting and Rearranging Slides, Paragraphs, and Text

PP2002-1-2
PP2002-4-8

In the **Outline** tab, you can select, edit, and rearrange slides, paragraphs, and text by using the Outlining toolbar buttons or by dragging the slides, paragraphs, or text. You can also create several new slides from one slide.

To edit or rearrange slides and paragraphs, you first select the text. To select a slide or paragraph, you click the corresponding slide icon or paragraph bullet. To select a word, you double-click the word. To select any portion of a title or paragraph, you can drag the I-beam pointer to highlight the text. In the **Outline** tab, you can also click the blank area at the end of a title or paragraph to select the entire line of text. This technique works especially well when selecting slide titles.

You can rearrange slides and paragraphs in the **Outline** tab by using the **Move Up** button and the **Move Down** button on the Outlining toolbar or by dragging selected slides and paragraphs to the desired location. You can also drag a paragraph so that it becomes part of another paragraph. To move selected words, you simply drag the selection to the new position.

ArrangeText

In this exercise, you select and delete a slide and a paragraph, and then you rearrange slides, paragraphs, and words using different methods.

1   On the Standard toolbar, click the **Open** button.

Open

The **Open** dialog box appears.

2   Navigate to the **SBS** folder on your hard disk, double-click the **PowerPoint** folder, double-click the **Outlining** folder, and then double-click the **Arrange-Text** file.

The ArrangeText presentation opens, displaying Slide 1 in Normal view.

Four-headed
arrow pointer
↔↕

3   In the **Outline** tab, scroll down to Slide 4, position the I-beam pointer (which changes to the four-headed arrow) over the icon for Slide 4, and then click the icon to select the slide.

The entire slide, including all text and graphic objects (even those that are not visible in the **Outline** tab), is selected.

4   Press the ⌈Del⌉ key.

PowerPoint deletes Slide 4 and renumbers the other slides.

Tip

You can also delete the currently selected or displayed slide in any view by clicking **Delete Slide** on the **Edit** menu or by selecting its title text and deleting it.

5   In the **Outline** tab, scroll to the top of the outline.

6 Position the I-beam pointer (which changes to the four-headed arrow) over the bullet next to the paragraph titled *Set an atmosphere* in Slide 3, and then click the bullet.

PowerPoint selects the paragraph, including all related indented paragraphs. After you select a paragraph or any text in Outline view, you can delete it at any time. Slide 3 contains information that was already covered in Slide 2, so you delete the repetitive information.

7 Press ⌷Del⌷.

PowerPoint deletes the paragraph.

8 Click the bullet next to the paragraph titled *Research your topic* in Slide 3 to select the paragraph.

9 Hold down the ⌷Shift⌷ key, and then click the bullet for the paragraph titled *Walk through your project*. The bulleted text in between is also selected.

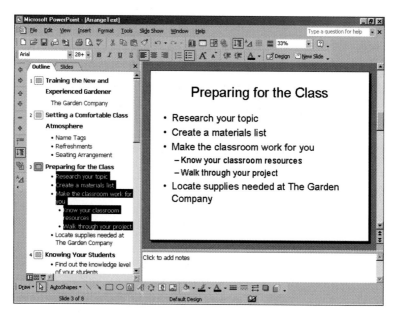

Tip

You can also select multiple paragraphs by dragging the mouse. Click the I-beam pointer where you want the selection to begin, and then drag the I-beam pointer down to where you want the selection to end. PowerPoint selects everything between the first click and the ending point of the drag action.

10 Position the I-beam pointer in the middle of the word *Locate* in the last paragraph in Slide 3.

I-beam pointer

11 Drag the I-beam pointer to the right, through the text *Locate supplies needed at the Garden Company*, to select all of the text that follows in the line.

When the Automatic Word Selection feature is turned on, PowerPoint selects the entire word even though you started the selection in the middle.

Tip

You can turn off the **Automatic Word Selection** command by clicking **Options** on the **Tools** menu, clicking the **Edit** tab, and then clearing the **When selecting, automatically select entire word** check box.

12 In Slide 3, double-click the word *needed*, and then drag it to the left of the word *supplies* on the same line.

Drag pointer

As you drag, a gray indicator line shows where PowerPoint will place the text. When you release the mouse button, the word *needed* moves to its new position.

13 In the **Outline** tab, scroll down so that Slide 5 is the top slide in the pane.

14 Position the four-headed arrow over the slide icon for Slide 5, *Providing Key Information on a Handout*.

15 Drag the slide icon down between Slides 6 and 7.

Vertical two-headed arrow

As you drag, the pointer changes to the vertical two-headed arrow, and a vertical placement line appears, showing you where you can place the slide.

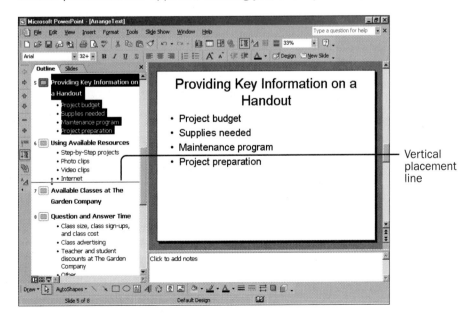

After you release the mouse button, PowerPoint reorders and renumbers the slides.

16 Click the bullet to the left of the paragraph *Project Preparation* in Slide 6 to select the text.

Move Up

17 On the Outlining toolbar, click the **Move Up** button three times.

The paragraph *Project Preparation* becomes the first bulleted item.

18 Scroll to the top of the outline, and then in Slide 3, position the four-headed arrow over the bullet next to the text *Know your classroom resources*.

19 Drag the text line horizontally to the left one level.

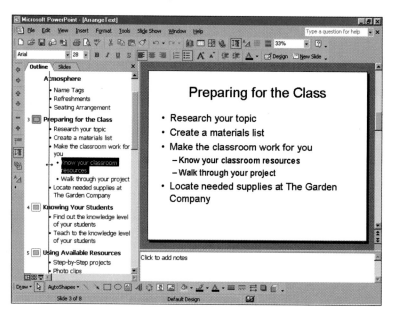

Horizontal two-headed arrow

As you drag, the pointer changes to the horizontal two-headed arrow again, and a vertical line indicates at what level PowerPoint will place the text. The text line moves one indent level to the left.

Move Down

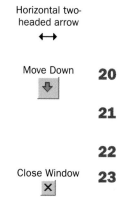

20 Drag the bulleted text *Walk through your project* horizontally to the left one level, and then click the **Move Down** button on the Outlining toolbar.

21 Click the bullet next to the text *Make the classroom work for you*, and then press [Del] to delete the bullet point.

22 On the Standard toolbar, click the **Save** button to save the presentation.

Close Window

23 Click the **Close Window** button in the presentation window.

The ArrangeText presentation closes.

Formatting Text in an Outline

PP2002-2-2

Approved Courseware

FormatText

After you finish entering and moving text in an outline, you can change the look of the text by applying character formatting, such as font type, size, and style. To format text, you first select it and then apply the specific formatting that you want, using the commands on the Formatting toolbar. The Formatting toolbar includes commands to change the font type and size and to apply the bold, italic, and underline styles.

In this exercise, you change the style, font, size, and color of text in an outline.

1 On the Standard toolbar, click the **Open** button.

Open

The **Open** dialog box appears.

2 Navigate to the **SBS** folder on your hard disk, double-click the **PowerPoint** folder, double-click the **Outlining** folder, and then double-click the **Format-Text** file.

The FormatText presentation opens, displaying Slide 1 in Normal view.

3 In the **Outline** tab, scroll to the top of the outline, if necessary.

4 Double-click the blank area to the right of the word *Gardener* in the title of Slide 1.

The title text is selected.

Bold

B

5 On the Formatting toolbar, click the **Bold** button.

PowerPoint changes the style of the selected text to bold.

Font Color

6 On the Drawing toolbar, click the **Font Color** down arrow, and then click the Bright Green color box on the far right side of the menu.

7 Select the text *The Garden Company* in Slide 1.

Italic

I

8 On the Formatting toolbar, click the **Italic** button.

PowerPoint changes the style of the selected text to italic.

Font Size

9 With the subtitle text still selected, on the Formatting toolbar, click the **Font Size** down arrow, and then click **36**.

The subtitle font changes from 32 points to 36 points.

10 In the **Outline** tab, double-click the blank area to the right of the slide title *Training the New and Experienced Gardener*.

The entire line is selected.

Increase Font Size

11 On the Formatting toolbar, click the **Increase Font Size** button.

The slide title font changes from 44 points to 48 points.

12 On the Formatting toolbar, click the **Font** down arrow, scroll down the font list, and then click **Times New Roman**.

The selected text changes from Arial to Times New Roman.

13   Select the text *The Garden Company* in Slide 1, click the **Font** down arrow again on the Formatting toolbar, and then click **Times New Roman**.

The **Times New Roman** font is now at the top of the font list, and is applied to the subtitle.

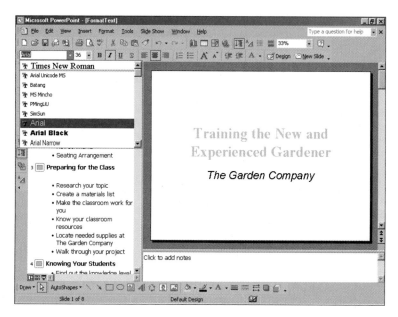

Tip

PowerPoint places recently used fonts at the top of the font list, separated from the rest of the list by a double line, so you don't have to scroll down the list of fonts to find your favorites.

14   In the **Outline** tab, click a blank area to deselect the text in the outline.

PowerPoint deselects the slide text.

15   On the Standard toolbar, click the **Save** button to save the presentation.

Close Window

![x]

16   Click the **Close Window** button in the presentation window.

The FormatText presentation closes.

Sending an Outline or Notes to Word

PP2002-6-4

Approved Courseware

PowerPoint allows you to reuse your presentation content in a Word document. As long as Word is installed on your computer, you can export a presentation outline or speaker notes directly from PowerPoint into a report in Word with the **Send To Microsoft Word** feature. PowerPoint launches Word and sends or copies the outline or notes pages in the presentation to a blank Word document. When you need the text portion of a presentation for use in another program, you can save the presentation text in a format called **Rich Text Format (RTF)**. Saving an outline in RTF allows you to save any formatting that you made to the presentation text in a common file format that you can open in other programs. There are many programs, such as Word for Macintosh or older versions of PowerPoint, that can import outlines saved in RTF format.

SendOutline

In this exercise, you send the presentation outline to Word and then save a presentation as an outline.

1   On the Standard toolbar, click the **Open** button.

Open

The **Open** dialog box appears.

2   Navigate to the **SBS** folder on your hard disk, double-click the **PowerPoint** folder, double-click the **Outlining** folder, and then double-click the **SendOutline** file.

The SendOutline presentation opens, displaying Slide 1 in Normal view.

3   On the **File** menu, point to **Send To**, and then click **Microsoft Word**.

The **Send To Microsoft Word** dialog box appears with five page layout options and two pasting options.

Important

The page layout options determine the type of information that you want to send to Word. The pasting options determine how you want to send the information.

4   Click the **Outline only** option, and then click **OK**.

PowerPoint launches Word and inserts the presentation slides with the title text and main text format into a blank Word document.

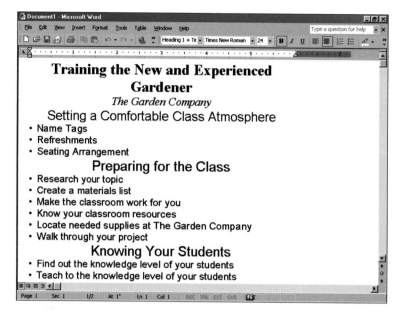

5 On the **File** menu in the **Word** window, click **Save As**.

The **Save As** dialog box appears.

6 In the **File name** box, type **PPTOutline**.

7 Navigate to the **SBS** folder, double-click the **PowerPoint** folder, and then double-click the **Outlining** folder.

8 Click **Save**.

Word saves the presentation slide text in a document called PPTOutline in the **Outlining** folder.

9 On the **File** menu in the **Word** window, click **Exit**.

Word closes, and PowerPoint appears.

10 On the **File** menu, click **Save As**.

The **Save As** dialog box appears.

11 In the **File name** box, type **RTFOutline**.

12 Click the **Save as type** down arrow, and then click **Outline/RTF**.

13 Navigate to the **SBS** folder, double-click the **PowerPoint** folder, and then double-click the **Outlining** folder.

14 Click **Save**.

PowerPoint saves the presentation slide text in RTF format in a document called **Outline RTF** in the **Outlining** folder.

15 On the Standard toolbar, click the **Save** button to save the presentation.

Close Window
[X]

16 Click the **Close Window** button in the presentation window.

The SendOutline presentation closes.

Chapter Wrap-Up

To finish the chapter:

Close
[X]

● On the **File** menu, click **Exit**, or click the **Close** button in the PowerPoint window.

PowerPoint closes.

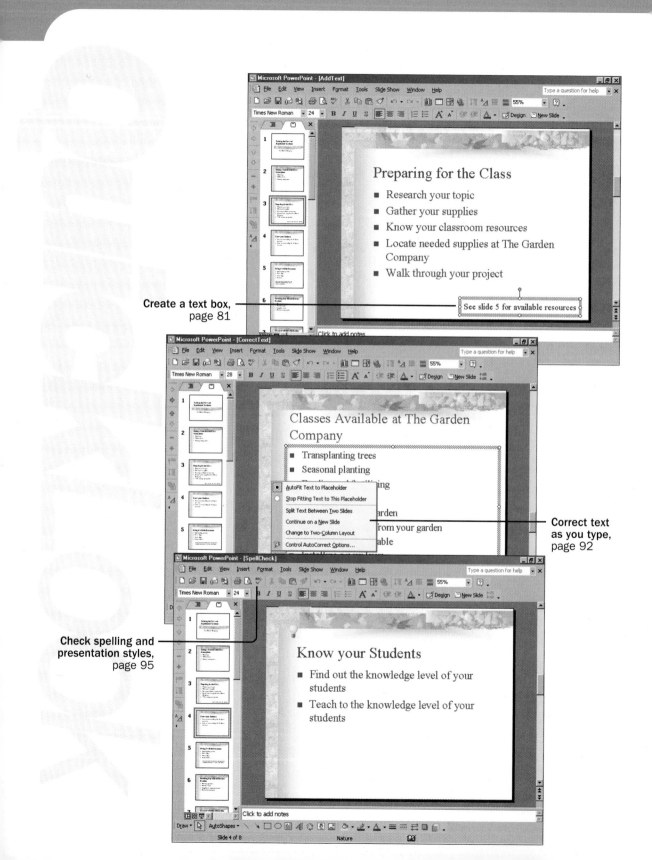

Create a text box,
page 81

Correct text
as you type,
page 92

Check spelling and
presentation styles,
page 95

Chapter 5
Adding and
Modifying Slide Text

After completing this chapter, you will be able to:

✔ Add and move text on slides.

✔ Change text alignment and spacing.

✔ Find and replace text and fonts.

✔ Correct text while typing.

✔ Check spelling and presentation styles.

In Microsoft PowerPoint, you can add text to your presentation and then modify it to fine-tune your message. You also have complete control over the placement and position of text. PowerPoint offers several alternatives for placing text on your slides: text placeholders for entering slide titles and subtitles, text labels for short notes and phrases, and text boxes for longer text. You can also place text inside objects, such as circles, rectangles, or stars.

The owner of The Garden Company has been working on a training presentation for new gardening class teachers and wants to add and modify supplementary text to fine-tune her message.

In this chapter, you'll create several kinds of text objects, edit text, change the appearance of text, find and replace text, replace fonts, let PowerPoint correct text while you type, check spelling, and check presentation style.

This chapter uses the practice files AddText, AlignText, ReplaceText, CorrectText, and SpellCheck that you installed from this book's CD-ROM. For details about installing the practice files, see "Using the Book's CD-ROM" at the beginning of this book.

Adding and Moving Text on Slides

PP2002-2-2

Approved Courseware

In addition to title and bulleted text, you can also add supplemental text to your slides. While the title and bulleted text appear in the outline and on the slide, the supplemental text appears only on the slide. Before you can add and move supplemental text on slides, you need to know how PowerPoint represents text on slides. An **object** is anything that you can manipulate, including text. For example, the title object on a slide is all of the text in the title, which is treated as a unit. To make formatting changes to all of the text in a text object, you need to first select the object. To select an object, you click a part of the object by using the pointer. To deselect an object, you move the pointer to a blank area of the slide and then click the blank area.

In PowerPoint, you can select a text object in two ways. The first way is to click the text in the text object, which displays a **slanted-line selection box**, consisting of gray slanted lines, around the text object. You can edit any content within the text object; for example, you can type or delete text. The second way is to click the edge of a slanted-line selection box, which selects the entire object. When you select the entire object, a fuzzy outline, called a **dotted selection box**, appears around the text object and is ready for you to edit as an object; that is, you can manipulate it as a unit. The white circles at each corner of either type of selection box are **resize handles**, which you can use to adjust and resize the object. A sample of each selection box is shown in the following illustrations:

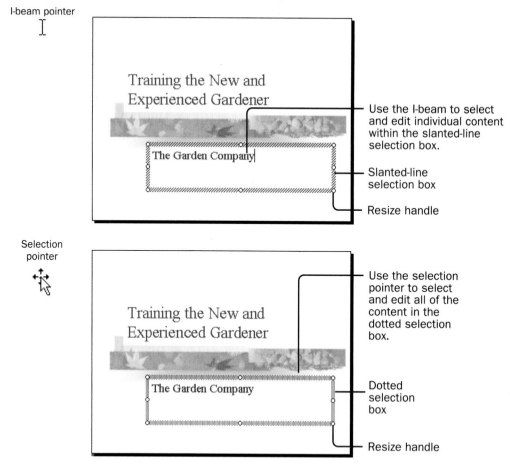

I-beam pointer

Use the I-beam to select and edit individual content within the slanted-line selection box.

Slanted-line selection box

Resize handle

Selection pointer

Use the selection pointer to select and edit all of the content in the dotted selection box.

Dotted selection box

Resize handle

Once you have selected a text object with the dotted selection box, you can move or copy the text object to any place on a slide to change the appearance of a presentation. Dragging a text object is the most efficient way to move or copy it on a slide. The mouse is used to drag a text object from one location to another on a slide. While you drag an object, you can hold down the [Ctrl] key to make a copy of it.

Slides usually contain text boxes for title and bulleted text into which you enter your main ideas. You can also place other text objects on a slide by using the Text Box button on the Drawing toolbar. Text boxes are used when you need to include annotations or minor points that do not belong in a list.

You can create two types of text objects: a **text label**, which is text that does not word wrap within a defined box; and a **word processing box**, which is text that word wraps inside the boundaries of an object. Text labels are usually used to enter short notes or phrases: you use a word processing box for longer text or sentences. You can create a text label on a slide by using the Text Box tool to select a place on the slide where you will begin typing your text. You can create a word processing box by using the Text Box tool to drag the pointer to create a text box of the appropriate width.

Once you have created a word processing box or a text label, you can change one object into the other by changing the word-wrap option and the fit text option in the **Format Text Box** dialog box. You can also reduce the size of a text label to create a word processing box by dragging one of the corner resize handles. The text rewraps to adjust to the new size.

AddText

In this exercise, you select and deselect a text object, move a text object by dragging the edge of the text object's selection box, add text in a text object, and then create a text label and a word processing box.

1   Start PowerPoint, if necessary.

Open

2   On the Standard toolbar, click the **Open** button.

The **Open** dialog box appears.

3   Navigate to the **SBS** folder on your hard disk, double-click the **PowerPoint** folder, double-click the **AddingText** folder, and then double-click **AddText**.

The AddText presentation opens, displaying Slide 1 in Normal view.

4   On Slide 1, click the subtitle object.

The text box is selected with the slanted-line selection box.

5   Position the pointer on top of an edge of the slanted-line selection box.

The pointer changes to the selection pointer, shown in the margin.

Selection
pointer

6   Click the edge of the slanted-line selection box.

The selection box changes to a dotted selection box.

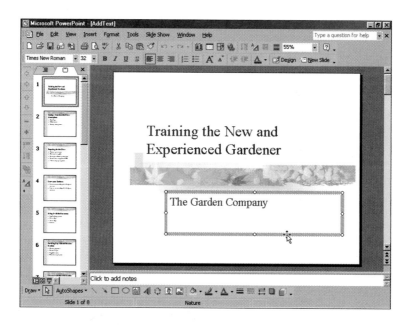

Tip

You can select an object with just one click. Position the pointer above or below the object until it changes to the selection pointer, and then click the slide. The dotted selection box appears.

7   Click outside the selection box in a blank area to deselect the text box.

Tip

To copy a text object, hold down the <kbd>Ctrl</kbd> key, and then drag the selection box of a text object to a new location on the slide.

8   In the Slide pane, drag the scroll box to Slide 3.

9   Double-click the text *TGC* in the bulleted list to select the text.

10   Type **The Garden Company**.

The paragraph wraps in the text object.

Text Box

11   Click in a blank area of the slide to deselect the text box.

12   On the Drawing toolbar, click the **Text Box** button.

Upside-down
T-pointer

The pointer changes to the upside-down T-pointer.

13   Position the pointer at the bottom left of the slide.

14 Click the slide to create a text label.

A small, empty selection box composed of gray slanted lines appears with the blinking insertion point in it.

15 Type **See slide 5 for available resources**.

16 Click the edge of the slanted-line selection box, and then drag the edge of the text to the right.

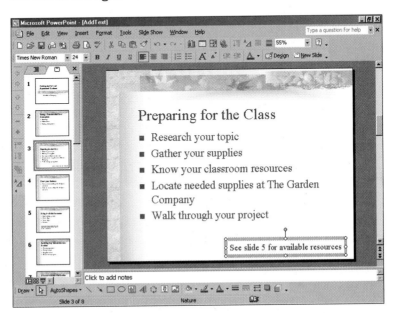

Tip

The text that you create on a slide using the Text Box tool does not appear in Outline view. Only text entered in a title or main text placeholder appears in Outline view.

17 Click a blank area of the slide to deselect the text box.

18 In the Slide pane, drag the scroll box to Slide 5.

Text Box

19 On the Drawing toolbar, click the **Text Box** button.

The pointer changes to the upside-down T-pointer.

20 Position the upside-down T-pointer below the last bullet, and then drag the pointer to create a box that extends approximately three-fourths of the way across the slide.

When you release the mouse button, a slanted-line selection box appears with the blinking insertion point in it.

21 Type **The Garden Company staff can create PowerPoint presentations for you prior to your class session.**

The width of the box does not change, but the words wrap, and the box height increases to accommodate the complete entry.

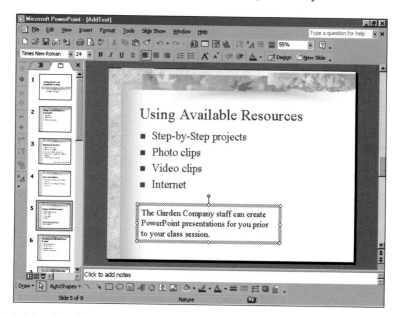

22 Click a blank area of the slide to deselect the text object.

23 On the Standard toolbar, click the **Save** button to save the presentation.

Close Window

24 Click the **Close Window** button in the presentation window.

The AddText presentation closes.

Changing Text Alignment and Spacing

PP2002-2-2

Approved Courseware

PowerPoint enables you to control the way text lines up on the slide. You can align text to the left or right or to the center in a text object. You can also adjust the alignment of text in an object by selecting the object and clicking an alignment button (Align Left, Center, or Align Right) on the Formatting toolbar. The **Align Left** button aligns text evenly along the left edge of the text box and is useful for paragraph text. The **Align Right** button aligns text evenly along the right edge of the text box and is useful for text labels. The **Center** button aligns text in the middle of the text box and is useful for titles and headings. You can also adjust the vertical space between selected lines and the space before and after paragraphs by selecting the object and clicking a line spacing button (Increase Paragraph Spacing or Decrease Paragraph Spacing) on the Formatting toolbar or by using the **Line Spacing** command on the **Format** menu.

A text object can be any size. Sometimes the text within a text object doesn't fill the entire object. PowerPoint allows you to adjust the text object to fit the amount of text. If you draw a shape and add text to it, you can adjust the text to fit inside the object. You can adjust the position of text in a text object by selecting or clearing the **Resize AutoShape to fit text** option on the **Text Box** tab in the **Format AutoShape** dialog box.

In this exercise, you adjust a text object and a text placeholder, change the alignment of text in a text object, decrease paragraph spacing, and adjust line spacing.

AlignText

1 On the Standard toolbar, click the **Open** button.

Open

The **Open** dialog box appears.

2 Navigate to the **SBS** folder on your hard disk, double-click the **PowerPoint** folder, double-click the **AddingText** folder, and then double-click **AlignText**.

The AlignText presentation opens, displaying Slide 1 in Normal view.

3 In the Slide pane, drag the scroll box to Slide 5.

4 Click the bottom text box on Slide 5, and then click the edge of the text box to select it with the dotted selection box.

Two-headed arrow pointer

5 Position the pointer (which changes to the two-headed arrow pointer) over the right middle resize handle of the text box.

6 Drag the resize handle to the right to extend the text box about an inch.

The text box enlarges, and the text wraps to the text object.

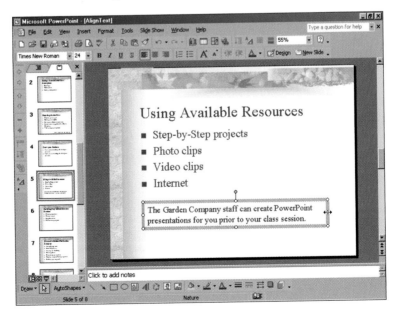

7 On the **Format** menu, click **Text Box**.

The **Format Text Box** dialog box appears.

8 Click the **Text Box** tab.

Format Text Box	? X

Colors and Lines	Size	Position	Picture	Text Box	Web

Text anchor point: Top

Internal margin

Left: 0.1" Top: 0.05"

Right: 0.1" Bottom: 0.05"

☑ Word wrap text in AutoShape

☑ Resize AutoShape to fit text

☐ Rotate text within AutoShape by 90°

OK   Cancel   Preview

9 Clear the **Word wrap text in AutoShape** check box.

10 Click **OK**.

The word processing box changes to a text label and stretches across the slider beyond the slide boundary.

Tip

You can also convert a text label to a word processing box by dragging a resize handle to reduce the width of the text box. The text inside wraps to adjust to the new dimensions of the text box.

Undo

11 On the Standard toolbar, click the **Undo** button.

The word processing box is restored.

Selection pointer

12 Position the pointer near the bulleted text on Slide 5 until it changes to the selection pointer, and then click to select the paragraph text object.

Notice that the dotted selection box is larger than it needs to be.

13 On the **Format** menu, click **Placeholder**.

The **Format AutoShape** dialog box appears.

Tip

The command on the **Format** menu changes, depending on the type of object selected. If you resize a text box, the command on the **Format** menu is **Text Box**, and the dialog box that opens is titled **Format Text Box**.

14 Click the **Text Box** tab to display text spacing and alignment options.

15 Select the **Resize AutoShape to fit text** check box, and then click **OK**.

The object adjusts to fit the size of the text.

16 Click a blank area of the slide to deselect the text box.

17 In the Slide pane, drag the scroll box to Slide 8, and then select the text box at the bottom of the slide.

Center

18 On the Formatting toolbar, click the **Center** button.

The text in the text object aligns to the center of the text box.

Increase Para-
graph Spacing

19 On the Formatting toolbar, click the **Increase Paragraph Spacing** button.

The paragraph spacing in the text box increases by increments of 0.1 lines, from 1.0 to 1.1.

Important

If the **Increase Paragraph Spacing** button is not available on the Formatting toolbar, click the **Toolbar Options** down arrow, and then point to **Add or Remove Buttons** to display a list of additional Formatting buttons, click the button to place it on the toolbar, and then click a blank area of the slide to deselect the menu.

20 Click a blank area of the slide to deselect the text box.

Selection
pointer

21 Click the edge of the bulleted paragraph text box on Slide 8 with the selection pointer.

The dotted selection box appears.

22 On the **Format** menu, click **Line Spacing**.

The **Line Spacing** dialog box appears.

Line Spacing

Line spacing
[1] Lines

Before paragraph
[0.2] Lines

After paragraph
[0] Lines

[OK] [Cancel] [Preview]

23 Click the **Before paragraph** down arrow until **0.1** appears, and then click **OK**.

The paragraph spacing before each paragraph decreases by 0.1 lines.

24 Click a blank area of the slide to deselect the text box.

Tip

Everything that you can do to manipulate a text label or word processing box you can also do to any text object, including title and paragraph text objects.

25 On the Standard toolbar, click the **Save** button to save the presentation.

Close Window

26 Click the **Close Window** button in the presentation window.

The AlignText presentation closes.

Finding and Replacing Text and Fonts

The **Find** and **Replace** commands on the **Edit** menu allow you to locate and change specific text in a presentation. **Find** helps you locate each occurrence of a specific word or set of characters, while **Replace** locates every occurrence of a specific word or set of characters and replaces it with a different one. You can change every occurrence of specific text all at once, or you can accept or reject each change individually. The **Find** and **Replace** commands also give you options for more detailed searches. If you want to search for whole words so that the search doesn't stop on a word that might contain only part of your search word, you select the **Find whole words only** check box. If you want to find a word or phrase that matches a certain capitalization exactly, you select the **Match case** check box. In addition to finding text, you can also find and replace a specific font in a presentation. The **Replace Fonts** command allows you to replace every instance of a font style that you have been using with another.

ReplaceText

In this exercise, you use the **Replace** command to find and replace a word and then replace a font.

1 On the Standard toolbar, click the **Open** button.

Open

The **Open** dialog box appears.

2 Navigate to the **SBS** folder on your hard disk, double-click the **PowerPoint** folder, double-click the **AddingText** folder, and then double-click **ReplaceText**.

The ReplaceText presentation opens, displaying Slide 1 in Normal view.

3 On the **Edit** menu, click **Replace**.

The **Replace** dialog box appears.

4 Click in the **Find what** box, if necessary, and then type **Supplies**.

5 Press the ⇥ key, or click in the **Replace with** box.

6 Type **Supplies and equipment**.

7 Select the **Match case** check box to find the text in the **Find what** box exactly as you typed it.

Replace	? X
Fi_nd what:	Find Next
Supplies ▼	Close
Re_place with:	
Supplies and equipment ▼	Replace
☑ Match case	Replace All
☐ Find whole words only	

8 Click **Find Next**.

PowerPoint finds and selects the word *Supplies* on Slide 6.

Tip

If the dialog box covers up the selected text, move the **Replace** dialog box out of the way by dragging its title bar.

9 Click **Replace**.

PowerPoint replaces the selected text *Supplies* with the text *Supplies and equipment*. An alert box appears, telling you that PowerPoint has finished searching the presentation.

10 Click **OK**, and then click **Close** to close the **Replace** dialog box.

11 Click a blank area of the slide to deselect any text boxes.

12 On the **Format** menu, click **Replace Font**.

The **Replace Font** dialog box appears.

13 Click the **Replace** down arrow, and then click **Arial**.

14 Click the **With** down arrow, scroll down, and then click **Impact**.

15 Click **Replace**.

Throughout the presentation, the text formatted with the Arial font changes to the Impact font.

16 Click **Close** in the **Replace Font** dialog box.

17 In the Slide pane, drag the scroll box to Slide 8.

The Arial font in the bottom text box is now Impact.

18 On the Standard toolbar, click the **Save** button to save the presentation.

Close Window

19 Click the **Close Window** button in the presentation window.

The ReplaceText presentation closes.

Correcting Text While Typing

PP2002-2-2

Approved Courseware

As you type text in a presentation, you might be aware of making typographical errors, but when you look at the text, some of the mistakes have been corrected. With AutoCorrect, PowerPoint corrects common capitalization and spelling errors as you type. For example, if you frequently type *tehm* instead of *them*, you can create an AutoCorrect entry named *tehm*. Then, whenever you type *tehm* followed by a space or a punctuation mark, PowerPoint replaces the misspelling with *them*. You can customize AutoCorrect to recognize or ignore misspellings that you routinely make or to ignore specific text that you do not want AutoCorrect to change. You can also use AutoCorrect to recognize abbreviations or codes that you create to automate typing certain text. For example, you could customize AutoCorrect to type your full name when you type in only your initials.

AutoCorrect Options
new for
OfficeXP

When you point to a word that AutoCorrect changed, a small blue box appears under the first letter. When you point to the small blue box, the **AutoCorrect Options** button appears. The **AutoCorrect Options** button gives you control over whether you want the text to be corrected. You can change text back to its original spelling, or you can stop AutoCorrect from automatically correcting text. You can also display the **AutoCorrect** dialog box and change AutoCorrect settings.

AutoFit Options
new for
OfficeXP

As you type text in a placeholder, PowerPoint uses AutoFit to resize the text, if necessary, to fit into the placeholder. The AutoFit Options button, which appears near your text the first time that it is resized, gives you control over whether you want the text to be resized. The **AutoFit Options** button displays a menu with options for controlling how the option works. For example, you can stop resizing text for the current placeholder while still maintaining your global AutoFit settings. You can also display the **AutoCorrect** dialog box and change the AutoFit settings so that text doesn't resize automatically.

CorrectText

In this exercise, you add an AutoCorrect entry, use AutoCorrect to fix a misspelled word, and then use AutoFit to resize a text box.

1   On the Standard toolbar, click the **Open** button.

Open

The **Open** dialog box appears.

2   Navigate to the **SBS** folder on your hard disk, double-click the **PowerPoint** folder, double-click the **AddingText** folder, and then double-click **CorrectText**.

The CorrectText presentation opens, displaying Slide 1 in Normal view.

3   On the **Tools** menu, click **AutoCorrect Options**, and then click the **AutoCorrect** tab, if necessary.

The **AutoCorrect** dialog box appears.

4   Click in the **Replace** box, if necessary, and then type **likns**.

The word *links* can be easily mistyped as *likns*.

5   Press [Tab], type **links**, and then click **Add**.

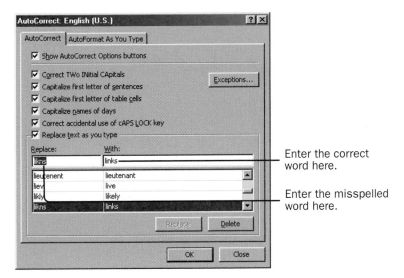

Enter the correct word here.

Enter the misspelled word here.

Now whenever you type *likns* in any presentation, PowerPoint replaces it with *links*.

6   Click **OK**.

7 In the Slide pane, drag the scroll box to Slide 5.

8 Click the blank area immediately after the word *Internet*, press [Space], and then type **likns**.

9 Press [Space].

PowerPoint corrects the word to *links*.

AutoCorrect
Options

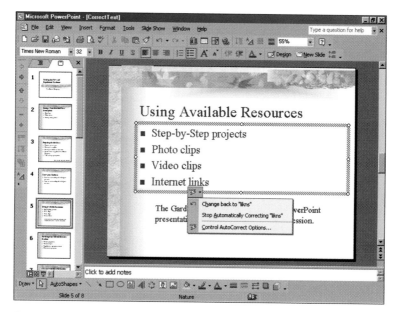

10 Point to the small blue box under the word *links* to display the **AutoCorrect Options** button, and then click the **AutoCorrect Options** down arrow.

11 Click a blank area of the slide to deselect the **AutoCorrect Options** menu.

12 In the Slide pane, drag the scroll box to Slide 7.

13 Click to the right of the word *table* in the last line of the text box, and then press the [Enter] key.

14 Type **Installing a new lawn**.

The text box automatically resizes to fit the text in the box. The **AutoFit Options** button appears to the left of the text box.

AutoFit Options

15 Point to the **AutoFit Options** button, and then click the **AutoFit Options** down arrow.

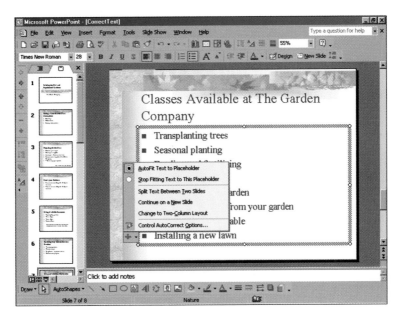

16 Click **Change to Two-Column Layout**.

Another bulleted list appears on the slide.

17 Type **Installing a sprinkler system** in the bulleted list on the right.

18 Click a blank area of the slide to deselect the text box.

19 On the Standard toolbar, click the **Save** button to save the presentation.

Close Window

20 Click the **Close Window** button in the presentation window.

The CorrectText presentation closes.

Checking Spelling and Presentation Styles

PowerPoint's spelling checker checks the spelling of the entire presentation, including all slides, outlines, notes pages, and handout pages. To help you identify misspelled words or words that PowerPoint's built-in dictionary does not recognize, PowerPoint underlines them with a wavy red line. To turn this feature off, you can clear the **Check spelling as you type** check box on the **Spelling and Style** tab of the **Options** dialog box (available on the **Tools** menu). PowerPoint includes several built-in dictionaries, so you can check presentations that use languages other than English. You can also create custom dictionaries in PowerPoint to check the spelling of unique words, or you can use custom dictionaries from other Microsoft programs. If a word is in a foreign language, you can mark it as such, and PowerPoint won't flag it as a misspelling anymore.

You can correct misspelled words in your presentation two different ways. You can use the **Spelling** button on the Standard toolbar to check the entire presentation, or when you encounter a wavy red line under a word, you can right-click the word and choose the correct spelling from the list on the shortcut menu.

PowerPoint's style checker works with the Office Assistant to help you correct common presentation style design mistakes so that your audience focuses on content, not visual mistakes. When the Office Assistant is visible, the style checker reviews the presentation for typical mistakes, such as incorrect font size, too many fonts, too many words, inconsistent punctuation, and other readability problems. The style checker then suggests ways to improve the presentation.

SpellCheck

In this exercise, you mark a word as a foreign language word, select and correct a misspelled word, check spelling in the entire presentation, and then set the style options and check the presentation style.

1   On the Standard toolbar, click the **Open** button.

Open

The **Open** dialog box appears.

2   Navigate to the **SBS** folder on your hard disk, double-click the **PowerPoint** folder, double-click the **AddingText** folder, and then double-click **SpellCheck**.

The SpellCheck presentation opens, displaying Slide 1 in Normal view.

3   In the Slide pane, drag the scroll box to Slide 8.

The words *Je*, *ne*, *saise*, and *quoi* appear with a wavy red underline, indicating that they are misspelled or not recognized by the dictionary.

4   Select the French phrase *Je ne saise quoi* in the text box.

5   On the **Tools** menu, click **Language**.

The **Language** dialog box appears.

6   Scroll down the list, click **French (France)**, click **OK**, and then click in the text box to deselect the French words.

PowerPoint marks the selected words as French words for the spelling checker.

The red lines under correctly spelled words no longer appear, indicating that the dictionary now recognizes the words. For misspelled words, the red lines still appear.

7   Right-click the word *saise*, and then click **sais** on the shortcut menu.

PowerPoint corrects the misspelled word.

Spelling

8   On the Standard toolbar, click the **Spelling** button.

PowerPoint begins checking the spelling in the presentation. The spelling checker stops and selects the proper name *Galos*.

Galos does not appear in your dictionary, but you know it is a proper name that is spelled correctly.

Tip

The custom dictionary allows you to add words that the standard dictionary doesn't recognize. *Galos* is a proper name that you can add to your custom dictionary.

9 Click **Add**.

The word *Galos* is added to the custom dictionary and the spelling checker continues to check the presentation.

Tip

If you do not want to add a name or word to the spelling checker, you can click **Ignore** or **Ignore All**. The spelling checker will ignore the word or all appearances of the word in the current presentation.

10 The spelling checker stops and selects the misspelled word *Saeting*. A list appears in the **Suggestions** box, showing possible correct spellings of the misspelled word. The correct word spelling, *Seating*, appears in the list.

Tip

Click **AutoCorrect** in the **Spelling** dialog box to add the misspelling and the correct spelling of a word to the AutoCorrect table of entries.

11 Click the suggested spelling *Seating*, if necessary, and then click **Change** to correct the spelling.

The spelling checker continues to check the presentation for misspelled words or words not found in the dictionary. A dialog box appears when PowerPoint completes checking the entire presentation.

12 Click **OK** to continue, and then drag the scroll box up to Slide 1.

13 On the **Tools** menu, click **Options**.

The **Options** dialog box appears.

14 Click the **Spelling and Style** tab to display a list of options.

15 Select the **Check style** check box, and then click **Style Options**.

The **Style Options** dialog box appears. If PowerPoint prompts you to enable the Office Assistant, click **Enable Assistant**.

16 Select the **Body punctuation** check box to check for consistent body punctuation in the presentation.

17 Click the **Body punctuation** down arrow, and then click **Paragraphs have consistent punctuation**.

Style Options	? X
Case and End Punctuation	Visual Clarity

Case
- ☑ Slide title style: Title Case ▼
- ☑ Body text style: Sentence case ▼

End punctuation
- ☐ Slide title punctuation: Paragraphs have punctuation ▼
- ☑ Body punctuation: Paragraphs have consistent punctuation ▼

To check for the consistent use of end punctuation other than periods, enter characters in the edit boxes below:

Slide title: [   ]   Body text: [   ]

[OK]   [Cancel]   [Defaults]

18 Click **OK** to close the **Style Options** dialog box, and then click **OK** again to close the **Options** dialog box.

Light bulb

19 In the Slide pane, drag the scroll box to Slide 4.

A light bulb appears on Slide 4.

20 Click the **light bulb**.

Office Assistant

A dialog balloon appears over the Office Assistant, as shown in the margin. The Office Assistant noticed that the text in the placeholder should be capitalized. The default style for title text is to capitalize all words in the title.

Tip

If you make a decision on a tip and then change your mind, you may need to display the tip again. To do this, you need to reset your tips so that the Office Assistant will display all of them again. To reset your tips, right-click the **Office Assistant**, click **Options**, click **Reset my tips**, and then click **OK**.

21 Click the **Change the text to title case** option.

PowerPoint capitalizes the word *Your* in the title. The dialog balloon disappears.

22 On the Standard toolbar, click the **Save** button to save the presentation.

Close Window

![X]

23 Click the **Close Window** button in the presentation window.

The SpellCheck presentation closes.

Changing Capitalization

As part of the style checking process, PowerPoint checks the text case, such as capitalization, of sentences and titles in the presentation, but you can independently change text case for selected text with a command on the **Format** menu. The **Change Case** command allows you to change text to sentence case, title case, uppercase, lowercase, or toggle case, which is a mixture of cases.

To change the text case:

1 Select the text that you want to change.

2 On the **Format** menu, click **Change Case**.

The **Change Case** dialog box appears with the **Sentence case** option set as the default.

3 Click the change case option that you want to apply to the selected text.

4 Click **OK** to apply the change option to the presentation.

Chapter Wrap-Up

To finish the chapter:

Close

![X]

● On the **File** menu, click **Exit**, or click the **Close** button in the PowerPoint window.

PowerPoint closes.

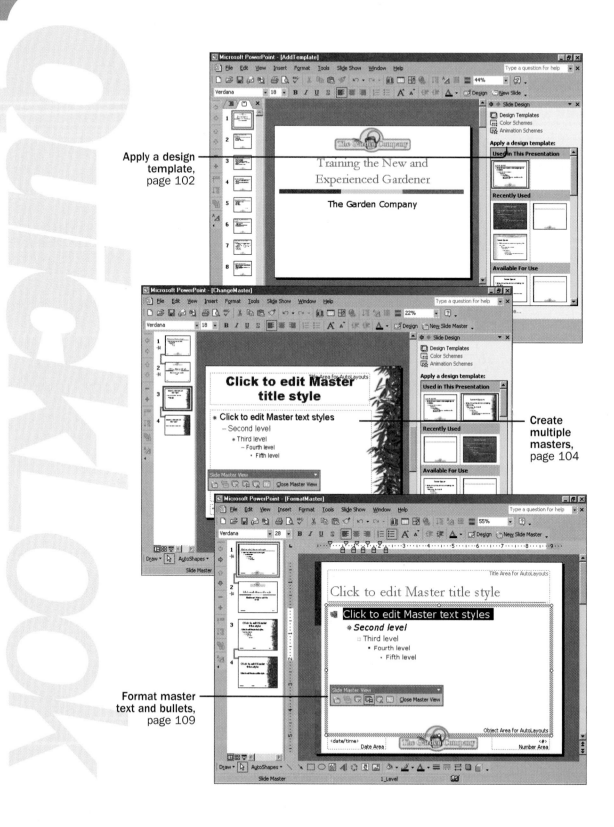

Apply a design template, page 102

Create multiple masters, page 104

Format master text and bullets, page 109

Chapter 6
Applying and Modifying Design Templates

After completing this chapter, you will be able to:

✔ **Apply a design template to a presentation.**

✔ **Make your presentation look consistent.**

✔ **Format master text and bullets.**

✔ **Save a presentation as a design template.**

A **template** is a presentation file that has a predefined set of color and text characteristics. You can create a presentation from a template, or you can apply a template to an existing presentation. When you apply a template to a presentation, the slides in the presentation take on the characteristics of the template, so you can maintain a uniform design throughout. PowerPoint uses masters that control the look of the individual parts of the presentation, including formatting, color, graphics, and text placement, to maintain a uniform design. Every presentation has a set of masters, one for each view.

The owner of The Garden Company has been working on a training presentation for new gardening class teachers and wants to apply an older company presentation design template to her new presentation. She then wants to make some modifications to update the design.

In this chapter, you'll apply a PowerPoint template, view and switch to various masters, change the display for master objects, modify and format the master text, and save a presentation as a template.

 This chapter uses the practice files AddTemplate, ApplyTemplate, ChangeMaster, FormatMaster, and SaveTemplate that you installed from this book's CD-ROM. For details about installing the practice files, see "Using the Book's CD-ROM" at the beginning of this book.

Applying a Design Template to a Presentation

PP2002-4-1

Approved Courseware

PowerPoint comes with a wide variety of professionally designed templates that can help you achieve the look that you want. When you apply a template to a presentation, PowerPoint copies the information from each master in the template to the corresponding masters in the presentation. All slides in a presentation will then acquire the look of the template.

You can use one of the many templates that come with PowerPoint, or you can create your own from existing presentations. Moreover, you can apply different templates throughout the development process until you find the look that you like best. To apply a template to an existing presentation, you open the presentation and then use the **Slide Design** task pane to locate and select the template that you want.

AddTemplate
ApplyTemplate

Open

In this exercise, you apply a template to an existing presentation.

1   Start PowerPoint, if necessary.

2   On the Standard toolbar, click the **Open** button.

The **Open** dialog box appears.

3   Navigate to the **SBS** folder on your hard disk, double-click the **PowerPoint** folder, double-click the **Applying** folder, and then double-click the **AddTemplate** file.

The AddTemplate presentation opens, displaying Slide 1 in Normal view.

Slide Design

Design

4   On the Formatting toolbar, click **Slide Design**.

The Slide Design task pane opens.

5   In the **Slide Design** task pane, click **Design Templates**.

6   At the bottom of the **Slide Design** task pane, click **Browse**.

The **Apply Design Template** dialog box appears.

7   Navigate to the **SBS** folder on your hard disk, double-click the **PowerPoint** folder, and then double-click the **Applying** folder.

8   In the list of file and folder names, click **ApplyTemplate**.

9   Click **Apply**.

PowerPoint applies, or copies, the information from the template file ApplyTemplate to the masters in the presentation. The text style and format, slide colors, and background objects change to match the template. Your content remains the same.

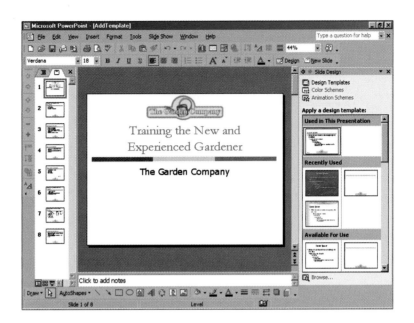

Close

10 In the **Slide Design** task pane, click the **Close** button to close the task pane.

11 On the Standard toolbar, click the **Save** button to save the presentation.

Close Window

12 Click the **Close Window** button in the presentation window.

The AddTemplate presentation closes.

Reapplying a Slide Layout

If you make changes to the layout of a slide but then decide you would rather use the original slide layout, you can reapply the original slide layout to that slide.

To reapply a slide layout:

1 Display the slide to which you want to reapply a slide layout.

2 On the **Format** menu, click **Slide Layout** to display the **Slide Layout** task pane.

3 Click the down arrow next to the original slide layout that you want to apply.

4 On the menu, click **Reapply Layout**.

PowerPoint reapplies the slide layout.

Making Your Presentation Look Consistent

PP2002-4-4
PP2002-4-5
PP2002-4-6

Approved Courseware

PowerPoint comes with two special slides called **masters**—Slide Master and Title Master. The Slide Master and Title Master for a template are called a slide-title master pair. You can create more than one Slide Master or Title Master within a presentation. This is useful for creating separate sections within the same presentation. To create multiple masters in a presentation, you can insert a new Slide Master and Title Master in a presentation or apply more than one template to your presentation.

Multiple masters
new for
OfficeXP

The **Slide Master** controls the properties of every slide in the presentation. All of the characteristics of the Slide Master (background color, text color, font, and font size) appear on every slide in the presentation. When you make a change on the Slide Master, the change affects every slide. For example, if you want to include your company logo, other artwork, or the date on every slide, you can place it on the Slide Master. The Slide Master contains master placeholders for title text, paragraph text, date and time, footer information, and slide numbers. The master title and text placeholders control the text format for every slide in a presentation. If you want to make a change throughout your presentation, you need to change each slide master or pair of masters. For example, when you change the master title text format to italic, the title on each slide changes to italic to follow the master. If, for a particular slide, you want to override the default settings on the Slide Master, you can use commands on the **Format** menu. For example, if you want to omit background graphics on a slide, you can use that option in the **Background** dialog box for the selected slide.

The title slide has its own master, called the **Title Master**. Changes that you make to the Title Master affect only the title slide of the presentation. Like the Slide Master, the Title Master contains placeholders. The main difference between the Slide Master and the Title Master is the Title Master's use of a master subtitle style instead of the master text style. The Slide Master and Title Master appear together in Slide Master view. You can select either master as a slide miniature in Slide Master view to make changes to it. When you view a master, the Master toolbar appears. This toolbar contains the **Close Master View** button, which returns you to the view you were in before you opened the Master. The Master toolbar also contains several buttons to insert, delete, rename, duplicate, and preserve masters. When you preserve a master, you protect it from being deleted.

Each master contains placeholders. Background objects, such as text and graphics, that are entered into placeholders will appear on every page associated with that master. Examples of objects that you may want to include are your company name, logo, or product name. You can modify and arrange placeholders on all of the master views for the date and time, footers, and slide numbers, all of which appear on the Slide Master in the default position. You can also customize the position of the placeholders. PowerPoint also comes with a Handout Master and a Notes Pages Master, where you can add text and graphics.

ChangeMaster

In this exercise, you view the Title Master and the Slide Master, switch between them, preserve the original masters, insert a second slide master and title master, switch to Handout Master and Notes Master, remove the footer from the title slides, and then edit the master placeholders on the Slide Masters.

Open

1 On the Standard toolbar, click the **Open** button.

The **Open** dialog box appears.

2 Navigate to the **SBS** folder on your hard disk, double-click the **PowerPoint** folder, double-click the **Applying** folder, and then double-click the **ChangeMaster** file.

The ChangeMaster presentation opens, displaying Slide 1 in Normal view.

3 On the **View** menu, point to **Master**, and then click **Slide Master**.

The Title Master appears along with the **Slide Master View** toolbar. Slide miniatures of the Title Master and Slide Master appear in the Slides pane on the left side of the presentation window.

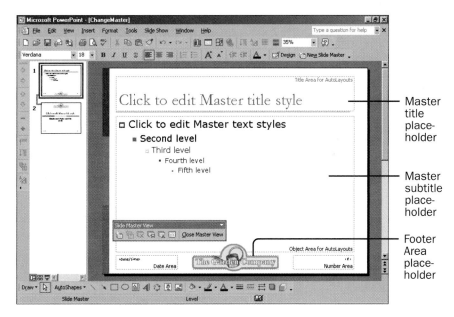

Troubleshooting

If you don't have a Title Master, you can create one by switching to the Slide Master and clicking **New Title Master** on the **Insert** menu.

4 In the Slides pane, click Slide 1.

The Slide Master slide appears.

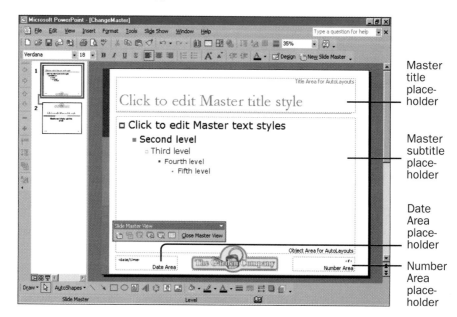

Master title place-holder

Master subtitle place-holder

Date Area place-holder

Number Area place-holder

Tip

You can allow or prevent multiple masters in a presentation. On the **Tools** menu, click **Options**, click the **Edit** tab. Under **Disable New Features**, clear the **Multiple masters** check box to allow multiple design templates to be applied, or select the **Multiple masters** check box to restrict design templates to one per presentation.

Preserve Master

5 On the **Slide Master View** toolbar, click the **Preserve Master** button.

A gray thumbtack appears next to both slide masters in the Slides pane, protecting them from being deleted or changed by PowerPoint.

Insert New Slide Master

6 On the **Slide Master View** toolbar, click the **Insert New Slide Master** button.

Slide 3 appears below Slide 2 with a blank slide design.

Insert New Title Master

7 On the **Slide Master View** toolbar, click the **Insert New Title Master** button.

Slide 4 appears below Slide 3 with a blank title slide design and the slide-title master pair is connected together.

8 On the **Slide Master View** toolbar, click the **Preserve Master** button.

An alert message appears, asking if you want to delete these masters since they are currently not used on any slides.

9 Click **No**.

The gray thumbtack next to both new slide masters disappears, and the masters are no longer protected from being deleted or changed.

Slide Design

![Design]

10 On the Formatting toolbar, click **Slide Design**, and then in the **Slide Design** task pane, click **Design Templates**, if necessary.

11 In the **Slide Design** task pane, under **Apply a design template**, scroll down to the **Bamboo** design, and then click the design template.

The new slide masters appear with the Bamboo design.

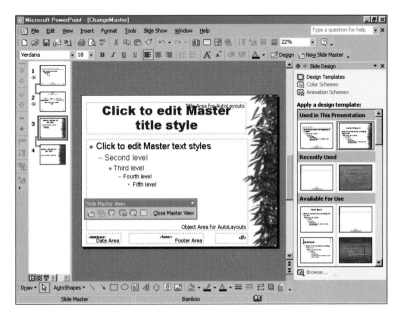

Troubleshooting

If the Bamboo design is not available, insert the Office XP CD-ROM into the drive, scroll to the bottom of the design templates in the **Slide Design** task pane, and then click **Additional Design Templates** or click **Browse** at the bottom of the **Slide Design** task pane, navigate to the **Applying** folder, and then double-click the **Bamboo** template file.

12 On the **View** menu, point to **Master**, and then click **Handout Master**.

The Handout Master and **Handout Master View** toolbar appear.

Show positioning of 3-per-page handouts

13 On the **Handout Master View** toolbar, click the **Show positioning of 3-per-page handouts** button.

The master changes to show three handouts per page.

Tip

Using the Handout Master View toolbar, you can show the positioning of one, two, three, four, six, or nine slides per page.

14 On the **View** menu, point to **Master**, and then click **Notes Master**.

The Notes Master appears, showing the slide and speaker note text positioning for the notes pages, along with the Notes Master View toolbar.

15 On the **Notes Master View** toolbar, click **Close Master View**.

PowerPoint returns you to the first slide in the presentation in Slide view.

Tip

You can also exit a master view and switch back to Normal view by clicking the **Normal View** button.

16 In the Slide pane, drag the scroll box to Slide 7.

17 In the **Slide Design** task pane, under **Used in This Presentation**, point to the **Bamboo** design scheme, click the down arrow on the scheme, and then click **Apply to Selected Slides**.

PowerPoint applies the Bamboo design to only Slide 7.

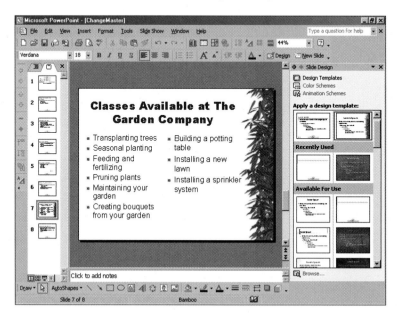

Slide Design

Design

18 In the **Slide Design** task pane, click the **Close** button to close the task pane.

19 On the **View** menu, click **Header and Footer**.

The **Header and Footer** dialog box appears.

20 Select the **Slide number** check box, and then select the **Don't show on title slide** check box.

21 Click **Apply to All**, and then scroll up to Slide 1 in the Slide pane.

The slide footer information disappears from the Slide 1, which is a title slide.

Next Slide

22 Click the **Next Slide** button to view Slide 2.

The slide footer information remains on the rest of the slides.

23 On the Standard toolbar, click the **Save** button to save the presentation.

Close Window

24 Click the **Close Window** button in the presentation window.

The ChangeMaster presentation closes.

Formatting Master Text and Bullets

PP2002-4-4

Approved Courseware

Formatting the placeholders in Slide Master view provides consistency to a presentation. The master placeholders for the title, bulleted text, date and time, slide number, and footer determine the style and position of those objects. To format master text, you first select the text placeholder and then alter the format to look the way you want. To format bulleted text, you have to place the insertion point in the line of the bulleted text that you want to change.

In addition to formatting text, PowerPoint allows you to customize the bullets in a presentation for individual paragraphs or entire objects. You can replace a bullet with a different font style and color, a picture, or a number.

PowerPoint uses indent markers to control the distance between bullets and text. Adjusting indents in PowerPoint works the same way it does in Microsoft Word. To change the distance between a bullet and its corresponding text, you first display the ruler, which shows the current bullet and text placement, and then adjust indent markers on the ruler. The indent markers on the ruler control the indent levels of the master text object. Each indent level consists of two triangles, called **indent markers**, and a small box, called a **margin marker**. The upper indent marker controls the first line of the paragraph; the lower indent marker controls the left edge of the paragraph. Each indent level is set so that the first line extends to the left of the paragraph, with the rest of the paragraph "hanging" below it. This indent setting is called a **hanging indent**. To adjust an indent marker, you move the triangle on the ruler to a new position. You can move the entire level—the bullet and text—by using the margin marker.

FormatMaster

In this exercise, you format a master text placeholder, format master bullets with a different symbol and picture, display the ruler, adjust indent markers, adjust the margin level, and hide the master objects on a slide background.

1 On the Standard toolbar, click the **Open** button.

Open

The **Open** dialog box appears.

2 Navigate to the **SBS** folder on your hard disk, double-click the **PowerPoint** folder, double-click the **Applying** folder, and then double-click **FormatMaster**.

The FormatMaster presentation opens, displaying Slide 1 in Normal view.

3 On the **View** menu, point to **Master**, and then click **Slide Master**.

The Slide Master view appears, displaying Slide 2, the Slide Master.

4 In the Slides pane, click Slide 1, and then click the **Number Area** placeholder to select the object.

5 On the Formatting toolbar, click the **Font Size** down arrow, and then click **18**.

6 Click a blank area outside of the master text placeholder to deselect it.

7 In the master text placeholder, position the I-beam cursor to the right of the text *Second level*, and then click a blank area to place the insertion point.

Italic

I

8 On the Formatting toolbar, click the **Italic** button.

The text *Second level* changes to italic.

9 Click a blank area outside of the master text placeholder to deselect it.

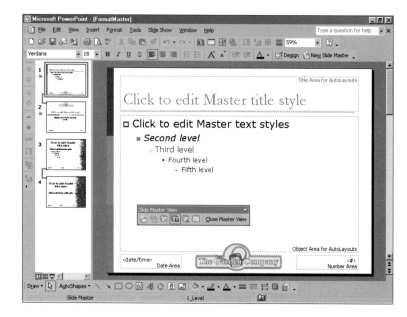

10 On the Slide Master, click the first line of text titled *Click to edit Master text styles* in the master text placeholder.

The first bullet in the lower master text placeholder is selected.

Tip

If you delete a placeholder by mistake, you can click **Master Layout** on the **Format** menu, click the appropriate placeholder check box, and then click **OK** to reapply the placeholder, or you can click the **Undo** button.

11 On the **Format** menu, click **Bullets and Numbering**.

The **Bullets and Numbering** dialog box appears, displaying the current bullet symbol.

12 Click the **Size** up arrow until **100** appears, increasing the size of the bullet.

Tip

You can click a different bullet color, adjust the size percentage, change the symbol by selecting another one or by using the **Picture** or **Customize** command, or change the bullets to numbers.

13 Click **Picture**.

The **Picture Bullet** dialog box appears.

14 Click the **Nature** bullet in the upper-left corner, if necessary, as shown in the following illustration:

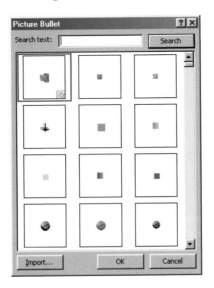

Tip

You can use a scanned image or other photograph to replace a bullet. In the **Picture Bullet** dialog box, click **Import**, select the image that you want to import in the **Add Clips To Organizer** dialog box, and then click **Add**. The image appears as one of the choices in the **Picture Bullet** dialog box.

15 Click **OK**.

16 Right-click the second line of text titled *Second level* in the master text place-holder.

PowerPoint selects the text, and a shortcut menu appears.

17 Click **Bullets and Numbering** on the shortcut menu.

18 Click **Customize**.

The **Symbol** dialog box appears.

19 Scroll down the font list, and then click the symbol shown in the following illustration:

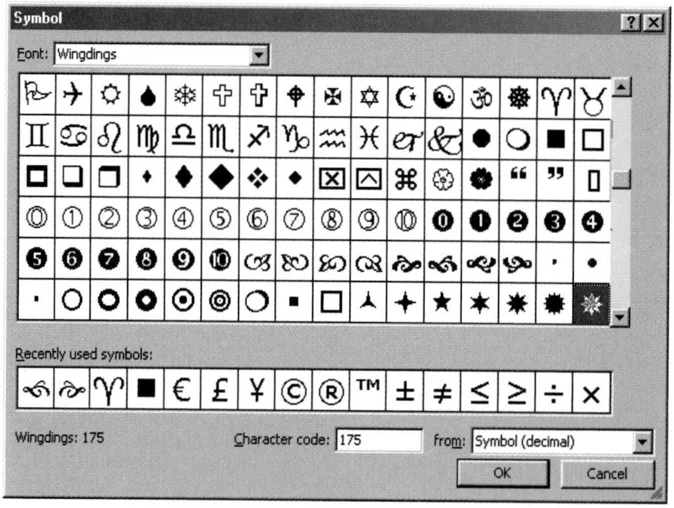

20 Click **OK** to display the **Bullets and Numbering** dialog box.

21 Click the **Size** up arrow until **85** appears, increasing the size of the bullet, and then click **OK**.

Slide Master view appears with the new bullets and sizes.

Tip

You can also hide master objects in PowerPoint. For individual slides, you may want to hide background objects, such as date and time, header and footer, slide number placeholders, graphics, shapes, and lines, so that they do not appear on the screen. On the **Format** menu, click **Background** to display the **Background** dialog box, select the **Omit background graphics from master** check box, and then click **Apply**.

22 On the **View** menu, click **Ruler**, if necessary, to display the ruler.

23 Click the master text placeholder titled *Click to edit Master title style*.

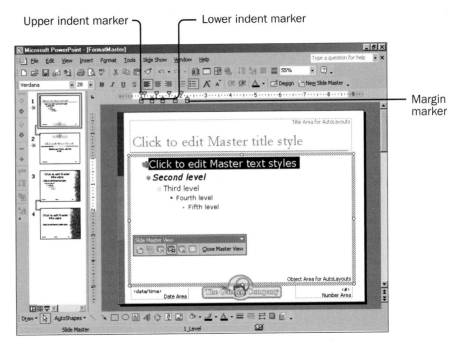

24 Click the line of text titled *Click to edit Master text styles* in the master text placeholder.

The ruler adds indent markers for each level of text represented in the bulleted list. Five pairs of indent markers appear—upper and lower.

Indent markers

25 Drag the indent marker of the first indent level on the left side of the ruler to the right, so that it is aligned with the lower indent marker, as shown in the illustration on the next page.

Move the upper indent marker to here.

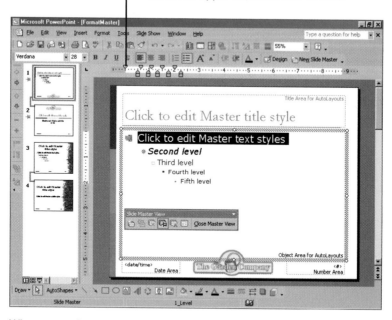

When you release the mouse button, the text for the first indent level moves to the right.

Margin marker

26 Slowly drag the **margin marker** of the first indent level on the left side of the ruler to the left margin of the ruler.

The bullet, text, and indent markers move to the left margin.

Important

If you drag an indent level or margin marker into another indent level, the first indent level (or marker) pushes the second indent level until you release the mouse button. To move an indent marker back to its original position, drag the indent level's margin marker, or click the **Undo** button.

Moving the first margin marker repositions the left margin of the master text object.

Tip

If the indent markers are not aligned over one another, drag one of the markers back to the other. Also, depending on the size of your monitor, indent changes may be subtle and hard to detect.

27 Drag the lower indent marker of the first indent level to the 0.5 inch mark on the ruler.

The first indent level of the ruler is formatted again as a hanging indent. Your presentation window should look like the following illustration:

Move the lower indent marker to here.

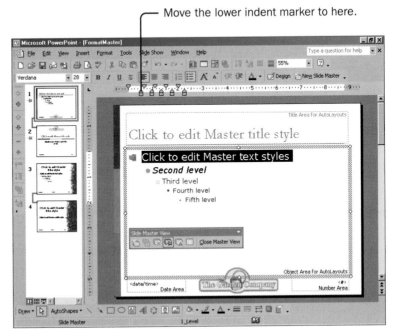

28 On the **Slide Master View** toolbar, click the **Close Master View** button.

PowerPoint returns you to Slide 1.

Next Slide

29 Click the **Next Slide** button to move to Slide 2.

30 On the Standard toolbar, click the **Save** button to save the presentation.

Close Window

31 Click the **Close Window** button in the presentation window.

The FormatMaster presentation closes.

Saving a Presentation as a Design Template

PP2002-4-5

Approved Courseware

After customizing the masters, you can save the presentation as a new design template, which you can apply to other presentations.

SaveTemplate

Open

In this exercise, you save a presentation as a design template.

1 On the Standard toolbar, click the **Open** button.

The **Open** dialog box appears.

2 Navigate to the **SBS** folder on your hard disk, double-click the **PowerPoint** folder, double-click the **Applying** folder, and then double-click the **SaveTemplate** file.

The SaveTemplate presentation opens, displaying Slide 1 in Normal view.

3 On the **File** menu, click **Save As**.

The **Save As** dialog box appears.

4 In the **File name** box, type **DesignTemplate**.

5 Click the **Save as type** down arrow, and then click **Design Template**.

PowerPoint displays the **Templates** folder.

Tip

Whenever you save a new template as a design template, it is included as a choice in the **Slide Design** task pane for future PowerPoint presentations.

6 Navigate to the **SBS** folder on your hard disk, double-click the **PowerPoint** folder, and then double-click the **Applying** folder.

7 Click **Save**.

PowerPoint saves the template in the **Applying** folder.

8 On the Standard toolbar, click the **Save** button to save the presentation.

Close Window

9 Click the **Close Window** button in the presentation window.

The SaveTemplate presentation closes.

Chapter Wrap-Up

To finish the chapter:

Close

● On the **File** menu, click **Exit**, or click the **Close** button in the PowerPoint window.

PowerPoint closes.

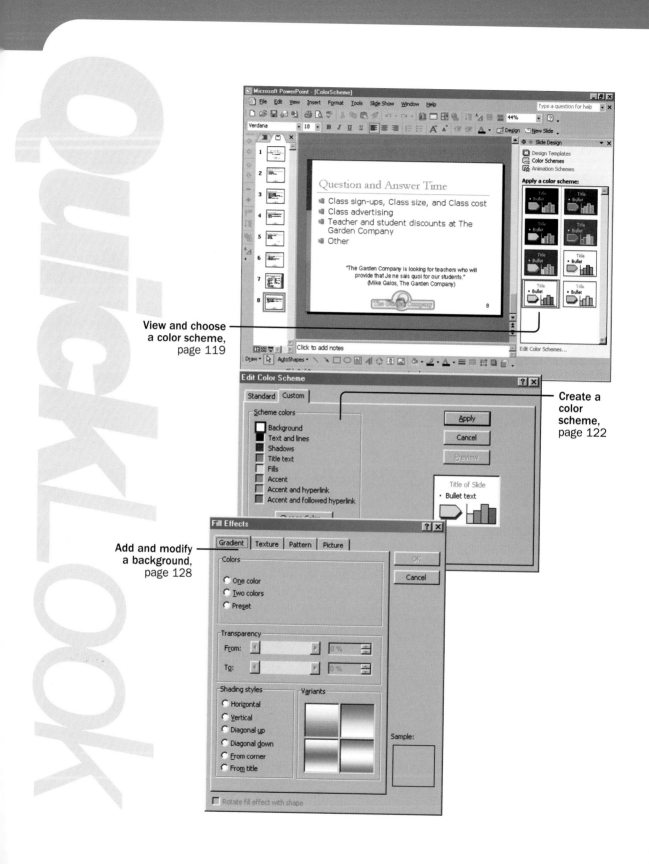

View and choose a color scheme, page 119

Create a color scheme, page 122

Add and modify a background, page 128

Chapter 7
Viewing and Changing Presentation Colors

After completing this chapter, you will be able to:

✔ View and choose a color scheme.

✔ Create a color scheme.

✔ Add colors to a presentation.

✔ Add and modify a slide background.

Every presentation, even a blank one, contains a set of colors called a color scheme. A **color scheme** is a set of eight colors designed to be used as the colors in slide presentations. The color scheme determines the colors for the background, text, lines, shadows, fills, and accents of slides. Using Microsoft PowerPoint's color scheme capabilities, you can experiment with different colors and schemes until you find the combination of colors that you like for an aesthetically pleasing design.

The owner of The Garden Company has been working on a training presentation for new gardening class teachers and wants to change the presentation colors to match the company colors.

In this chapter, you'll view and choose a color scheme, change colors in a color scheme, create a color scheme, add more colors, add a background to a slide, copy a color scheme to a slide, and create a textured background.

This chapter uses the practice files ColorScheme, CreateScheme, AddColor, and AddBackgrnd that you installed from this book's CD-ROM. For details about installing the practice files, see "Using the Book's CD-ROM" at the beginning of this book.

Viewing and Choosing a Color Scheme

Every presentation has at least one color scheme. A presentation with more than one set of slide masters can have more than one color scheme. A color scheme can be a set of custom colors that you choose, or it can be the default color scheme. Understanding color schemes helps you create professional-looking presentations that use an appropriate balance of color for your presentation content.

Slide Design task pane

new for OfficeXP

To view your presentation's color scheme, click **Color Schemes** in your **Slide Design** task pane. The **Slide Design** task pane displays your presentation's current color scheme with a selection rectangle and other custom color schemes that you can apply to your presentation. To edit a color scheme, click **Edit Color Schemes** at the bottom of the task pane. The **Edit Color Scheme** dialog box allows you to change the colors in your color scheme, choose a different color scheme, or create your own color scheme. Once you find the look that you want, you can apply the color scheme to one or all of the slides in a presentation.

The default color schemes in PowerPoint are made up of a palette of eight colors. These colors appear on the menu when you click the **Fill Color** or **Font Color** down arrow on the Drawing toolbar. These eight colors correspond to the following elements in a presentation:

- **Background** This color is the canvas, or drawing area, color of the slide.
- **Text and lines** This color contrasts with the background color. It is used for typing text and drawing lines.
- **Shadows** This color is generally a darker shade of the background.
- **Title text** This color contrasts with the background color.
- **Fills** This color contrasts with both the Background color and the Text and lines color.
- **Accent** This color is designed to work as a complementary color for objects in the presentation.
- **Accent and hyperlink** This color is designed to work as a complementary color for objects and hyperlinks.
- **Accent and followed hyperlink** This color is designed to work as a complementary color for objects and visited hyperlinks.

ColorScheme

In this exercise, you examine the current color scheme of a presentation and then choose another color scheme.

1 Start PowerPoint, if necessary.

Open

2 On the Standard toolbar, click the **Open** button.

The **Open** dialog box appears.

3 Navigate to the **SBS** folder on your hard disk, double-click the **PowerPoint** folder, double-click the **Coloring** folder, and then double-click **ColorScheme**.

The ColorScheme presentation opens, displaying Slide 1 in Normal view.

4 In the Slide pane, drag the scroll box to Slide 8.

Slide Design

5 On the Formatting toolbar, click the **Slide Design** button, and in the **Slide Design** task pane, click **Color Schemes**.

Color Scheme choices appear in the task pane, showing a preview of the current color scheme used in the slide master, indicated by the box surrounding it, and other available presentation color schemes.

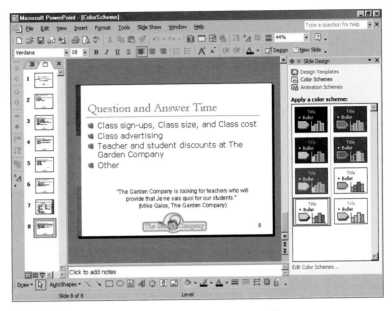

6 In the Slide pane, drag the scroll box to Slide 7.

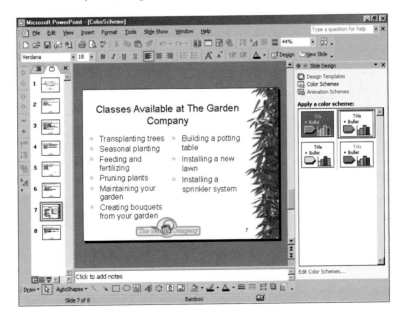

7 In the **Slide Design** task pane, click the last color scheme on the right.

The colors on Slide 7 now correspond to the new color scheme. The colors on the other slides remain the same.

Close

8 In the **Slide Design** task pane, click the **Close** button to close the task pane.

9 On the Standard toolbar, click the **Save** button to save the presentation.

Close Window

10 Click the **Close Window** button in the presentation window.

The ColorScheme presentation closes.

Creating a Color Scheme

You can modify any or all of the colors within a color scheme to create your own color combinations. You can apply your color scheme changes to the current slide or to the entire presentation. For example, you might want to create a customized color scheme that complements your company's logo. To change colors, you open the **Edit Color Schemes** dialog box from the Color Schemes section of the Slide Design task pane and then use the **Change Color** feature available on the **Custom** tab. You can select colors from a standard color palette or specify a color based on **RGB** (Red, Green, and Blue) values. A large percentage of the visible spectrum is represented by mixing red, green, and blue colors. When you specify a value for Red, Green, and Blue, the mixing of the shades creates a color.

You can create a new color scheme by changing the existing color scheme and then adding the color scheme to the standard set of color schemes available. The color schemes are available on the **Slide Design** task pane and the **Standard** tab of the **Edit Color Scheme** dialog box.

CreateScheme

In this exercise, you change a color in a color scheme, add a new color scheme to the presentation's set of color schemes, and then delete a color scheme.

1 On the Standard toolbar, click the **Open** button.

Open

The **Open** dialog box appears.

2 Navigate to the **SBS** folder on your hard disk, double-click the **PowerPoint** folder, double-click the **Coloring** folder, and then double-click **CreateScheme**.

The CreateScheme presentation opens, displaying Slide 1 in Normal view.

3 In the Slide pane, drag the scroll box to Slide 8.

Slide Design

4 On the Formatting toolbar, click the **Slide Design** button to open the **Slide Design** task pane.

5 In the **Slide Design** task pane, click **Color Schemes**.

Color Scheme choices appear in the task pane.

6 Click **Edit Color Schemes** at the bottom of the **Slide Design** task pane.

The **Edit Color Scheme** dialog box appears, showing the **Custom** tab. The **Custom** tab displays a grid of eight colored boxes that correspond to the selected color scheme. These eight colors make up the presentation's current color scheme.

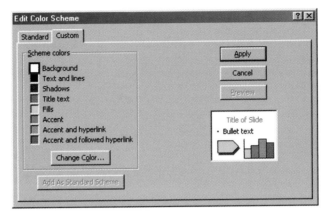

7   In the **Scheme colors** area, click the **Title text** color box to select the color.

8   Click **Change Color**.

The **Title Text Color** dialog box appears, showing the **Standard** tab, which displays a color palette of standard colors from which to choose.

9   In the color palette, click the green color, as shown in the following illustration:

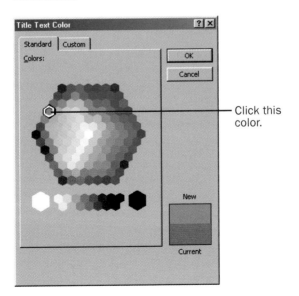

Click this color.

The current color and the new color appear in the lower right-corner of the **Title Text Color** dialog box.

10 Click **OK**.

The **Title Text** color box changes to green in the color scheme.

11 Click **Apply**.

The new color scheme appears at the bottom of the **Slide Design** task pane. The slide titles are now green. PowerPoint applies the change to all of the slides, except Slide 7, which uses a different master slide.

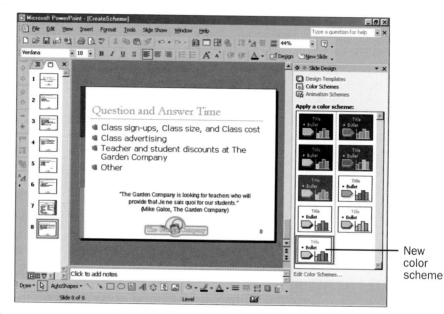

New color scheme

12 In the **Slide Design** task pane, click **Edit Color Schemes**.

The **Edit Color Scheme** dialog box appears, showing the **Custom** tab.

13 Double-click the **Fills** color box, and then click the **Custom** tab.

The **Fill Color** dialog box appears, showing the **Custom** tab.

14 In the **Green** box, type **243**.

The RGB setting 255, 243, 0 appear in the **Fill Color** dialog box. This RGB color matches the yellow color in the company logo.

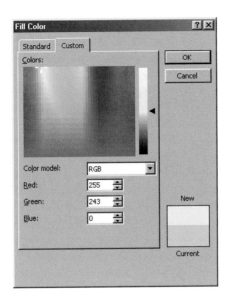

15 Click **OK**.

The **Edit Color Scheme** dialog box appears, and the **Fills** color box changes to yellow.

16 Click **Add As Standard Scheme** to create a new color scheme.

The **Add As Standard Scheme** button is dimmed, indicating that the color scheme has been added to the color scheme list.

17 Click the **Standard** tab.

The new color scheme appears with a selection box.

18 Click the color scheme box in the third row and third column.

The **Edit Color Scheme** dialog box should look like the following illustration:

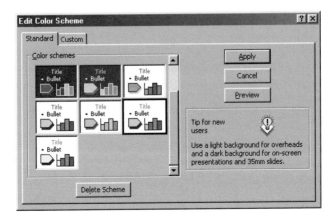

19 Click **Delete Scheme**.

The color scheme is deleted.

Tip

When you delete a color scheme, you cannot undo the operation and retrieve the color scheme.

20 Click **Apply**.

A new color scheme appears in the **Slide Design** task pane while an existing one is removed. The fill color for drawn shapes is now yellow to match the company logo. PowerPoint applies the change to all of the slides, except Slide 7.

Close

21 In the **Slide Design** task pane, click the **Close** button to close the task pane.

Tip

You can reuse color schemes without having to recreate them. You simply select the slide in the **Slides** tab with the color scheme that you want to reuse, click the **Format Painter** button on the Standard toolbar to copy or pick up the color scheme, and then click another slide to apply the color scheme. You can also use the Format Painter to copy a color scheme from one presentation and apply it to another.

22 On the Standard toolbar, click the **Save** button to save the presentation.

Close Window

23 Click the **Close Window** button in the presentation window.

The CreateScheme presentation closes.

Adding Colors to a Presentation

In addition to the eight basic color scheme colors, PowerPoint allows you to add more colors to your presentation. **More colors** are additional colors that you can add to each of the toolbar button **color menus**—the **Font Color** button menu, for example. More colors are useful when you want an object or picture to always have the same color. They are also useful when you want to change the color of an object to a specific color but the presentation color scheme does not have that color. Colors that you add to a specific color menu appear in all color menus and remain in the menu even if the color scheme changes.

AddColor

In this exercise, you add a color to the menus.

1 On the Standard toolbar, click the **Open** button.

Open

The **Open** dialog box appears.

2 Navigate to the **SBS** folder on your hard disk, double-click the **PowerPoint** folder, double-click the **Coloring** folder, and then double-click **AddColor**.

The AddColor presentation opens, displaying Slide 1 in Normal view.

3 In the Slide pane, drag the scroll box to Slide 5.

Selection pointer

4 Move the pointer to the edge of the text object above the logo so that the pointer changes to the selection pointer, and then select the text object to display the dotted selection box.

Font Color

5 On the Drawing toolbar, click the **Font Color** down arrow.

A menu appears.

6 On the menu, click **More Colors**.

7 In the color palette, click the dark maroon color, as shown in the following illustration:

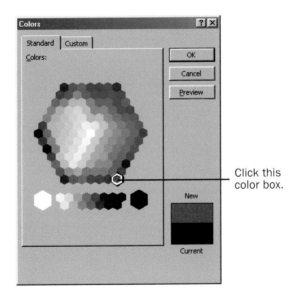

Click this color box.

8 Click **OK**.

The text in the selected object changes to the dark maroon color, and the colored bar on the **Font Color** button appears with the currently selected color—in this case, dark maroon.

Font Color

9 On the Drawing toolbar, click the **Font Color** down arrow.

The color that you just added appears on the second line of color choices and is now available to use throughout the presentation.

The **Font Color** menu should look like the following illustration:

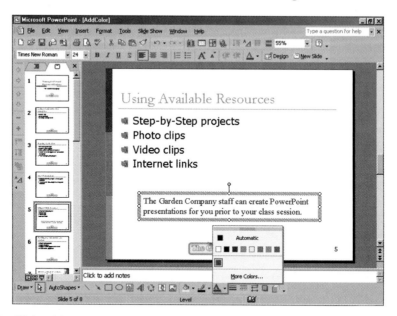

10 Click a blank area in the presentation window to close the menu.

11 On the Standard toolbar, click the **Save** button to save the presentation.

Close Window

12 Click the **Close Window** button in the presentation window.

The AddColor presentation closes.

Adding and Modifying a Slide Background

PP2002-3-2

Approved Courseware

In PowerPoint, you can create a special **background** on a slide by adding a shade, a texture, a pattern, or even a picture. A shaded background is a visual effect in which a solid color gradually changes from light to dark or dark to light. PowerPoint offers one-color and two-color shaded backgrounds with six styles: horizontal, vertical, diagonal up, diagonal down, from corner, and from title. For a one-color shaded background, the shading color can be adjusted lighter or darker, depending on your needs. You can also choose a preset color background, one of 24 professionally designed backgrounds in which the color shading changes direction according to the shading style selected.

In addition to a shaded background, you can also have a background with a texture, a pattern, or a picture. PowerPoint has several different textures, patterns, and pictures that you can apply to a presentation.

AddBackgrnd

Open

In this exercise, you add a shade to a slide background and then change the background from shaded to textured.

1 On the Standard toolbar, click the **Open** button.

The **Open** dialog box appears.

2 Navigate to the **SBS** folder on your hard disk, double-click the **PowerPoint** folder, double-click the **Coloring** folder, and then double-click **AddBackgrnd**.

The AddBackgrnd presentation opens, displaying Slide 1 in Normal view.

3 In the Slide pane, drag the scroll box to Slide 7.

4 On the **Format** menu, click **Background**.

The **Background** dialog box appears.

5 Click the **Background fill** down arrow, as shown in the following illustration:

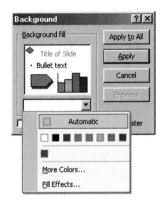

6 On the **Background Fill** menu, click **Fill Effects**.

The **Fill Effects** dialog box appears, showing four tabs: **Gradient**, **Texture**, **Pattern**, and **Picture**, with the **Gradient** tab on top. This tab shows three color options, six shading styles, and four variants for the selected colors. Currently, no colors or shading style are selected.

7 In the **Colors** area, click the **One color** option.

The **Color 1** list appears.

8 Click the **Color 1** down arrow, and then click the Green color box on the submenu.

9 In the **Colors** area, drag the scroll box all the way to the right, the lightest range.

10 In the **Shading styles** area, click the **Vertical** option.

The Shading variant boxes to the right change to vertical styles.

11 In the **Variants** area, click the upper-right shading box.

The **Sample** box shows you a preview of your selection.

12   Click **OK**.

The **Background** dialog box appears.

13   Click **Apply**.

PowerPoint applies the shaded background only to the current slide.

Tip

You can add or change a slide background picture. On the **Format** menu, click **Background**, click the **Background fill** down arrow, click **Fill Effects**, click the **Picture** tab, click **Select Picture**, find the folder that contains the picture that you want, double-click the file name, and then click **OK**. To apply the change to the current slide, click **Apply**. To apply the change to all slides, click **Apply to All**.

14   In the Slide pane, drag the scroll box to Slide 1.

15   On the **Format** menu, click **Background**.

The **Background** dialog box appears.

16   Click the **Background fill** down arrow, and then click **Fill Effects**.

The **Fill Effects** dialog box appears.

17   Click the **Texture** tab, and then click the **White marble** textured fill in the second row and second column.

The **White marble** name appears at the bottom of the dialog box.

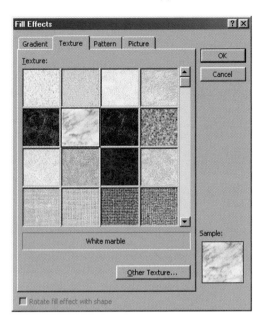

18 Click **OK** to display the Background dialog box, and then click **Apply**.

PowerPoint applies the textured background only to the current slide.

19 On the **Format** menu, click **Background**.

The **Background** dialog box appears.

20 Click the **Background fill** down arrow, and then click the White color box.

The textured background changes back to white.

21 Click **Apply to All**.

PowerPoint applies the background to all of the slides in the presentation.

22 On the Standard toolbar, click the **Save** button to save the presentation.

Close Window

23 Click the **Close Window** button in the presentation window.

The AddBackgrnd presentation closes.

Chapter Wrap-Up

To finish the chapter:

Close

● On the **File** menu, click **Exit**, or click the **Close** button in the PowerPoint window.

PowerPoint closes.

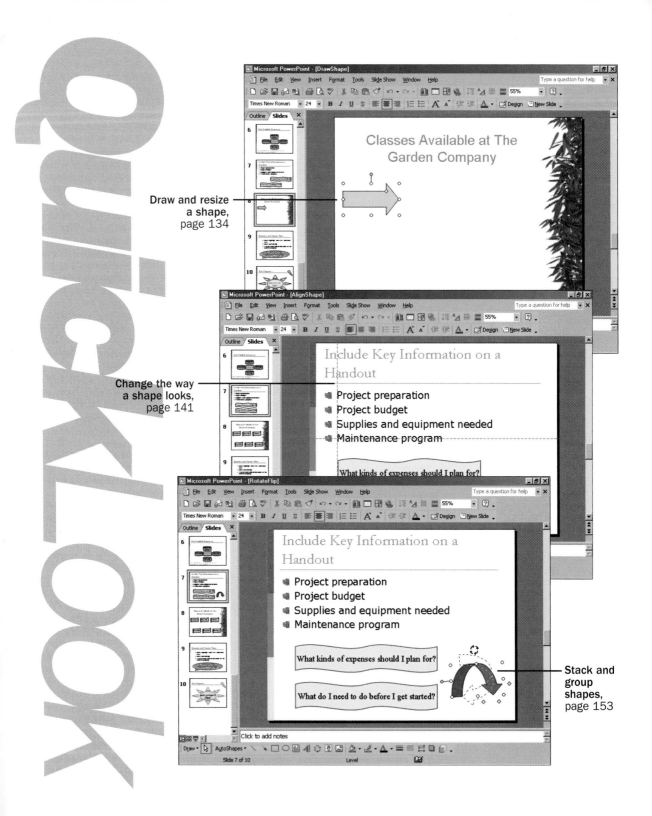

Draw and resize a shape, page 134

Change the way a shape looks, page 141

Stack and group shapes, page 153

Chapter 8
Drawing and Modifying Shapes

After completing this chapter, you will be able to:

✔ Draw and resize a shape.
✔ Copy and move a shape.
✔ Change the way a shape looks.
✔ Align shapes.
✔ Connect shapes.
✔ Add 3-D effects to shapes.
✔ Change the stacking order of shapes.
✔ Rotate and flip shapes.
✔ Draw and edit an arc shape.
✔ Group and ungroup shapes.

In addition to meaningful text, an effective presentation also includes shapes and pictures that complement and enhance the message. You can use PowerPoint to draw objects and modify their attributes, which include size, line style, color, and shading.

The owner of The Garden Company has been working on a training presentation for gardening teachers and is now ready to draw and modify shapes to enhance the text.

In this chapter, you'll draw and resize shapes, copy and move shapes, change the way a shape looks, align, connect, and add 3-D effects to shapes, change the stacking order of shapes, rotate and flip shapes, draw and edit arcs, and group and ungroup shapes.

This chapter uses the practice files DrawShape, CopyMove, ChangeShape, Align-Shape, ConnectShape, 3DShape, StackShape, RotateFlip, DrawArc, and GroupShape that you installed from this book's CD-ROM. For details about installing the practice files, see "Using the Book's CD-ROM" at the beginning of this book.

Drawing and Resizing a Shape

The shapes that you draw, the pictures that you import from other programs, and the text that you type are all examples of objects. You draw all objects in PowerPoint using the same technique, except for freeform objects, which are made up of multiple lines and curves. To draw an object, you select a drawing tool from the Drawing toolbar or **AutoShapes** menu, and then you drag the pointer to create the object.

Resizing, copying, pasting, moving, cutting, and deleting are editing commands that you can use on any object. To edit an object, you must first select it. After you draw an object, it appears selected. To select another object, you click any visible part of that object. To deselect an object, you move the pointer off the object and click in a blank area of the slide. You can apply attributes only to objects that are selected.

Banner

Often you'll draw an object or import a picture that isn't the right size for the slide. To change the size of an object, you drag the white squares, called **resize handles** or sizing handles. Some PowerPoint objects—such as triangles, parallelograms, rounded rectangles, and arrows—are adjustable. **Adjustable objects** have an adjustment handle (which looks like a small, yellow diamond) positioned on one side of the object next to a resize handle. This handle allows you to alter the appearance of the object without changing its size. The banner in the margin illustrates an object with two adjustment handles.

DrawShape

In this exercise, you draw an object using a drawing tool from the **AutoShapes** menu, and then you select, deselect, resize, and adjust an object.

1 Start PowerPoint, if necessary.

2 On the Standard toolbar, click the **Open** button.

Open

The **Open** dialog box appears.

3 Navigate to the **SBS** folder on your hard disk, double-click the **PowerPoint** folder, double-click the **Drawing** folder, and then double-click the **DrawShape** file.

The DrawShape presentation opens, displaying Slide 1 in Normal view.

4 In the Slide pane, drag the scroll box to Slide 2.

5 On the Drawing toolbar, click **AutoShapes**.

6 Point to **Stars and Banners**, and then point to the **5-Point Star** in the first row.

5-Point Star

7 Click the **5-Point Star** button.

In the presentation window, the pointer changes to the cross-hair pointer.

Tip

You can draw a proportional object by holding down the [Shift] key or the [Ctrl] key while you draw. Holding down [Shift] maintains the proportions of the object while holding down [Ctrl] draws the object from its center outward.

Cross-hair
pointer

+

8   Position the cross-hair pointer in the lower-right corner of the slide, hold down [Shift] (which maintains the proportions of the object), and then drag to draw a 5-point star shape, as shown in the following illustration:

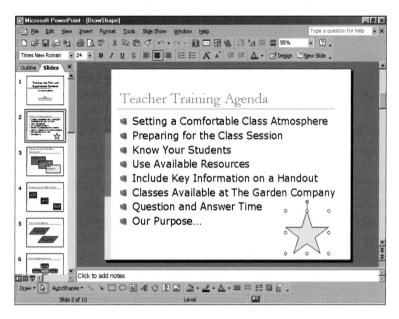

Tip

You can turn off a drawing tool by clicking its button on the Drawing toolbar or by pressing the [Esc] key.

The 5-point star shape appears with white circles on each side of the object, indicating that the object is selected.

Tip

When you draw an object, PowerPoint uses the colors from the current color scheme for the fill and line colors. You can change the default settings for the object, such as line style or fill color. Select the object with the default settings that you want to change, click **Draw** on the Drawing toolbar, and then click **Set AutoShape Defaults**.

9 In the Slide pane, drag the scroll box to Slide 8.

10 Click the arrow object.

The arrow object is selected.

11 Click outside of the arrow object in a blank area of the slide.

The arrow object is deselected.

12 Select the arrow object.

Resize handles appear around the edges of the object.

13 Drag the arrow's right-middle resize handle to match the following illustration:

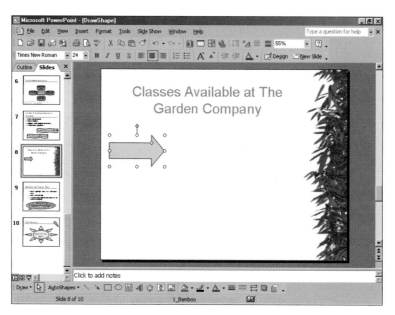

Horizontal two-headed arrow

↔

When you position the pointer over a resize handle, the pointer changes to a small two-headed arrow, indicating the directions in which you can resize the object. As the object is resized, a dotted outline of the object appears, indicating what the object will look like when you release the mouse button.

Adjustment pointer

▷

14 Position the pointer on the arrow object's adjustment handle (the yellow diamond).

The pointer changes to the adjustment pointer.

15 Drag the adjustment handle to the left, but do not release the mouse button.

Notice that dragging the adjustment handle changes the shape of the arrowhead but leaves the size of the arrow the same. As you adjust the object, a dotted outline of the object appears, indicating what the object will look like when you release the mouse button.

136

16 Drag the adjustment handle back to its approximate original position.

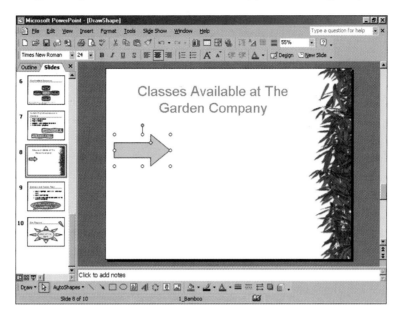

Tip

PowerPoint allows you to work with objects outside of the slide area in the background portion of the presentation window. This can be helpful if you want to include special instructions or sidebar information in the presentation. Any objects in the gray area will not print or display during a slide show.

17 On the Standard toolbar, click the **Save** button to save the presentation.

Close Window
☒

18 Click the **Close Window** button in the presentation window.

The DrawShape presentation closes.

Copying and Moving a Shape

Office
Clipboard task
pane
new for
OfficeXP

You can copy a selected object or multiple objects to the **Office Clipboard** and then paste the objects in other parts of the presentation. You can use the Office Clipboard in the task pane to store multiple items of information from several different sources in one storage area shared by all Office programs. Unlike the Windows Clipboard, which stores only a single item of information at a time, the Office Clipboard allows you to copy multiple items of text or pictures from one or more presentations. When you copy multiple items, the Office Clipboard in the task pane appears and shows all of the items that you stored there. You can paste these items of information into any Office program, either individually or all at once.

Clipboard icon

If you prefer, you can change the way the Office Clipboard works by turning on and off the Office Clipboard options in the task pane. Changing the options allows you to display the Office Clipboard when copying items, copy items to the Office Clipboard without displaying the Office Clipboard, display the **Clipboard** icon in the status area of the taskbar when the Office Clipboard is turned on, and display the collected item ScreenTip in the status area of the taskbar when copying items to the Office Clipboard. To access these options, you click **Options** at the bottom of the **Office Clipboard** task pane. To manually open the Office Clipboard, you click **Office Clipboard** on the **Edit** menu or double-click the **Clipboard** icon on the taskbar.

You can also copy an object to another location in a single movement by using the Ctrl key or by using the **Duplicate** command on the **Edit** menu. To use the Ctrl key, select the object that you want to copy, hold down Ctrl, and then drag; as you drag, a copy of the original object follows the mouse pointer.

CopyMove

In this exercise, you copy and move an object and then select, deselect, and copy multiple objects.

1 On the Standard toolbar, click the **Open** button.

Open

The **Open** dialog box appears.

2 Navigate to the **SBS** folder on your hard disk, double-click the **PowerPoint** folder, double-click the **Drawing** folder, and then double-click the **CopyMove** file.

The CopyMove presentation opens, displaying Slide 1 in Normal view.

3 In the Slide pane, drag the scroll box to Slide 8.

4 Click the arrow to select the object.

Copy

5 On the Standard toolbar, click the **Copy** button.

A copy of the arrow is stored on the Office Clipboard.

Paste

6 On the Standard toolbar, click the **Paste** button.

A copy of the arrow is pasted on the slide and overlaps the original arrow.

Tip

If the Office Clipboard already contains one or more items, it appears when you copy another item.

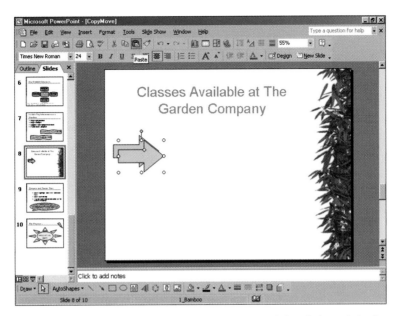

7   Drag the new arrow about half an inch to the right of the original arrow and up to align the two objects.

As the object moves, a dotted outline of the arrow appears, indicating where the new location will be when you release the mouse button.

Tip

To constrain an object's movement horizontally or vertically, hold down `Shift` while you drag the object.

Copy pointer

8   Hold down `Ctrl`, position the mouse pointer over the second arrow, and then hold down the mouse button.

The pointer changes to the Copy pointer.

9   While still holding down `Ctrl`, drag the arrow about a half an inch to the right of the second arrow.

Tip

You can work with several objects at once by selecting all of them. You can select and deselect multiple objects by using `Shift` or by using a selection box.

A copy of the object appears to the right of the other two.

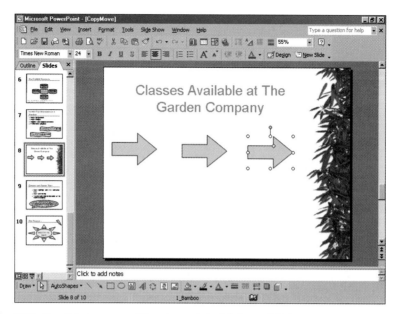

10 With the third arrow still selected, hold down [Shift], and then click the first two arrows.

The initially selected object remains selected, and the first two objects are added to the selection.

11 Hold down [Shift], and then click the middle object again.

The object is removed from the selection.

12 Click a blank area of the slide to deselect the arrow objects.

13 Position the pointer on the left edge of the slide, just below the title.

14 Drag a selection box to the bottom-right corner, enclosing and selecting all three objects within the marquee.

All three objects are selected.

15 On the Standard toolbar, click the **Copy** button.

The Office Clipboard appears in the **Clipboard** task pane.

Troubleshooting

Clipboard icon

If the Office Clipboard doesn't appear, you can double-click the **Clipboard** icon on the taskbar, or on the **Edit** menu, click **Office Clipboard**.

16 In the **Office Clipboard** task pane, click the item with the three arrows.

A copy of the three arrows is pasted on the slide, overlapping the original arrows.

Selection pointer

17 With all three copy arrows still selected, position the pointer over one of the arrows so that the pointer changes to the selection pointer, and then drag the copied arrows down and to the right, as shown in the following illustration:

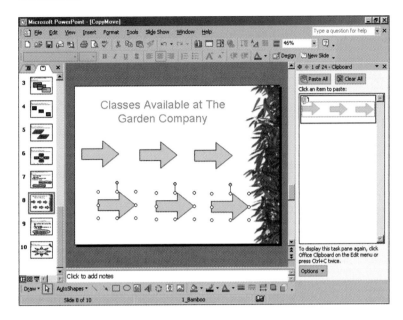

Tip

Multiple copies of the same object appear only once in the Office Clipboard.

18 In the **Office Clipboard** task pane, click **Clear All** to remove all of the items in the Office Clipboard.

19 Click the **Close** button in the **Office Clipboard** task pane.

20 On the Standard toolbar, click the **Save** button to save the presentation.

Close Window

[X]

21 Click the **Close Window** button in the presentation window.

The CopyMove presentation closes.

Changing the Way a Shape Looks

Objects have attributes that define how they appear on the slide. An object has graphic attributes—such as fill, line, shape, and shadow—and text attributes—such as style, font, color, embossment, and shadow. Objects that you draw usually have a fill and a border or frame. Before you can modify these attributes, you must first select the objects that you want to change.

For example, you can change the line style of the frame of the object to complement the textured fill for the presentation, or you can give an object a shadow to help create a three-dimensional appearance. When you give an object a shadow, you can also choose the color of the shadow and its **offset**, the direction in which it falls from the object. As part of the text attributes, you can add text to an object. When you add text to an object, PowerPoint centers the text as you type, and the text becomes part of the object. You can add text to only one object at a time. You can format text in an object by selecting the object and then using the formatting buttons to achieve the look that you want. Using the **Format Painter** command, you can copy a set of styles from selected text and objects and apply them to other selected text and objects.

If you created an object using an AutoShape, PowerPoint allows you to change the shape to another shape with one easy command. With the shape selected, you click **Change AutoShape** on the **Draw** menu on the Drawing toolbar.

ChangeShape

In this exercise, you change the shape of an object and add text to it, modify an object's fill and frame, add and modify an object's shadow, change the text color and style, and format text with the Format Painter command.

1   On the Standard toolbar, click the **Open** button.

Open

The **Open** dialog box appears.

2   Navigate to the **SBS** folder on your hard disk, double-click the **PowerPoint** folder, double-click the **Drawing** folder, and then double-click the **Change-Shape** file.

The ChangeShape presentation opens, displaying Slide 1 in Normal view.

3   In the Slide pane, drag the scroll box to Slide 8.

4   Click the first arrow to select the object.

5   Hold down ⇧ Shift , and then click each of the arrows on the slide to select them.

All six arrows are selected.

Draw

Draw ▾

6   On the Drawing toolbar, click **Draw**, point to **Change AutoShape**, and then point to **Stars and Banners**. The **Stars and Banners** submenu appears.

7   On the submenu, click the **Change Shape to Horizontal Scroll** shape in the fourth row.

The selected arrow shapes change to the scroll shape. The new scroll shape fits in the same area and keeps the same attributes as the original arrow shape.

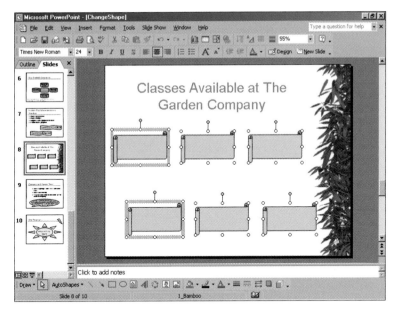

8   Click a blank area of the slide to deselect the objects.

9   Click the top-left scroll object, and then type **Trees/Shrubs**.

When you click an object, a slanted-line selection box appears around it, indicating that the object is ready for you to enter or edit text, as shown in the following illustration:

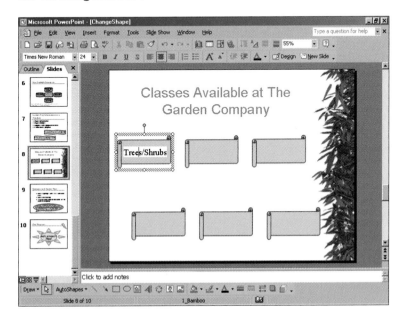

10 Click the top-middle object, and then type **Lawn Care** to enter text into the object.

A slanted-line selection box appears around the object.

11 Click the top-right object, and then type **Flowers** to enter text into the object.

12 In the lower-left object, type **Indoor Plants**; in the lower-middle object, type **Transplanting**; and then in the lower-right object, type **Landscaping**.

13 Click a blank area of the slide to deselect the object.

14 In the Slide pane, drag the scroll box to Slide 10.

15 Select the sun object.

The sun object is selected with the dotted selection box.

Fill Color

16 On the Drawing toolbar, click the **Fill Color** down arrow.

A drop-down menu appears with a number of fill options.

17 On the **Fill Color** menu, click **Fill Effects**.

The **Fill Effects** dialog box appears.

18 Click the **Texture** tab to display a list of textured fills.

19 Click the **Water Droplets** textured fill (the first box in the fifth row), as shown in the following illustration:

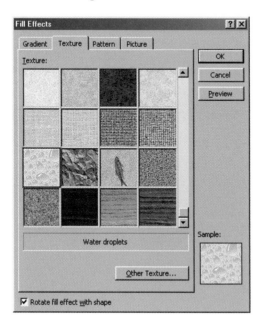

Tip

You can click **Other Texture** to add new textures from the installation CD-ROM or the Web to the list of current textured fills.

20 Click **OK**.

The sun is filled with the new texture and remains selected.

Line Color

21 On the Drawing toolbar, click the **Line Color** down arrow.

A drop-down menu appears with a selection of line colors.

22 On the **Line Color** menu, click the Orange **Follow Accent Scheme Color** box.

The new line color is applied to the object and remains selected.

Shadow Style

23 On the Drawing toolbar, click the **Shadow Style** button.

The **Shadow** drop-down menu appears with a selection of shadow styles.

Shadow Style 6

24 On the **Shadow** menu, click **Shadow Style 6** button (the second box in the second row), as shown in the following illustration:

The shadow is applied to the object.

Shadow Style

25 On the Drawing toolbar, click the **Shadow Style** button, and then click **Shadow Settings**.

The **Shadow Settings** toolbar appears.

Nudge Shadow
Down

26 On the **Shadow Settings** toolbar, click the **Nudge Shadow Down** button five times.

The shadow increases incrementally.

Shadow Color

27 On the **Shadow Settings** toolbar, click the **Shadow Color** down arrow, and then click the Orange **Follow Accent Scheme Color**.

The shadow color changes to a semitransparent orange to match the outline.

Tip

Shadow
On/Off

To turn off a shadow, you can either click the **Shadow On/Off** button on the **Shadow Settings** toolbar or click **No Shadow** on the **Shadow** drop-down menu.

28 On the **Shadow Settings** toolbar, click the **Close** button.

The **Shadow Settings** toolbar closes.

Font Color

29 On the Drawing toolbar, click the **Font Color** down arrow, and then click in the Blue **Custom Color** box.

The text inside the object turns blue.

Bold

30 On the Formatting toolbar, click the **Bold** button.

The text inside the object becomes bold.

31 On the Formatting toolbar, click the **Font** down arrow, scroll down the font list, and then click **Comic Sans MS**.

The text inside the object changes to the Comic Sans MS font.

Format Painter

32 On the Standard toolbar, click the **Format Painter** button.

Format Painter
pointer

PowerPoint copies and stores the specific text and object styles of the selected text object. The standard pointer changes to the Format Painter pointer, as shown in the left margin.

33 Click the lightning bolt object to copy the format to the object.

PowerPoint applies all of the formats from the sun object to the lightning bolt object.

Tip

To apply the Format Painter to multiple items throughout the presentation, double-click the **Format Paint** button. When you finish applying the Format Painter, press `Esc`.

34 Click a blank area of the slide to deselect the object.

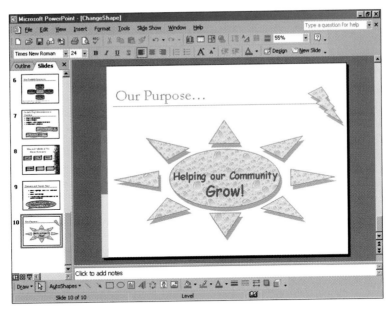

35 On the Standard toolbar, click the **Save** button to save the presentation.

Close Window

36 Click the **Close Window** button in the presentation window.

The ChangeShape presentation closes.

Aligning Shapes

PowerPoint uses two fundamentally different ways of aligning a group of objects: aligning objects to each other or aligning them to a guide.

The **Align or Distribute** command aligns two or more objects relative to each other vertically to the left, center, or right. You can also align objects horizontally to the top, middle, or bottom. To align several objects to each other, you select them and then choose an alignment option.

Visible grid
new for
OfficeXP

PowerPoint guides can align an individual object or a group of objects to a vertical or horizontal guide. Turning on the visible grid or visible guides option makes it easier to create, modify, and align a shape. Within the **Grid and Guides** dialog box, you can select from a variety of options, such as snapping objects to the grid or to other objects and displaying drawing guides on-screen. To align several objects to a guide, you first turn the guides on. Then you adjust the guides and drag the objects to align them to the guide.

AlignShape

In this exercise, you align an object to another object and then align an object to guides.

1 On the Standard toolbar, click the **Open** button.

Open

The **Open** dialog box appears.

2 Navigate to the **SBS** folder on your hard disk, double-click the **PowerPoint** folder, double-click the **Drawing** folder, and then double-click the **AlignShape** file.

The AlignShape presentation opens, displaying Slide 1 in Normal view.

3 In the Slide pane, drag the scroll box to Slide 7.

4 In the Slide pane, hold down ⌈shift⌋, and then select both double wave shapes.

Draw

Draw ▾

5 On the Drawing toolbar, click **Draw**, point to **Align or Distribute**, and then click **Align Center**.

The objects align vertically to each other at their centers.

6 On the **View** menu, click **Grid and Guides**.

The **Grid and Guides** dialog box appears.

7 Select the **Display grid on screen** check box, and then click **OK** to close the **Grid and Guides** dialog box.

8 If necessary, reselect the two objects, hold down ⌈shift⌋, and then drag the selected objects to the left until their left edges touch or snap to the grid.

9 On the **View** menu, click **Grid and Guides**.

The **Grid and Guides** dialog box appears.

10 Clear the **Display grid on screen** check box, select the **Display drawing guides on screen** check box, and then click **OK** to close the **Grid and Guides** dialog box.

Vertical and horizontal dotted lines appear in the center of the slide, indicating that the guides are turned on.

Tip

You can press ⌈Alt⌋+⌈F9⌋ to quickly turn the guides on and off and press ⌈shift⌋+⌈F9⌋ to quickly turn the grid on and off.

11 Position the pointer on the vertical guide in a blank area of the slide, and then drag the guide to the left of the objects.

As you drag, the pointer changes to a Guide indicator, and a number appears, shown in inches, indicating how far you are from the center of the slide.

12 Drag the vertical guide left until the Guide indicator is aligned with the bulleted text.

Tip

If the Guide indicator skips numbers as you drag the guides across the slide, you can clear the **Snap objects to grid** check box in the **Grid and Guides** dialog box. When you select the **Snap objects to grid** check box, objects snap to a grid of evenly spaced lines, helping you align the objects.

13 If necessary, reselect the two objects, hold down $\boxed{\text{Shift}}$, and then drag the selected objects to the right until their left edges touch or snap to the vertical guide.

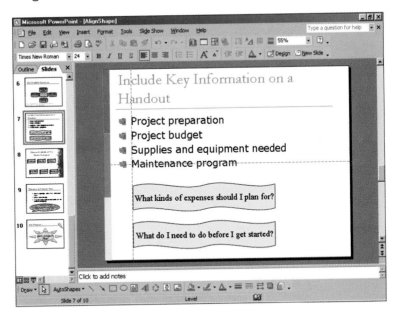

14 Press $\boxed{\text{Alt}}$+$\boxed{\text{F9}}$ to turn off the guides.

15 On the Standard toolbar, click the **Save** button to save the presentation.

Close Window

16 Click the **Close Window** button in the presentation window.

The AlignShape presentation closes.

Connecting Shapes

Connection
pointer

PowerPoint makes it easy to draw and modify flow charts and diagrams. Flow charts and diagrams consist of shapes connected together to indicate a sequence of events. With PowerPoint, you can join two objects with a connecting line. Once two objects are joined, the connecting line moves when you move either object. The connecting line touches special connection points on the objects. When you position the pointer over an object, small blue handles, known as **connection sites**, appear, and the pointer changes to a small box, called the **connection pointer**, shown in the left margin. You can drag a connection end point to another connection point to change the line or drag the adjustment handle to change the shape of the connection line.

ConnectShape

In this exercise, you connect two objects and then change and format a connector line.

1   On the Standard toolbar, click the **Open** button.

Open

The **Open** dialog box appears.

2   Navigate to the **SBS** folder on your hard disk, double-click the **PowerPoint** folder, double-click the **Drawing** folder, and then double-click the **Connect-Shape** file.

The ConnectShape presentation opens, displaying Slide 1 in Normal view.

3   In the Slide pane, drag the scroll box to Slide 4.

Elbow
Double-Arrow
Connector

4   On the Drawing toolbar, click **AutoShapes**, point to **Connectors**, and then click the **Elbow Double-Arrow Connector** button in the second row.

5   Position the pointer over the top object.

Small, blue handles appear, and the pointer changes to a small box, called the connection pointer.

6   Position the center of the pointer halfway up the right side of the top object (over the outer blue handle), and then click the object to select a connection point.

7   Position the pointer halfway up the left side of the middle object (over the outer blue handle), and then click the object to select another connection point.

Round, red handles appear at each end of the line, indicating that the objects are connected. A yellow, diamond-shaped handle appears in the middle of the connector lines so that you can resize the curve of the line.

Tip

If green, square handles appear at the end, the objects are not connected.

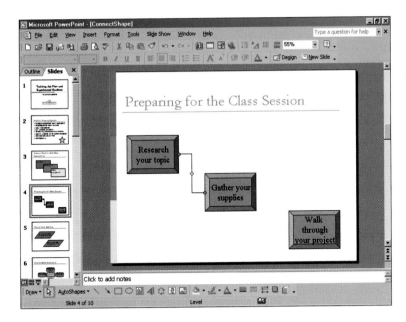

Elbow
Double-Arrow
Connector

8   On the Drawing toolbar, click **AutoShapes**, point to **Connectors**, and then click the **Elbow Double-Arrow Connector** button in the second row.

9   Draw a connection line between the right side of the middle object (the outer blue handle) and the left side of the right object (the outer blue handle).

A double-arrow line connects the objects.

Tip

After you connect objects, you can change the connector line at any time.

10   Drag the red handle on the right side of the middle connector line to the bottom of the middle object.

The line reconnects to a different point on the object.

11   Select the left connector line that connects the top and middle objects.

12   Drag the red handle on the left side of the middle connector line to the top of the middle object.

The line reconnects in a different position.

13   With the top connector line still selected, hold down ⎈Shift⎉, and then click the bottom connector line.

The two connector lines are selected.

Dash Style

14   On the Drawing toolbar, click the **Dash Style** button, and then click the **Round Dot** line style, the second line from the top, to change the line style.

Line Style

15 On the Drawing toolbar, click the **Line Style** button, and then click the **3 pt** line style.

The connector lines are dashed and three points in size.

16 On the Standard toolbar, click the **Save** button to save the presentation.

Close Window

17 Click the **Close Window** button in the presentation window.

The ConnectShape presentation closes.

Adding 3-D Effects to Shapes

Once you draw an object, you can change the object to look three-dimensional. With PowerPoint's 3-D options, you can change the depth of the object and its color, rotation, angle, direction of lighting, and surface texture.

3DShape

In this exercise, you change an object to look 3-D and change an object's 3-D settings.

1 On the Standard toolbar, click the **Open** button.

Open

The **Open** dialog box appears.

2 Navigate to the **SBS** folder on your hard disk, double-click the **PowerPoint** folder, double-click the **Drawing** folder, and then double-click the **3DShape** file.

The 3DShape presentation opens, displaying Slide 1 in Normal view.

3 In the Slide pane, drag the scroll box to Slide 5.

4 Click the top object, hold down [shift], and then click the bottom object to select both objects.

3-D Style 6

5 On the Drawing toolbar, click the **3-D Style** button, and then click **3-D Style 6** to add a 3-D style to the selected objects.

3-D Style

6 On the Drawing toolbar, click the **3-D Style** button, and then click **3-D Settings**.

The **3-D Settings** toolbar appears.

Lighting

7 On the **3-D Settings** toolbar, click the **Lighting** button, and then click the **Lighting Direction** button in the first row and third column.

Tilt Left

8 On the **3-D Settings** toolbar, click the **Tilt Left** button five times to adjust the lighting angle.

Depth

9 On the **3-D Settings** toolbar, click the **Depth** button, and then click **144 pt**.

The objects now look like pedestals.

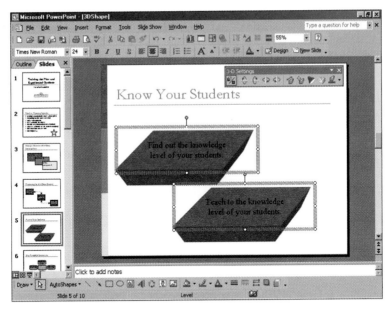

10 Click the **Close** button on the **3-D Settings** toolbar to close the toolbar.

11 Click a blank area of the slide to deselect the objects.

12 On the Standard toolbar, click the **Save** button to save the presentation.

Close Window

13 Click the **Close Window** button in the presentation window.

The 3DShape presentation closes.

Changing the Stacking Order of Shapes

Stacking is the placement of objects one on top of another. The drawing order determines the object stacking order: the first object that you draw is on the bottom, and the last object that you draw is on the top. But you can change the placement of the objects by using the **Bring to Front**, **Send to Back**, **Bring Forward**, and **Send Backward** commands on the **Draw** menu on the Drawing toolbar.

Tip

If you cannot see an object in a stack, you can press the Tab key or Shift+Tab to cycle forward or backward through the objects until you select the object that you want.

StackShape

In this exercise, you change the stacking order of objects.

1 On the Standard toolbar, click the **Open** button.

The **Open** dialog box appears.

2 Navigate to the **SBS** folder on your hard disk, double-click the **PowerPoint** folder, double-click the **Drawing** folder, and then double-click the **Stack-Shape** file.

The StackShape presentation opens, displaying Slide 1 in Normal view.

3 In the Slide pane, drag the scroll box to Slide 3.

4 Click the middle rectangle object to select it.

Draw

Dr̲aw ▾

5 On the Drawing toolbar, click **Draw**, point to **Order**, and then click **Send to Back**.

The middle rectangle object appears behind the other objects.

6 On the Drawing toolbar, click **Draw**, point to **Order**, and then click **Bring to Front**.

The middle rectangle object appears on top of the other objects.

7 On the Drawing toolbar, click **Draw**, point to **Order**, and then click **Send Backward**.

The middle rectangle object appears between the other objects.

8 Click a blank area of the slide to deselect the object.

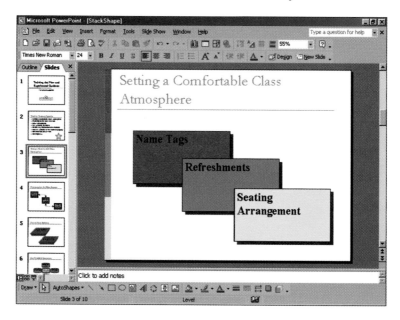

Close Window

9   On the Standard toolbar, click the **Save** button to save the presentation.

10   Click the **Close Window** button in the presentation window.

The StackShape presentation closes.

Rotating and Flipping Shapes

Picture rotation

new for
OfficeXP

Once you create an object, you can change its orientation on the slide by rotating or flipping it. Rotating turns an object 90 degrees to the right or left; flipping turns an object 180 degrees horizontally or vertically. If you need a more exact rotation, which you cannot achieve in 90 or 180 degree increments, you can drag the green rotate lever at the top of an object to rotate it to any position. You can also rotate and flip any type of picture—including bitmaps—in a presentation. This is useful when you want to change the orientation of an object or image, such as changing the direction of an arrow.

RotateFlip

In this exercise, you rotate and flip an object.

1   On the Standard toolbar, click the **Open** button.

The **Open** dialog box appears.

Open

2   Navigate to the **SBS** folder on your hard disk, double-click the **PowerPoint** folder, double-click the **Drawing** folder, and then double-click the **RotateFlip** file.

The RotateFlip presentation opens, displaying Slide 1 in Normal view.

3   In the Slide pane, drag the scroll box to Slide 7.

4   Select the curved arrow object.

Draw

Dr̲aw ▾

5   On the Drawing toolbar, click **Draw**, point to **Rotate or Flip**, and then click **Rotate Right**.

The object rotates right 90 degrees.

6   On the Drawing toolbar, click **Draw**, point to **Rotate or Flip**, and then click **Flip Horizontal**.

The object flips horizontally.

Free Rotate
pointer

7   Position the pointer (which changes to the Free Rotate pointer) over the green rotate lever at the top of the object, and then drag right to rotate the arrow object to the point at the lower double wave object.

The object rotates freely.

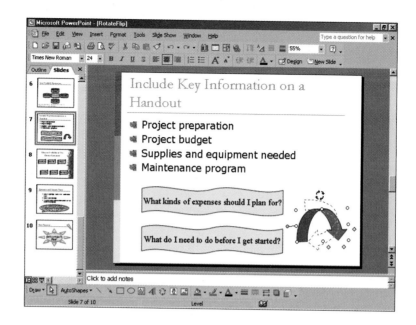

Tip

You can also use the **Free Rotate** command on the **Flip and Rotate** submenu on the **Draw** menu to rotate an object to any angle. The **Free Rotate** command changes the resize handles to green rotate levers, which allows you to drag any of the green rotate levers to rotate the object to any position.

8 On the Standard toolbar, click the **Save** button to save the presentation.

Close Window

![x]

9 Click the **Close Window** button in the presentation window.

The RotateFlip presentation closes.

Drawing and Editing an Arc Shape

With PowerPoint, you can draw and edit curved lines, called **arcs**. You can change the shape of any arc by resizing it or by moving its control handles. The direction in which you drag the arc determines whether the arc opens up or down, and the distance you drag the arc determines its size.

To draw an arc, you use the Arc tool just like any other drawing tool. Once you draw an arc, you can change its angle by dragging one of its adjustment handles. You can also change the roundness or size of the arc by resizing the object. Once you edit the size and shape, you can format the arc by changing the line thickness or adding an arrowhead or fill. If you need to create more than one arc, you can duplicate an arc and then rotate and flip it to position it correctly.

DrawArc

In this exercise, you draw an arc, edit the angle and roundness of the arc, format the arc, and then duplicate and rotate the arc.

1 On the Standard toolbar, click the **Open** button.

Open

The **Open** dialog box appears.

2 Navigate to the **SBS** folder on your hard disk, double-click the **PowerPoint** folder, double-click the **Drawing** folder, and then double-click the **DrawArc** file.

The DrawArc presentation opens, displaying Slide 1 in Normal view.

3 In the Slide pane, drag the scroll box to Slide 6.

Tip

To make it easier to connect the arc to the shapes, you can turn on the Snap objects to other objects feature, which aligns objects together, and turn off the Snap objects to frid feature. To do this, click **Draw** on the Drawing toolbar, click **Grid and Guides** to open the dialog box, clear the **Snap objects to grid** check box, and then select the **Snap objects to other objects** check box.

Arc

4 On the Drawing toolbar, click **AutoShapes**, point to **Basic Shapes**, and then click the **Arc** button.

In the presentation window, the pointer changes to the cross-hair pointer.

Tip

You cannot change lines, arcs, and freeforms by using the **Change AutoShape** command.

Cross-hair
pointer

5 Position the cross-hair pointer on the right-middle edge of the object labeled *Step-by-step project*.

+

6 Drag the cross-hair pointer down to the top center of the cylinder object labeled *Photo clips*.

Two adjustment handles appear at each end of the arc, as shown in the following illustration:

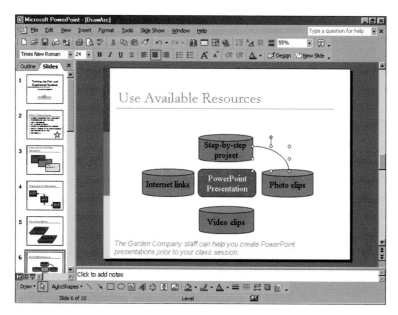

7 Drag the bottom adjustment handle until you draw a half circle, as shown in the following illustration:

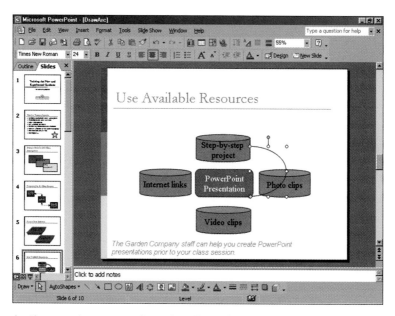

As the arc changes, a dotted outline of the arc appears, indicating what the arc will look like when you release the mouse button.

8   Hold down ⌈Shift⌉, and then drag the lower-middle resize handle down so the end of the arc touches to the middle of the cylinder object labeled *Video clips*.

As the arc changes, a dotted outline of the arc appears, indicating what the arc will look like when you release the mouse button.

Line Style

9   On the Drawing toolbar, click the **Line Style** button.

The **Line Style** menu appears, showing a variety of line widths and styles.

10   On the menu, click the **3 pt** line.

The arc line changes to a thicker point size.

Arrow Style

11   On the Drawing toolbar, click the **Arrow Style** button.

The **Arrow Style** menu appears, showing a variety of arrowhead styles.

12   On the menu, click **Arrow Style 5**.

The arc line changes to an arrow style.

13   Hold down ⌈Ctrl⌉ and ⌈Shift⌉, and then drag the arc object to the left side of the screen.

A copy of the arc appears as you drag.

Free Rotate
pointer

14   Position the pointer, which changes to the Free Rotate pointer, over the green rotate lever at the top of the object, and then drag to rotate the object and flip it horizontally.

The arrow is now pointing upwards.

15   Hold down ⌈Shift⌉, and then drag the arc to the right until it reaches the left edge of the objects labeled *Step-by-step project* and *Video clips*.

16   Hold down ⌈Shift⌉, and then click the arc object on the right.

Both arc objects are selected.

17   On the Drawing toolbar, click **Draw**, point to **Order**, and then click **Send to Back**.

Both arc objects are moved behind the other objects.

18   Click a blank area of the presentation window to deselect the objects.

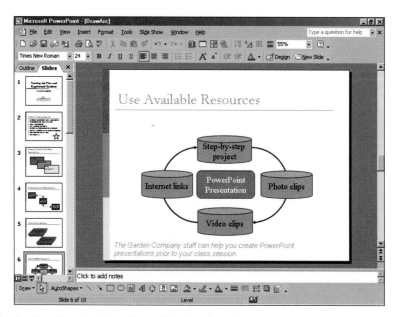

19   On the Standard toolbar, click the **Save** button to save the presentation.

Close Window

20   Click the **Close Window** button in the presentation window.

The DrawArc presentation closes.

Grouping and Ungrouping Shapes

Single selection in a group
new for
OfficeXP

Objects can be grouped together, ungrouped, and regrouped in PowerPoint to make editing and moving information easier. Rather than moving several objects one at a time, you can group the objects and move them all together. Grouped objects appear as one object, but each object in the group maintains its individual attributes. You can change an individual object within a group without ungrouping. This is useful when you need to make only a small change to a group, such as changing the color of a single shape in the group. You can also format specific AutoShapes, drawings, or pictures within a group without ungrouping. Simply select the object within the group, change the object or edit text within the object, and then deselect the object.

However, if you need to move an object in a group, you need to first ungroup the objects, make the change, and then group the objects together again. After you ungroup a set of objects, PowerPoint remembers each object in the group and in one step regroups those objects when you use the **Regroup** command. Before you regroup a set of objects, make sure that at least one of the grouped objects is selected.

GroupShape

In this exercise, you group, ungroup, and regroup objects.

1   On the Standard toolbar, click the **Open** button.

The **Open** dialog box appears.

Open

2   Navigate to the **SBS** folder on your hard disk, double-click the **PowerPoint** folder, double-click the **Drawing** folder, and then double-click the **Group-Shape** file.

The GroupShape presentation opens, displaying Slide 1 in Normal view.

3   In the Slide pane, drag the scroll box to Slide 5.

4   Drag a selection marquee around the two objects.

Each object has its own dotted selection box.

Draw

5   On the Drawing toolbar, click **Draw**, and then click **Group**.

The objects are grouped together as one object with one set of resize handles around the edge of the grouped object.

6   Click the upper object to select it.

The resize handles around the object change to gray with x's inside, indicating that an individual object in a group is selected.

Fill Color

7   On the Drawing toolbar, click the **Fill Color** button, and then click the Blue Custom Color box on the submenu.

The object changes to the color blue without ungrouping.

8   On the Drawing toolbar, click **Draw**, and then click **Ungroup**.

The object is ungrouped into individual objects.

9   Click a blank area of the slide to deselect the objects.

10   Drag the upper object to the right about a half an inch.

11   On the **Draw** menu, click **Regroup** to regroup the objects.

12   On the Standard toolbar, click the **Save** button to save the presentation.

Close Window

13   Click the **Close Window** button in the presentation window.

The GroupShape presentation closes.

Chapter Wrap-Up

To finish the chapter:

Close

●   On the **File** menu, click **Exit**, or click the **Close** button in the PowerPoint window.

PowerPoint closes.

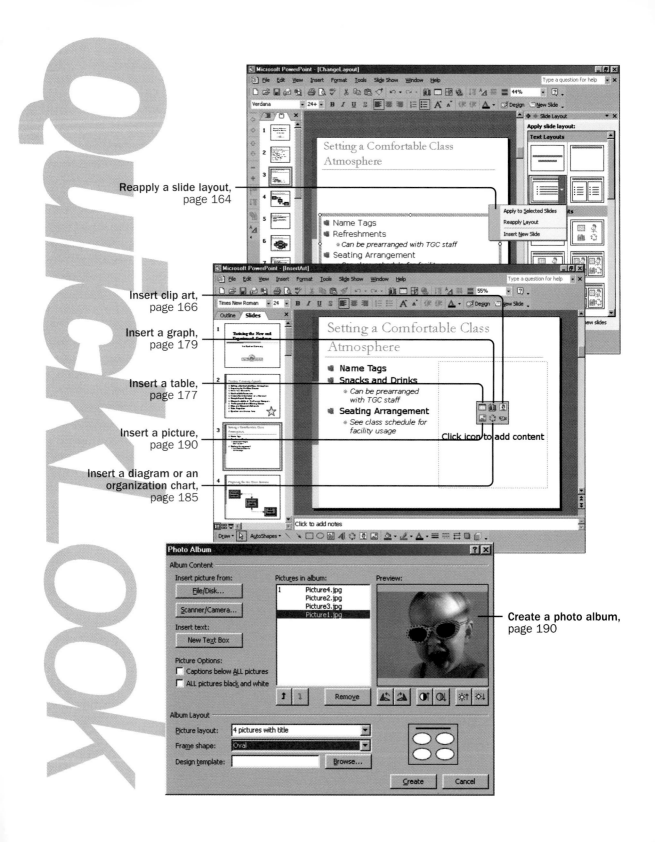

Reapply a slide layout, page 164

Insert clip art, page 166

Insert a graph, page 179

Insert a table, page 177

Insert a picture, page 190

Insert a diagram or an organization chart, page 185

Create a photo album, page 190

Chapter 9
Inserting Information into PowerPoint

After completing this chapter, you will be able to:

✔ Change the layout of a slide.

✔ Insert clip art.

✔ Change the size of an image.

✔ Change colors in a clip art image.

✔ Insert and format a table.

✔ Insert a Microsoft Excel chart.

✔ Insert and format a graph.

✔ Insert and modify an organization chart.

✔ Insert and modify a diagram.

✔ Insert a picture.

✔ Modify a picture.

✔ Insert and modify stylized text.

You can insert graphical and numerical information into a PowerPoint presentation to help you communicate your message in several ways. The most direct way is to copy and paste information such as text, objects, and slides within a presentation, among presentations, and into other Microsoft Windows–based programs. Another way to insert information into PowerPoint is to use commands on the **Insert** menu and the Standard and Drawing toolbars. These commands allow you to insert clip art, tables, charts, diagrams, pictures, or objects.

The owner of The Garden Company has been working on a training presentation and is now ready to add clip art, pictures, tables, and charts to her presentation to enhance her message.

In this chapter, you'll insert, modify, and resize clip art images; scale an image; recolor a clip art image; and insert and modify a table, a Microsoft Excel chart, a Microsoft Graph chart, an organization chart, a picture, and WordArt.

This chapter uses the practice files ChangeLayout, InsertArt, Logo, SizeImage, ColorImage, InsertTable, InsertExcel, Budget, InsertGraph, Sales, InsertOrg, InsertDiagrm, InsertPic, InsertPhoto, Picture1, Picture2, Picture3, Picture4, ModifyPic, and InsertWrdArt that you installed from this book's CD-ROM. For details about installing the practice files, see "Using the Book's CD-ROM" at the beginning of this book.

Changing the Layout of a Slide

PP2002-4-9

Approved Courseware

When inserting clip art, tables, and other information into PowerPoint, you often need to make a change to the slide layout. If you make changes to the layout of a slide but then decide you would rather use the original slide layout, you can reapply it using the **Slide Layout** command. You can also change the current layout of a slide by selecting a new layout from the **Slide Layout** task pane.

When you insert clip art, tables, charts, pictures, or objects, PowerPoint applies an **automatic layout behavior** that recognizes when you have inserted an object onto a slide with the bulleted list layout applied, and also changes the layout to the Text and Object layout so that the table and text are side by side. A Smart Tag icon also appears below the table to enable you to undo the automatic layout or to access more **AutoCorrect** options.

ChangeLayout

In this exercise, you reapply a layout to a slide and then apply a different layout to a slide.

1 Start PowerPoint, if necessary.

The PowerPoint program window opens.

2 On the Standard toolbar, click the **Open** button.

Open

The **Open** dialog box appears.

3 Navigate to the **SBS** folder on your hard disk, double-click the **PowerPoint** folder, double-click the **Inserting** folder, and then double-click the **ChangeLayout** file.

The ChangeLayout presentation opens, displaying Slide 1 in Normal view.

4 In the Slide pane, drag the scroll box to Slide 3.

5 Click in the bulleted text box, and then select the edge of the bulleted text object with the dotted-line selection box.

The bulleted text object is selected.

6 Drag the bulleted text object to the bottom of the slide.

7 On the **Format** menu, click **Slide Layout**.

The **Slide Layout** task pane opens with the current slide layout style selected.

8 Click the down arrow on the selected slide layout.

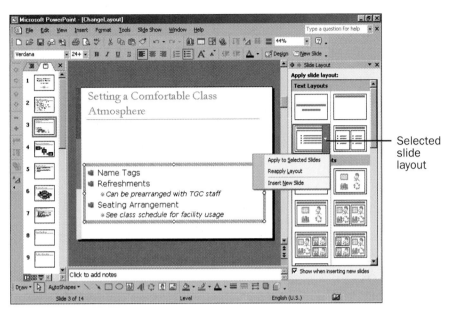

Selected slide layout

9 On the menu, click **Reapply Layout**.

PowerPoint uses the slide layout to reposition the title object to its original position on the slide.

10 In the **Slide Layout** task pane, scroll down until you reach the **Text and Content Layouts** heading.

11 Under the **Text and Content Layouts** heading, click the **Title, Text, and Content** slide layout.

The layout of Slide 3 changes. The bulleted list occupies only the left half of the screen; a content placeholder occupies the right half. The slide is now ready for you to insert a table, a chart, a piece of clip art, a picture, a diagram or organization chart, or a media clip.

Close

12 In the **Slide Layout** task pane, click the **Close** button.

13 On the Standard toolbar, click the **Save** button to save the presentation.

Close Window

14 Click the **Close Window** button in the presentation window.

The ChangeLayout presentation closes.

Inserting Clip Art

PP2002-3-1

Approved Courseware

PowerPoint provides access to hundreds of professionally designed pieces of clip art. To add a clip art image to a slide, you can use an AutoLayout with a content placeholder and simply click the **Insert Clip Art** icon, which opens the **Select Picture** dialog box. You can also click **Insert Clip Art** on the Drawing toolbar or point to **Picture** on the **Insert** menu and then click **Clip Art** to open the **Insert Clip Art** task pane, which assists you in searching for clip art.

Insert Clip Art
task pane
new for
OfficeXP

The Microsoft Clip Organizer sorts clip art images, pictures, sounds, and motion clips into categories. The Clip Organizer allows you to organize and select clips from Microsoft Office, from the Web, and from your personal collection of clips. With the **Search** button, you can search for specific media types, such as movies or clip art.

If you can't find the image that you want in the Clip Organizer, you can search for additional images in Clips Online, a clip gallery that Microsoft maintains on its Web site. To access Clips Online, you click the **Clips Online** button on the Clip Organizer toolbar or select the link at the bottom of the **Insert Clip Art** task pane. This launches your Web browser and navigates you directly to the Clips Online Web page, where you can access thousands of free clip art images.

If you do not find a shape that you want under **AutoShapes**, you can use the **More AutoShapes** command on the **AutoShapes** menu to open the **Insert Clip Art** task pane and display additional shapes.

You might want to add pictures and categories to the Clip Organizer for easy access in the future. You can import new images into the Clip Organizer by using **Add Clips to Organizer** on its **File** menu or by clicking the **Import** button at the bottom of the **Select Picture** dialog box.

InsertArt
Logo

In this exercise, you insert clip art images from Microsoft sources and then add a picture to the Clip Organizer.

Open

1   On the Standard toolbar, click the **Open** button.

The **Open** dialog box appears.

2   Navigate to the **SBS** folder on your hard disk, double-click the **PowerPoint** folder, double-click the **Inserting** folder, and then double-click the **InsertArt** file.

The InsertArt presentation opens, displaying Slide 1 in Normal view.

3   In the Slide pane, drag the scroll box to Slide 3.

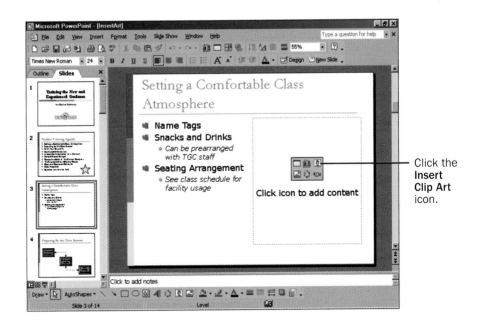

Click the
**Insert
Clip Art**
icon.

Insert Clip Art

4 In the Content placeholder, click the **Insert Clip Art** icon.

The **Select Picture** dialog box appears.

5 In the **Search text** box, type **food**, and then click **Search**.

All clip art pertaining to food appears.

6 In the first row, click the third piece of clip art titled *Apple for the Teacher*.

Important

If you are connected to the Internet, additional clip art appears in the **Select Picture** dialog box. The clip art from the Clip Organizer appears with a small globe icon in the lower-left corner of the image.

7   Click **OK**.

The **Select Picture** dialog box closes, and the clip art appears on the slide along with the **Picture** toolbar. When a picture is selected, PowerPoint opens the **Picture** toolbar.

Troubleshooting

If the **Picture** toolbar does not appear, right-click the clip art image, and then click the **Show Picture Toolbar** on the shortcut menu.

8   Click a blank area of the slide to deselect the image.

9   In the Slide pane, drag the scroll box to Slide 7.

10 On the **Insert** menu, point to **Picture**, and then click **Clip Art**.

The **Insert Clip Art** task pane appears with search options.

11 In the **Search text** box, type **equipment**, and then click **Search**.

All clip art pertaining to *equipment* appears.

12 Scroll down, if necessary, and then click the blue computer clip art.

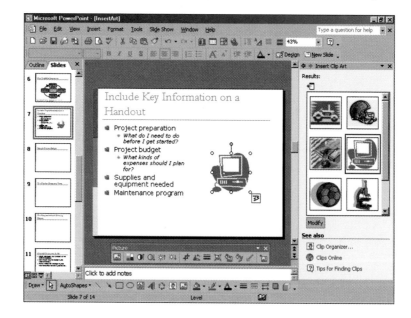

Automatic
Layout Options

PowerPoint inserts the clip art and reformats the slide with a new slide lay-out. An **Automatic Layout Options** button appears in the lower-right corner of the image, allowing you to undo the automatic layout, disable the auto-matic layout feature, or change AutoCorrect options.

13 Click the down arrow on the **Automatic Layout Options** button, and then click **Undo Automatic Layout**.

The clip art image moves to the center of the slide, overlapping the text.

14 Drag the clip art image to the lower-right corner of the slide.

15 Click outside of the image to deselect it.

The **Picture** toolbar is hidden.

16 In the Slide pane, drag the scroll box to Slide 2.

AutoShapes

AutoShapes ▼

17 On the Drawing toolbar, click **AutoShapes**, and then click **More AutoShapes**.

The **Insert Clip Art** task pane appears, showing available AutoShapes.

18 In the **Insert Clip Art** task pane, scroll down, and then click the tree AutoShape.

The tree appears in the middle of the slide.

19 Drag the image to the lower-right corner of the slide.

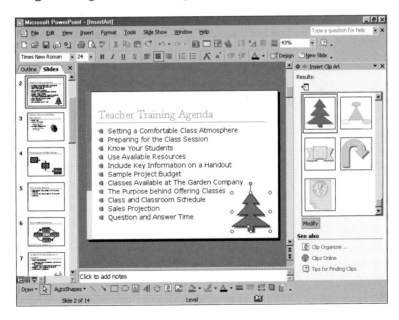

Insert Clip Art

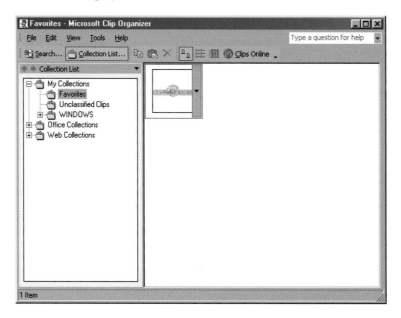

20 On the Drawing toolbar, click the **Insert Clip Art** button.

The **Insert Clip Art** task pane appears.

21 In the **Insert Clip Art** task pane, click **Clip Organizer**.

The **Microsoft Clip Organizer** window opens.

22 In the **Collections List**, under **My Collection**, click **Favorites**.

23 On the **File** menu, point to **Add Clips to Organizer,** and then click **On My Own**.

The **Add Clips to Organizer** dialog box appears.

24 Navigate to the **SBS** folder on your hard disk, double-click the **PowerPoint** folder, double-click the **Inserting** folder, and then click the **Logo** file.

Tip

To place images into a new or existing category, click **Add To** in the **Add to Clips Organizer** dialog box.

25 Click **Add**.

The **Microsoft Clip Organizer** window appears, displaying the logo under the **Favorites** category.

Tip

If the thumbnail view is not showing, click the **Thumbnails** button on the Clip Organizer toolbar.

26 Click the down arrow on the thumbnail of your Logo clip art, and then click **Edit Keywords**.

The **Keywords** dialog box appears.

27 In the **Keyword** box, type *logo*, and then click **Add**.

The keyword *logo* is added to the **Keywords for current clip** list.

28 Click **OK** to close the **Edit Keywords** dialog box, and then click the **Close** button in the **Microsoft Clip Organizer** window.

The **Microsoft Clip Organizer** closes, and the presentation window appears, showing the **Insert Clip Art** task pane.

29 In the **Search text** box, type *logo*, and then click **Search**.

The Garden Company logo appears in the clip art list.

Tip

To delete clip art from the Clip Organizer, click the down arrow next to the clip art image, click **Delete from Clip Organizer**, and then click **Yes** to confirm the deletion.

30 In the **Insert Clip Art** task pane, click the **Close** button.

31 On the Standard toolbar, click the **Save** button to save the presentation.

Close Window

×

32 Click the **Close Window** button in the presentation window.

The InsertArt presentation closes.

Changing the Size of an Image

Scaling changes the size of an entire object by a set percentage. With the **Picture** command on the **Format** menu, you can resize an object numerically instead of dragging its resize handle. You can scale an object by a set percentage relative to the original picture size if you select the appropriate check box on the **Size** tab in the **Format Picture** dialog box. Otherwise the picture is scaled relative to the current picture size. If you create a presentation specifically for giving a slide show, you can also optimize the size of an image for the size of the slide show screen by selecting the **Best scale for slide show** check box on the **Size** tab in the **Format Picture** dialog box.

Sizelmage

Open

In this exercise, you scale an object.

1 On the Standard toolbar, click the **Open** button.

The **Open** dialog box appears.

2 Navigate to the **SBS** folder on your hard disk, double-click the **PowerPoint** folder, double-click the **Inserting** folder, and then double-click the **Sizelmage** file.

The SizeImage presentation opens, displaying Slide 1 in Normal view.

3 In the Slide pane, drag the scroll box to Slide 7.

4 Double-click the clip art image.

The **Format Picture** dialog box appears.

5 Click the **Size** tab.

6 In the **Scale** area, select the number in the **Height** box.

7 Type **110**.

8 Click **Preview** to view the object before you close the dialog box.

The image width scale changes to 110%. Because the **Lock aspect ratio** check box is selected, the **Width** option setting changes to 110%.

9 Click **OK** to close the **Format Picture** dialog box.

The image height and width are scaled to 110% of the original size.

Tip

PowerPoint retains the original size of a picture or text object. If you accidentally change an object to the wrong size, you can set the scale back to 100% relative to its original size or click **Reset** in the dialog box.

10 On the Standard toolbar, click the **Save** button to save the presentation.

Close Window

11 Click the **Close Window** button in the presentation window.

The SizeImage presentation closes.

Changing Colors in a Clip Art Image

You can change the color of clip art images to create a different look or to match the current color scheme. The **Recolor Picture** command displays a dialog box with a preview of the picture and a list of all of the colors in the picture. You can change any color in the list.

ColorImage

In this exercise, you recolor an image that you have inserted from the Clip Gallery.

1 On the Standard toolbar, click the **Open** button.

The **Open** dialog box appears.

Open

2 Navigate to the **SBS** folder on your hard disk, double-click the **PowerPoint** folder, double-click the **Inserting** folder, and then double-click the **ColorImage** file.

The ColorImage presentation opens, displaying Slide 1 in Normal view.

3 In the Slide pane, drag the scroll box to Slide 13.

4 Select the clip art object.

5 On the **View** menu, point to **Toolbars**, and then click **Picture** to display the Picture toolbar, if necessary.

Recolor Picture

6 On the **Picture** toolbar, click the **Recolor Picture** button.

The **Recolor Picture** dialog box appears with the **Colors** option selected in the **Change** area.

7 Click the **Fills** option to display the fill colors in the image.

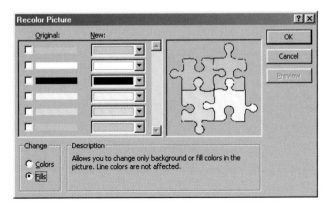

8 Under **New**, click the down arrow next to the lavender color (the sixth item in the **New** list of colors), and then click the Red color box (the eighth item in the color scheme).

The color swatch changes to red, and the preview box on the right shows that all parts of the image that had been lavender are now red.

9 Under **New**, click the down arrow next to the Light Green color box (the fifth item in the **New** list of colors).

10 Click in the Green color box (the fourth item in the color scheme).

11 Under **New**, click the down arrow next to the Orange color (the first item in the **New** list of colors).

12 Click in the Yellow color box (the fifth item in the color scheme).

13 Under **New**, click the down arrow next to the Tan color (the fourth item in the **Original** list of colors).

14 Click in the Brown color box (the seventh item in the color scheme).

15 Click **OK** to close the **Recolor Picture** dialog box.

PowerPoint recolors the clip art image.

16 Click a blank area of the slide to deselect the object.

The **Picture** toolbar is hidden.

17 On the Standard toolbar, click the **Save** button to save the presentation.

Close Window

18 Click the **Close Window** button in the presentation window.

The ColorImage presentation closes.

Inserting and Formatting a Table

PP2002-3-1
PP2002-3-4

Approved Courseware

A table organizes information neatly into rows and columns. The intersection of a row and a column is called a **cell**. You can create a table with standard-sized cells, or you can draw a custom table with various-sized cells. Once you create a table, you enter text into the cells just as you would in a paragraph, except that using the [Tab] key moves the insertion point from cell to cell instead of indenting text. The first row in the table is commonly used for column headings; the leftmost column is ideal for row labels. You can customize and format individual cells as well as the entire table. To accommodate the text that you enter in the table, you can merge, or combine, cells to form one long cell. This is useful when you want to spread the text across the top of a table. You can also split, or divide, a cell into two. With the Formatting and **Tables and Borders** toolbars, you can add color, add borders, and change text alignment in a table.

InsertTable

In this exercise, you insert and format a table.

Open

1 On the Standard toolbar, click the **Open** button.

The **Open** dialog box appears.

2 Navigate to the **SBS** folder on your hard disk, double-click the **PowerPoint** folder, double-click the **Inserting** folder, and then double-click the **InsertTable** file.

The InsertTable presentation opens, displaying Slide 1 in Normal view.

3 In the Slide pane, drag the scroll box to Slide 11.

4 Double-click the table placeholder.

The **Insert Table** dialog box appears.

5 Click the **Number of rows** up arrow until the number reaches **4**.

6 Click **OK**.

A blank table with two columns and four rows and the Tables and Borders toolbar appears.

Troubleshooting

If the **Automatic Layout Options** button appears, you can ignore it.

7 Click in the top left cell of the table to select it, if it is not already selected.

The **Tables and Borders** toolbar appears in the presentation window as soon as you click within the table.

Troubleshooting

If the **Tables and Borders** toolbar doesn't appear, on the **View** menu, point to **Toolbars**, and then click **Tables and Borders**.

8 Type the following text in the table, using [Tab] to move from cell to cell; after the word *Shrubs* press [Enter]:

Class	Classroom
Trees and Shrubs Lawn Care	Rear Patio
Flowers	Room 1
Indoor Plants	Greenhouse

Bold

9 Select the column titles *Class* and *Classroom* in the table, and then click the **Bold** button on the Formatting toolbar.

The column titles appear bold.

Center Vertically

10 On the Formatting toolbar, click the **Center** button to center the text in the cell, and then click **Center Vertically** on the **Tables and Borders** toolbar.

The column titles appear centered vertically in the cell.

Fill Color

11 On the **Tables and Borders** toolbar, click the **Fill Color** down arrow, and then click the Red color box (the eighth item in the color scheme).

The cells with the column titles are filled with red.

Draw Table

12 On the **Tables and Borders** toolbar, click the **Draw Table** button, and then draw a horizontal line under the text *Trees and Shrubs* and above the text *Lawn Care.*

A dotted line appears as you draw the line. The cell is split into two cells.

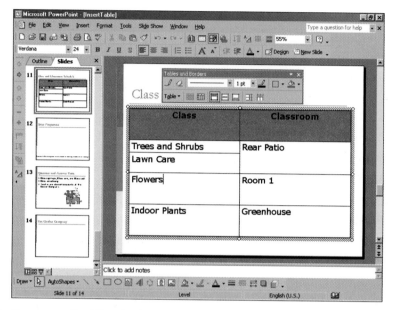

13 Draw a vertical line in the middle of the cell which contains the text *Room 1.*

The cell is split into two cells.

Eraser

14 On the **Tables and Borders** toolbar, click the **Eraser** button, and then click the vertical line next to the text *Room 1.*

The cell merges from two cells into one cell.

Tip

To add a column or row to a table, click in a cell next to where you want to insert the column or row, click **Table** on the **Tables and Borders** toolbar, and then click **Insert Columns to the Right**, **Insert Columns to the Left**, **Insert Rows Above**, or **Insert Rows Below**. To delete a column or row, click anywhere in a column or row, click **Table** on the **Tables and Borders** toolbar, and then click **Delete Rows** or **Delete Columns**.

15 On the **Tables and Borders** toolbar, click the **Eraser** button to turn the tool off.

16 Click in a blank area of the slide (not in the table) to deselect the table.

17 On the Standard toolbar, click the **Save** button to save the presentation.

Close Window

18 Click the **Close Window** button in the presentation window.

The InsertTable presentation closes.

Inserting a Microsoft Word Table

PP2002-6-3

Approved Courseware

You can insert a Word table into PowerPoint by inserting the table as an embedded object in a slide. (See "Inserting a Microsoft Excel Chart" in this chapter for more information about an embedded object.) If you do not have Word installed on your computer, skip this task.

To insert a Word table:

1 In PowerPoint, on the **Insert** menu, click **Object**.

2 In the **Insert Object** dialog box, click **Create New**.

3 In the **Object type** box, click **Microsoft Word Document**, and then click **OK**.

A Microsoft Word document opens in the PowerPoint slide.

4 Use the commands on the **Table** menu to create the table that you want.

5 Click outside of the table to return to Microsoft PowerPoint.

Inserting a Microsoft Excel Chart

PP2002-6-1

Approved Courseware

PowerPoint simplifies the process of inserting an Excel chart into a presentation by embedding the chart as an object in the slide. An **embedded object** is an object that maintains a direct connection to its original program, known as the **source program**. After you insert an embedded object, you can easily edit it by double-clicking it, which opens the program in which it was originally created.

Embedding objects increases the file size of a presentation because the embedded object is stored in the presentation. To reduce the file size of the presentation, you can link an object instead of embedding it. A **linked object** appears in the slide, but it actually contains a "link" back to the original document, known as the **source document**. When you link an object, the original object is stored in its source document, where it was created. The presentation stores only a representation of the original. The source program will update the object when you modify the source document.

InsertExcel
Budget

In this exercise, you insert an Excel chart object into a slide and then edit an embedded Excel object.

1 On the Standard toolbar, click the **Open** button.

The **Open** dialog box appears.

Open

2 Navigate to the **SBS** folder on your hard disk, double-click the **PowerPoint** folder, double-click the **Inserting** folder, and then double-click the **InsertExcel** file.

The **InsertExcel** presentation opens, displaying Slide 1 in Normal view.

3 In the Slide pane, drag the scroll box to Slide 8.

4 On the **Insert** menu, click **Object**.

The **Insert Object** dialog box appears.

5 Click the **Create from File** option, and then click **Browse**.

The **Browse** dialog box appears. It is similar to the **Open** dialog box.

6 Navigate to the **SBS** folder on your hard disk, double-click the **PowerPoint** folder, and then double-click the **Inserting** folder.

7 In the list of file and folder names, click **Budget**, and then click **OK** to close the **Browse** dialog box.

Name of
file to be
embedded

Click to link
instead of
embed.

Important

When working with a linked object, you need to remember to make any modifications in the source document, not in PowerPoint. Although you can make changes to the image in the presentation, they will be temporary, and you will lose them when you close the presentation. The next time that you open the presentation, the object will be updated (linked) to the version of the source document in the source program. To link an object, you select the **Link** check box in the **Insert Object** dialog box.

8 Click **OK**.

PowerPoint embeds the chart (a pie chart) into the new slide.

9 Double-click the embedded Excel chart.

The Excel workbook opens in PowerPoint and displays the **Chart2 worksheet** tab. The Standard and Formatting toolbars and menus change to the Excel toolbars, and the Excel Chart toolbar appears.

10 Click the **Sheet1** tab.

The **Sheet1** tab appears, displaying the worksheet data for the charts.

11   Click the **Chart1** tab.

The **Chart1** tab appears, displaying a chart.

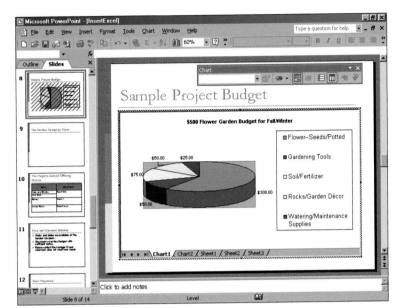

12   Click a blank area of the slide.

Excel closes, and the PowerPoint toolbars and menus return, and the embedded Excel object is updated on the slide.

13   On the Standard toolbar, click the **Save** button to save the presentation.

Close Window

14   Click the **Close Window** button in the presentation window.

The InsertExcel presentation closes.

Inserting and Formatting a Graph

PP2002-3-1

Approved Courseware

Microsoft Graph is a program that PowerPoint uses to insert a chart into a presentation slide. When you start Graph, create a chart, and return to the presentation slide, the chart becomes an embedded object in the slide. You can start Graph by double-clicking a chart placeholder, clicking the **Insert Chart** button on the Standard toolbar, or clicking **Chart** on the **Insert** menu.

In Graph, data is displayed in a datasheet and represented in a chart. The **datasheet** is composed of individual cells that form rows and columns, which in turn make up a group of related data points called a **data series**. A **data series marker** is a graphical representation in the chart of the information in the data series. Along the left and top edges of the datasheet are gray boxes, called control boxes. **Control boxes** correspond to the different data series in the datasheet. The first row and column of the datasheet contain names or labels for each data series. The data series labels appear in the chart. The chart is made up of different elements that help display the data from the datasheet. The chart shown above has an X-axis (horizontal axis) and a Y-axis (vertical axis), which serve as reference lines for the plotted data. (In a 3-D chart, the vertical axis is the Z-axis.) Along each axis are labels, called **tick-mark labels**, which identify the data plotted in the chart. There is also a **legend** in the chart that identifies each data series in the datasheet.

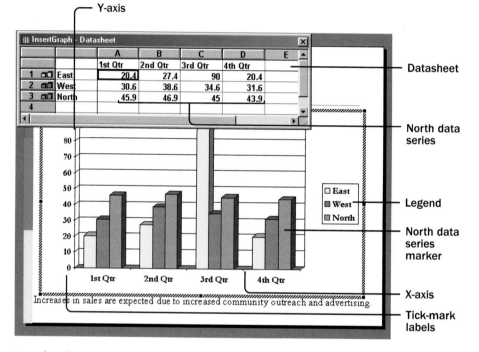

In a datasheet, you can use the mouse or keyboard commands to work with selected data by selecting an individual cell, a range of cells, or an entire row or column. A cell is identified by its row and column location in the datasheet. A selected cell, called the **active cell**, has a heavy border around it. When more than one cell is selected, the active cell is highlighted with a heavy border, and all other selected cells are highlighted in black. To perform most tasks on the datasheet, you must first select a specific cell or range of cells.

Tip

To select a single cell in the datasheet, simply click it. To select a range of cells, hold down the [Shift] key, and then click the first and last cells, which highlights the selected area. To select a row or column, click the row or column control box. To select the entire datasheet, click the control box in the upper-left corner.

Row control box

InsertGraph - Datasheet

		A	B	C	D	E
		1st Qtr	2nd Qtr	3rd Qtr	4th Qtr	
1	East	20.4	27.4	90	20.4	
2	West	30.6	38.6	34.6	31.6	
3	North	45.9	46.9	45	43.9	
4						

Column control box

Tick-mark label

Active cell

Chart icon

To enter data into the datasheet, you can perform one or more of the following: type your own data into the datasheet, import information directly from another program, such as Microsoft Excel, or copy and paste a specified range of data or a complete worksheet into Graph. Once the data is entered into the datasheet, you can easily modify and format the associated chart. Graph comes with a gallery that lets you change the chart type and then format the chart to get the results that you want. There are 14 chart categories, containing both two-dimensional and three-dimensional charts.

InsertGraph
Sales

In this exercise, you insert a Graph chart, import and enter data, and format the chart.

1 On the Standard toolbar, click the **Open** button.

The **Open** dialog box appears.

Open

2 Navigate to the **SBS** folder on your hard disk, double-click the **PowerPoint** folder, double-click the **Inserting** folder, and then double-click the **InsertGraph** file.

The InsertGraph presentation opens, displaying Slide 1 in Normal view.

3 In the Slide pane, drag the scroll box to Slide 12, and then double-click the chart placeholder.

The Chart AutoLayout already appears on Slide 12. When you double-click the chart placeholder, PowerPoint launches Microsoft Graph. The Graph Standard and Formatting toolbars and menus replace the PowerPoint toolbars and menus. The datasheet and chart windows appear with default data that you can replace with your own data.

Tip

If the datasheet obstructs the chart, you can move the datasheet window out of the way by dragging its title bar or by clicking its **Close** button. If the datasheet is closed, you can click the **View Datasheet** button on the Graph Standard toolbar to open it.

4 Click the blank cell above the data label *East*.

Graph will import the data into the datasheet, starting at the currently selected cell.

181

Import File

5 On the Graph Standard toolbar, click the **Import File** button.

The **Import File** dialog box appears. This dialog box functions just like the **Open** dialog box.

6 Navigate to the **SBS** folder on your hard disk, double-click the **PowerPoint** folder, double-click the **Inserting** folder, and then double-click the **Sales** file.

The **Import Data Options** dialog box appears. **Sheet1** from the Excel file is selected by default to be imported into the Graph chart.

7 Click **OK** to overwrite the current data in the datasheet.

Tip

To resize the datasheet, drag the lower-right corner of the datasheet window.

8 Click cell **A4**, scroll down if necessary, type **40000**, and then press [Tab].

Tip

You can use the drag-and-drop method to cut data from a datasheet and paste the information in a new location.

Graph accepts the new entry and moves the selection to cell B4.

9 In cell **B4**, type **46000**, and then press the [Enter] key.

Graph accepts the new entry and moves the selection down to cell B5.

InsertGraph - Datasheet		A	B	C	D	E	
	Sales Quar	2001	2002				
2	Spring	$100,000	$110,000				
3	Summer	$200,000	$224,000				
4	Fall	$40,000	$46,000				
5							

Chart Type

10 On the Graph Standard toolbar, click the **Chart Type** down arrow, and then click the **3-D Bar Chart** (the second chart down in the center column).

The chart changes to the 3-D Bar Chart type.

Tip

You can give your chart a dynamic look by changing the 3-D view. With Graph, you can control the elevation, rotation, position, and perspective for a 3-D chart by using the **3-D View** command on the **Chart** menu.

11 On the **Chart** menu, click **Chart Type**.

The **Chart Type** dialog box appears with standard and custom chart types and formats.

Tip

By default, Graph plots the chart so that the chart gives you information about the rows in the datasheet. In other words, the columns in the column chart represent the row names. You can change this to plot the data by the column names instead.

12 Click the **Custom Types** tab.

The **Custom Types** settings appear.

13 Click **Columns with Depth** in the **Chart type** list, and then click **OK**.

The chart changes to the Columns with Depth chart type.

14 Click the **Close** button on the Datasheet window to close the window.

15 On the Graph Standard toolbar, click the **Chart Objects** down arrow, and then click **Chart Area**, if necessary, to select the entire chart.

16 On the Graph Formatting toolbar, click the **Font Size** down arrow, and then click **18**.

The X-axis and Y-axis data labels and the legend font size change to 18 points.

17 On the **Chart** menu, click **Chart Options**, and then click the **Gridlines** tab.

The **Chart Options** dialog box appears with the Gridlines settings.

18 In the **Value (Z) axis** area, select the **Major gridlines** check box, and then click **OK**.

Gridlines appear on the chart.

19 In the chart, click the Y-axis with the dollar values.

Black handles appear at the end of the Y-axis.

Decrease
Decimal

20 On the Graph Formatting toolbar, click the **Italic** button, and then click the **Decrease Decimal** button twice to remove the decimal places in the Y-axis values.

21 Click the X-axis with the category values.

Black handles appear at the end of the X-axis.

Angle Counter-
clockwise

22 On the Graph Formatting toolbar, click the **Angle Counterclockwise** button.

The X-axis text angle changes to a 45-degree angle.

Tip

You can double-click almost any object in the chart window to edit its attributes. For example, you can double-click the Y-axis to display the **Format Axis** dialog box, where you can access patterns, font type and style, number format, and alignment.

23 Click a blank area of the presentation window outside of the Graph chart to quit Graph.

The PowerPoint toolbars and menus replace the Graph toolbar and menus, and the chart is embedded in the presentation slide.

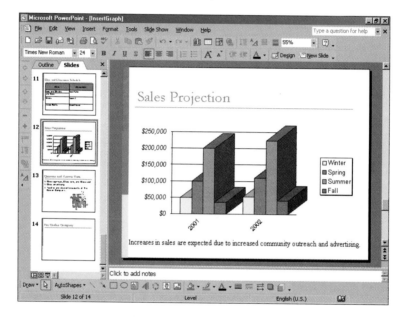

Tip

Once you create an embedded graph object, you can edit it by double-clicking the object. The embedded graph object opens in Microsoft Graph so that you can make changes.

24 On the Standard toolbar, click the **Save** button to save the presentation.

Close Window

25 Click the **Close Window** button in the presentation window.

The InsertGraph presentation closes.

Inserting and Modifying an Organization Chart

PP2002-3-1
PP2002-3-3

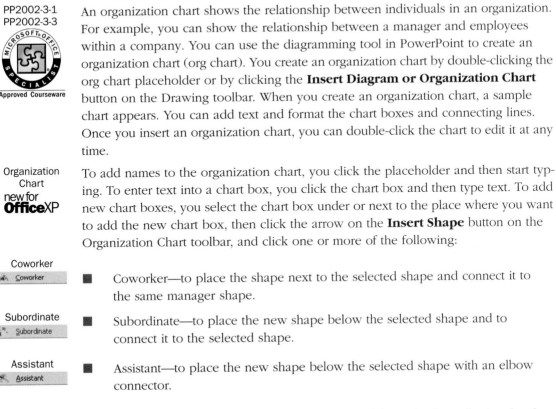

Approved Courseware

An organization chart shows the relationship between individuals in an organization. For example, you can show the relationship between a manager and employees within a company. You can use the diagramming tool in PowerPoint to create an organization chart (org chart). You create an organization chart by double-clicking the org chart placeholder or by clicking the **Insert Diagram or Organization Chart** button on the Drawing toolbar. When you create an organization chart, a sample chart appears. You can add text and format the chart boxes and connecting lines. Once you insert an organization chart, you can double-click the chart to edit it at any time.

Organization
Chart
new for
OfficeXP

To add names to the organization chart, you click the placeholder and then start typing. To enter text into a chart box, you click the chart box and then type text. To add new chart boxes, you select the chart box under or next to the place where you want to add the new chart box, then click the arrow on the **Insert Shape** button on the Organization Chart toolbar, and click one or more of the following:

Coworker

Coworker

- Coworker—to place the shape next to the selected shape and connect it to the same manager shape.

Subordinate

Subordinate

- Subordinate—to place the new shape below the selected shape and to connect it to the selected shape.

Assistant

Assistant

- Assistant—to place the new shape below the selected shape with an elbow connector.

If you add a chart box in the wrong place, you can delete it by first selecting the chart box and then pressing the [Del] key.

You can change the chart style, rearrange chart boxes, or edit names in the chart boxes to match the organization of the company. The current chart type appears in the traditional style, one manager at the top with subordinates below. You can use the **AutoFormat** button on the Organization Chart toolbar to change the chart style.

You can change the chart box color, shadow, border style, border color, or border line style by clicking commands on the Drawing toolbar. When you're finished working with the organization chart, you simply deselect the object.

Tip

PowerPoint can convert existing organization charts from previous versions of PowerPoint to Office diagrams and take advantage of the enhanced functionality and benefits of the current version. To convert an existing organization chart from a previous version of Organization Chart, simply double-click the chart, and PowerPoint converts it.

InsertOrg

Open

In this exercise, you insert an Organization Chart, enter text, add a chart box, and then change the chart style.

1   On the Standard toolbar, click the **Open** button.

The **Open** dialog box appears.

2   Navigate to the **SBS** folder on your hard disk, double-click the **PowerPoint** folder, double-click the **Inserting** folder, and then double-click the **InsertOrg** file.

The InsertOrg presentation opens, displaying Slide 1 in Normal view.

3   In the Slide pane, drag the scroll box to Slide 9.

4   Double-click the org chart placeholder.

The **Diagram Gallery** dialog box appears with the Organization Chart selected.

5   Click **OK**.

PowerPoint launches Organization Chart. The default chart displayed in the Organization Chart window represents the chart that Organization Chart will embed in the PowerPoint presentation. By default, the top chart box text is open. The **Organization Chart** toolbar is also displayed.

6   Type **Catherine Turner.**

Tip

To edit the chart's title text, select the text that you want to edit, and then type the new text.

7   Press ⌷Enter⌷, and then type **Owner.**

As you type, the chart box expands to fit the text.

8   Click a blank area in the organization chart area to deselect the chart box, and then click the lower-left chart box.

9   Enter chart box text to match the following illustration:

10 Click in the lower-left chart box.

11 On the **Organization Chart** toolbar, click the **Insert Shape** down arrow, and then click **Subordinate**.

A subordinate chart box is placed below the left chart box.

12 Click the subordinate chart box, and then type **Office Staff**.

13 Add chart boxes and enter text to match the following illustration:

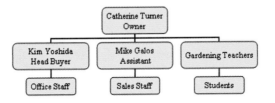

Autoformat

14 On the **Organization Chart** toolbar, click the **Autoformat** button.

The **Organization Chart Style Gallery** dialog box appears.

15 Under **Select a Diagram Style**, click **Brackets**, and then click **Apply**.

The style of the organization chart changes.

16 On the Formatting toolbar, click the **Font Size** down arrow, and then click **20**.

All text in the organization chart is resized to 20 points.

17 Click Kim Yoshida's chart box to select it.

18 On the **Organization Chart** toolbar, click the **Select** down arrow, and then click **Level**.

All chart boxes at the same level as Kim Yoshida's are selected.

19 Hold down [Shift], click Catherine Turner's chart box, and then click the **Bold** button on the Formatting toolbar.

The first two chart levels are now bold.

20 Click outside of the organization chart to deselect it.

Organization Chart embeds the chart into PowerPoint.

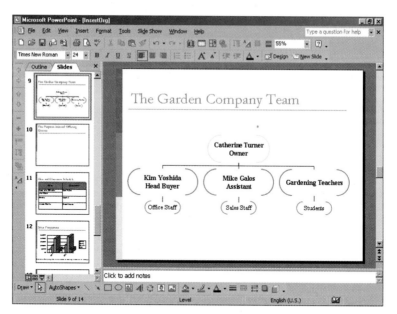

21 On the Standard toolbar, click the **Save** button to save the presentation.

Close Window

22 Click the **Close Window** button in the presentation window.

The InsertOrg presentation closes.

Inserting and Modifying a Diagram

PP2002-3-1
PP2002-3-3

Approved Courseware

PowerPoint offers a variety of built-in diagrams from which to choose, including pyramid, cycle, radial, and Venn diagrams as well as organization charts. Using built-in diagrams makes it easy to create and modify charts without having to create them from scratch. To use the built-in diagrams, click the **Insert Diagram or Organization Chart** button on the Drawing toolbar or click **Diagram** on the **Insert** menu, and then select a diagram.

InsertDiagrm

In this exercise, you insert a Venn diagram, enter data, and then format the diagram.

1 On the Standard toolbar, click the **Open** button.

Open

The **Open** dialog box appears.

2 Navigate to the **SBS** folder on your hard disk, double-click the **PowerPoint** folder, double-click the **Inserting** folder, and then double-click the **InsertDiagrm** file.

Insert
diagrams
new for
OfficeXP

The InsertDiagrm presentation opens, displaying Slide 1 in Normal view.

3 In the Slide pane, drag the scroll box to Slide 10.

Insert Diagram
or Organiza-
tion Chart

4 On the Drawing toolbar, click the **Insert Diagram or Organization Chart** button.

The **Diagram Gallery** dialog box appears.

5 Select the Venn diagram in the lower middle, and then click **OK**.

A Venn diagram appears on your slide with text boxes next to each circle.

6 Click the top text box, and then type **Create Loyal Customers**.

7 Click the right text box, and then type **Educate the Community**.

8 Click the left text box, and then type **Increase Sales**.

9 Click a blank area of the diagram to deselect the text box.

10 Drag the right middle sizing handle (black bar) to the right and drag the left middle sizing handle (black bar) to the left to resize the diagram as shown in the following illustration.

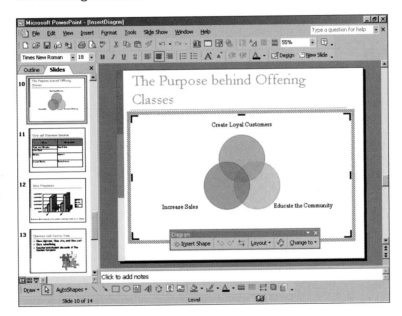

AutoFormat

11 On the **Diagram** toolbar, click the **AutoFormat** button.

The **Diagram Style Gallery** dialog box appears.

12 Under **Select a Diagram Style**, click **Primary Colors**, and then click **Apply**.

The colors of the Venn diagram change to primary colors.

13 On the Standard toolbar, click the **Save** button to save the presentation.

Close Window

14 Click the **Close Window** button in the presentation window.

The InsertDiagrm presentation closes.

Inserting a Picture

PP2002-3-1

Approved Courseware

PowerPoint makes it possible for you to insert pictures, graphics, scanned photographs, art, photos, or artwork from a CD-ROM or other program into a slide. When you use the **Picture** submenu on the **Insert** menu, you specify the source of the picture—a file, Word's clip art collection, or a scanner.

To insert a picture from a file on your hard disk, removable disk, or network, you use the **From File** command on the **Picture** submenu. To insert a picture from the clip art collection that comes with PowerPoint, you click the **Clip Art** command, which opens the **Insert Clip Art** task pane. Microsoft Office XP provides hundreds of professionally designed pieces of clip art that you can use in your documents. For example, you can insert clip art images of scenic backgrounds, maps, buildings, or people. If you have a scanner connected to the computer you are using, you can scan and insert a picture using the **From Scanner or Camera** command. Once you insert clip art or any picture into your document, you can modify it by using the Picture toolbar.

Photo album
new for
OfficeXP

If you have a large collection of pictures, you can use PowerPoint to create a photo album. PowerPoint allows you to insert multiple pictures from your hard disk into your photo album. You can also customize the photo album using special layout options, such as oval frames and captions under each picture.

Insert multiple pictures
new for
OfficeXP

When you insert pictures from files on your hard disk drive, scanner, digital camera, or Web camera, PowerPoint allows you to select multiple pictures, view thumbnails of them, and insert them all at once, which speeds up the process.

InsertPic
InsertPhoto

In this exercise, you insert a picture, open a new photo album, and insert multiple pictures into the photo album.

1 On the Standard toolbar, click the **Open** button.

Open

The **Open** dialog box appears.

2 Navigate to the **SBS** folder on your hard disk, double-click the **PowerPoint** folder, double-click the **Inserting** folder, and then double-click the **InsertPic** file.

The InsertPic presentation opens, displaying Slide 1 in Normal view.

3 In the Slide pane, drag the scroll box to Slide 5.

4 On the **Insert** menu, point to **Picture**, and then click **From File**.

The **Insert Picture** dialog box appears.

5 Navigate to the **SBS** folder on your hard disk, double-click the **PowerPoint** folder, and then double-click the **Inserting** folder.

6 In the list of file and folder names, click **InsertPhoto**, and then click **Insert**.

The picture and the **Picture** toolbar appear.

7 Drag the picture to the right corner of the slide.

8 On the **Insert** menu, point to **Picture**, and then click **New Photo Album**.

The **Photo Album** dialog box appears.

9 Click **File/Disk**.

The **Insert New Pictures** dialog box appears.

10 Navigate to the **SBS** folder on your hard disk, double-click the **PowerPoint** folder, and then double-click the **Inserting** folder.

You can now view and select thumbnails of all pictures in this folder.

Tip

Views

If you cannot see thumbnails of the pictures in this file, click the **Views** down arrow on the **Insert New Pictures** toolbar, and then select **Thumbnails**.

11 In the list of file and folder names, click **Picture1**, hold down the Ctrl key, and then click **Picture2**, **Picture3**, and **Picture4**.

All four pictures are selected.

12 Click **Insert**.

The **Photo Album** dialog box appears with the four pictures listed under **Pictures in Album**.

13 Under **Album Layout**, click the **Picture layout** down arrow, and then click **4 pictures with title**.

14 Click the **Frame shape** down arrow, and then click **Oval**.

The pictures in the photo album appear with oval frames.

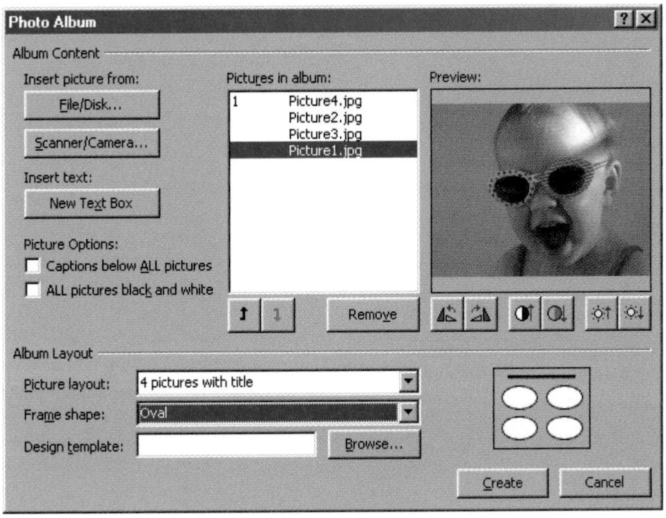

15 Click **Create**.

The **Photo Album** dialog box closes, and a new PowerPoint presentation opens with a title slide and your new four-picture slide.

16 On the **File** menu, click **Save As**, navigate to the **Inserting** folder in the **PowerPoint** folder, and then click **Save**.

PowerPoint saves the Photo Album file in the **Inserting** Folder.

Close Window

☒

17 Click the **Close Window** button in the Photo Album presentation window to return to your InsertPic presentation.

Tip

You can save a slide as a picture to use in other programs. Display or select the slide that you want to save, and then click **Save As** on the **File** menu. Click the **Save as type** down arrow, click **Windows Metafile**, and then click **Save**.

18 On the Standard toolbar, click the **Save** button to save the presentation.

Close Window

☒

19 Click the **Close Window** button in the presentation window.

The InsertPic presentation closes.

Modifying a Picture

If you insert a photograph or scanned image into a slide, you can enhance the image with brightness, contrast, and conversion controls. After you make changes, you can click the **Reset Picture** button on the **Picture** toolbar to reverse all changes. Sometimes you need only a portion of a picture in the presentation. With the **Crop Picture** command, you can mask portions of a picture so that you do not see all of it on the screen. The picture is not altered, just covered up. To rotate a picture, you select the object, position the pointer (which changes to the Free Rotate pointer) over the green rotate lever at the top of the object, and then drag to rotate the object to any angle.

Compress picture
new for
OfficeXP

You can also compress pictures with PowerPoint in order to minimize the file size of the image. In doing so, however, you many lose some visual quality, depending on the compression setting. You can pick the resolution that you want for the pictures in a presentation based on where or how they'll be viewed (for example, on the Web or printed), and you can set other options, such as delete cropped areas of picture, to get the best balance between picture quality and file size.

ModifyPic

In this exercise, you resize, enhance, move, crop, and then compress a picture.

1 On the Standard toolbar, click the **Open** button.

Open

🗁

The **Open** dialog box appears.

2 Navigate to the **SBS** folder on your hard disk, double-click the **PowerPoint** folder, double-click the **Inserting** folder, and then double-click the **ModifyPic** file.

The ModifyPic presentation opens, displaying Slide 1 in Normal view.

3 In the Slide pane, drag the scroll box to Slide 5.

4 Select the picture on the slide.

5 Hold down [Shift], and then drag the corner resize handles on the picture to enlarge the picture on the slide.

Important

If you are having trouble resizing the picture, you can press the [Alt] key while dragging the resize handles to turn off the **Snap objects to grid** feature, which aligns objects to an equally spaced grid on the slide.

Color

6 On the **Picture** toolbar, click the **Color** button, and then click **Washout**.

The picture is converted to a watermark.

Less Brightness

7 On the **Picture** toolbar, click the **Less Brightness** button four times.

The picture brightness decreases to enhance the look of the picture.

More Contrast

8 On the **Picture** toolbar, click the **More Contrast** button twice.

The picture contrast increases to enhance the look of the picture.

9 Drag the picture until it is aligned with the top of the bulleted text.

Crop

10 On the **Picture** toolbar, click the **Crop** button.

The pointer changes to the cropping tool.

Cropping Tool

11 Position the center of the cropping tool over the lower-middle resize handle, and then drag up to crop the bottom of the picture to the boy's knee.

Constrain pointer

While you are dragging, a dotted outline appears to show you the area that remains after cropping. The cropping tool also changes to a constrain pointer, indicating the direction in which you are cropping.

12 On the **Picture** toolbar, click the **Crop** button, or click a blank portion of the slide.

The cropping tool changes back to the pointer.

Compress Pictures

13 On the **Picture** toolbar, click the **Compress Pictures** button.

The **Compress Pictures** dialog box appears. The current settings fit your needs.

Compress Pictures [?] [X]

Apply to
- ( ) Selected pictures
- ( ) All pictures in document

Change resolution
- ( ) Web/Screen
- ( ) Print   Resolution: 200 dpi
- ( ) No Change

Options
- [✓] Compress pictures
- [✓] Delete cropped areas of pictures

[OK] [Cancel]

14 Click **OK**.

A warning box appears, letting you know that compressing pictures may reduce the quality of your images.

15 Click **Apply** to compress the image.

16 Drag the picture up in line with the top of the text box, and then deselect the picture.

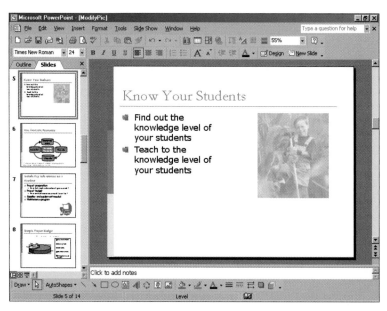

17 On the Standard toolbar, click the **Save** button to save the presentation.

Close Window [X]

18 Click the **Close Window** button in the presentation window.

The ModifyPic presentation closes.

Inserting and Modifying Stylized Text

PP2002-3-3

Approved Courseware

You can insert fancy or stylized text into a presentation with WordArt. WordArt allows you to add visual enhancements to your text that go beyond changing a font or font size. Most users apply WordArt to emphasize short phrases, such as *Our Customers Come First*, or to a single word, such as *Welcome*. You do not have to be an artist to create stylized text—WordArt provides you with a gallery of choices that stretches your text horizontally, vertically, or diagonally. You can also change the character spacing and reshape the text. You insert stylized text by first clicking the **Insert WordArt** button on the Drawing toolbar and then selecting a style.

InsertWrdArt

Open

In this exercise, you insert WordArt into a slide and format the WordArt text.

1 On the Standard toolbar, click the **Open** button.

   The **Open** dialog box appears.

2 Navigate to the **SBS** folder on your hard disk, double-click the **PowerPoint** folder, double-click the **Inserting** folder, and then double-click the **InsertWrdArt** file.

   The InsertWrdArt presentation opens, displaying Slide 1 in Normal view.

3 In the Slide pane, drag the scroll box to Slide 14.

Insert WordArt

4 On the Drawing toolbar, click the **Insert WordArt** button.

   The **WordArt Gallery** dialog box appears, displaying a list of styles.

5 Click the style in the third column, third row, as shown in the following illustration:

6 Click **OK**.

The **Edit WordArt Text** dialog box appears.

7 In the **Text** box, type **Helping our community grow!**

The WordArt text defaults to the Times New Roman font at 36 points.

8 Click **OK**.

The text that you typed and the **WordArt** toolbar appear.

9 Hold down ⎡shift⎤, and then drag the lower-left resize handle to the left to increase the size of the WordArt object until it reaches across the slide.

WordArt Shape

10 On the **WordArt** toolbar, click the **WordArt Shape** button, and then click the **Triangle Up** symbol in the first row.

The WordArt text appears as a triangle.

WordArt Character Spacing

11 On the **WordArt** toolbar, click the **WordArt Character Spacing** button.

A submenu appears with character spacing types.

12 On the **Character Spacing** submenu, click **Loose** to add space between the characters.

Format WordArt

13 On the **WordArt** toolbar, click the **Format WordArt** button.

The **Format WordArt** dialog box appears.

14 Click the **Size** tab.

15 In the **Size and rotate** area, click the up arrow until it reaches approximately 2" in the **Height** box.

16 Click **OK**.

The WordArt height increases to approximately 2 inches.

Shadow Style

17 On the Drawing toolbar, click the **Shadow Style** button, and then click **Shadow Settings**.

The **Shadow Settings** toolbar appears.

Nudge Shadow Up

18 On the **Shadow Settings** toolbar, click the **Nudge Shadow Up** button five times.

The WordArt shadow is adjusted upward.

19 Click the **Close** button on the **Shadow Settings** toolbar.

20 Drag the WordArt text object to the center of the slide, and then click a blank area of the presentation window.

The **WordArt** toolbar closes.

21 On the Standard toolbar, click the **Save** button to save the presentation.

Close Window

22 Click the **Close Window** button in the presentation window.

The InsertWrdArt presentation closes.

Chapter Wrap-Up

To finish the chapter:

Close

● On the **File** menu, click **Exit**, or click the **Close** button in the PowerPoint window.

PowerPoint closes.

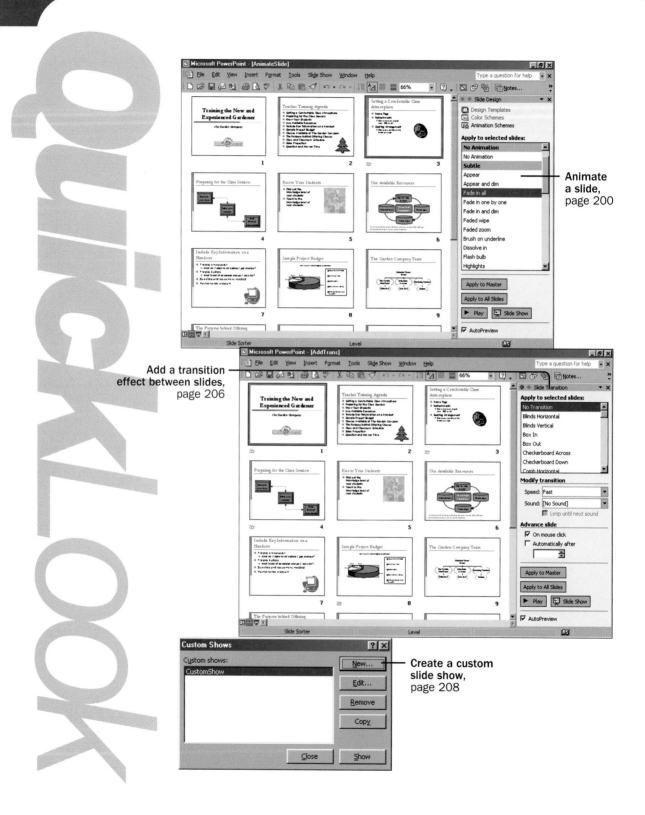

Animate a slide, page 200

Add a transition effect between slides, page 206

Create a custom slide show, page 208

Chapter 10
Setting Up and Delivering a Slide Show

After completing this chapter, you will be able to:

✔ Animate a slide during a slide show.
✔ Add transition effects between slides.
✔ Create and edit a custom show.
✔ Deliver a slide show.
✔ Take notes during a slide show.

In Microsoft PowerPoint, you can display presentations on your computer monitor using Slide Show view. Slide Show uses your computer like a projector to display a presentation on one or two monitors using the full screen or, using special hardware, on an overhead screen. You can set up a slide show to operate manually or continuously, unattended. To make your slide shows more exciting and engaging, you can add animation to text and graphics on the slide to display during a slide show. As you present a slide show, you can also take notes to document discussion points that members of your audience express during the presentation.

The owner of The Garden Company has been working on a training presentation for gardening teachers. She is ready to rehearse the slide show with Kim Yoshida and Mike Galos, two employees who will assist her in the teacher training session in two weeks.

In this chapter, you'll navigate through a slide show, draw on a slide during a slide show, add slide transitions, create custom animation, animate text, change animation settings, animate objects, hide a slide during a slide show, create and edit a custom slide show, and take notes during a slide show.

 This chapter uses the practice files AnimateSlide, AddTrans, CustomShow, Deliver-Show, and TakeNotes that you installed from this book's CD-ROM. For details about installing the practice files, see "Using the Book's CD-ROM" at the beginning of this book.

Animating a Slide During a Slide Show

PP2002-4-2

Approved Courseware

You can make a slide show more exciting and engaging by adding animation to the text and graphics on your slides. PowerPoint allows you to animate text and graph objects in a presentation. During a slide show, slide text can appear on the screen one paragraph, word, or letter at a time. A slide with text that you set to appear incrementally is called a **text animation slide**. You can determine which text indent levels to animate. For example, if a slide has multiple paragraphs and more than one level of bulleted text, you can customize the animation so that the levels of text in each bulleted item are animated separately.

In addition to animating text in a slide show, you can customize the animation of slide objects, such as drawn objects. To set custom animation effects, you must be in the Slide pane of Normal view. If you have an object with text, you can animate the text and the object separately or together. The default is for the object and its text to be animated at the same time. If you want, you can animate only the text in an object. Another way to customize object animation on a slide is to change the order of appearance for text or shapes on the screen during a slide show. You can also enhance a presentation by animating charts that are created with Microsoft Graph or imported from Microsoft Excel. For example, you can animate each data series in a chart to appear at a different time.

Animation Schemes

new for **Office**XP

The easiest way to apply animation effects to a slide show is to use **Animation Schemes** in the **Slide Design** task pane. **Animation Schemes** gives you one-click access to professionally designed animations divided into three categories: **Subtle**, **Moderate**, and **Exciting**. Most of these have sound connected to them. To preview each animation scheme, you can cycle through the various options until you find the animation that you want.

You can apply animation effects in Slide Sorter view or in Normal view. If you apply an animation effect in Slide Sorter view, PowerPoint applies the effect to every object on the slide except the title and background objects. If you apply an animation effect in Normal view, you need to select the objects that you want to animate on the current slide and then apply the effect.

If you would rather create your own animation scheme, you can customize the animation of an object by selecting the **Custom Animation** command on the **Slide Show** menu. Custom animations include moving multiple objects simultaneously, moving objects along a path, and applying sequencing for all effects on the slide. You can add animation schemes to each slide, or with one click, you can apply an animation scheme to all slides in a presentation.

AnimateSlide

In this exercise, you open **Animation Schemes** in the **Slide Design** task pane, apply an animation scheme to a slide, animate multiple slides, animate the text in a slide, change the text animation slide settings and text animation levels for a slide, animate the text in a slide object, change the order in which objects animate, and animate a chart in a slide.

1 Start PowerPoint, if necessary.

Open

2 On the Standard toolbar, click the **Open** button.

The **Open** dialog box appears.

3 Navigate to the **SBS** folder on your hard disk, double-click the **PowerPoint** folder, double-click the **ShowingSlides** folder, and then double-click the **AnimateSlide** file.

The AnimateSlide presentation opens, displaying Slide 1 in Normal view.

4 Click the **Slide Sorter View** button, and then click Slide 3 in Slide Sorter view.

5 On the **Slide Show** menu, click **Animation Schemes**.

The **Slide Design** task pane opens with a selection of animation schemes.

6 In the **Slide Design** task pane, under **Apply to selected slides**, click **Fade in all**.

PowerPoint applies the animation effect to the slide. An animation symbol appears below the left corner of Slide 3.

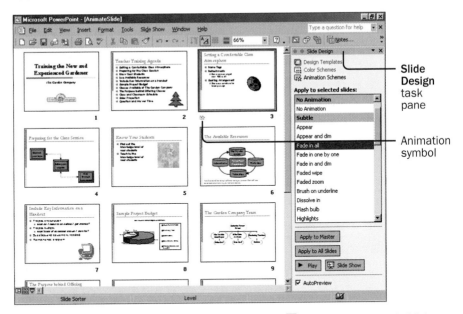

Slide Design task pane

Animation symbol

7 In Slide Sorter view, click Slide 2, hold down the Ctrl key, and then click Slides 5 and 6.

8 In the **Slide Design** task pane, under **Apply to selected slides**, click **Faded wipe**.

PowerPoint applies the animation effect to all three slides. An animation symbol appears below the left corner of each slide.

9 In Slide Sorter view, double-click Slide 1 to switch to Normal view and to display Slide 1.

10 On the **Slide Show** menu, click **Custom Animation**.

The **Custom Animation** task pane opens with the text prompt *Select an element of the slide, then click "Add Effect" to add animation.*

11 Click the title text *Training the New and Experienced Gardener*, and then click **Add Effect** in the **Custom Animation** task pane.

The **Add Effect** submenu appears with four effect categories: **Entrance**, **Emphasis**, **Exit**, and **Motion Paths**.

12 Point to **Entrance**, and then click **Fly In**.

The animation effect is demonstrated on Slide 1. In the **Custom Animation** task pane, the title text (item number 1), and a description of the effect appear in the **Animation Order** list.

13 Click the subtitle text *The Garden Company*.

14 In the **Custom Animation** task pane, click **Add Effect**, point to **Emphasis**, and then click **Spin**.

The animation effect is demonstrated. In the **Custom Animation** task pane, the subtitle text (item number 2), and a description of the effect appear in the **Animation Order** list.

Slide Show

15 Click the **Slide Show** button.

Slide 1 appears without the title.

16 Click anywhere on the screen to display the Fly In effect, and then click the screen a second time.

The company name spins.

17 Press the [Esc] key to end the slide show.

Slide 1 appears in Normal view.

18 In the **Custom Animation** task pane, click the first animated item in the **Animation Order** list to select it.

A down arrow appears when the item is selected.

19 Click the first animated item down arrow, click **Effect Options** to display the **Fly In** dialog box, and then click the **Effect** tab, if necessary.

The **Fly In** (your effect of choice) dialog box appears, showing the **Effect** tab.

20 In the **Enhancements** area, click the **Sound** down arrow, and then click **Camera**.

This option plays a sound during the slide animation.

21 Click the **Animate text** down arrow, and then click **By letter**.

This option animates the selected text one letter at a time.

Tip

You can enhance an animation by dimming out text after displaying it in a slide show. In the **Custom Animation** task pane, click the down arrow of the selected item in the **Animation Order** list, click **Effect Options**, click the **Effect** tab, click the **After animation** down arrow, and then click a color box or animation effect, such as hide after animation.

22 Click **OK**.

The animation effect and the sound play.

23 In the **Custom Animation** task pane under **Modify: Fly In**, click the **Start** down arrow, and then click **With Previous**.

The animation effect is set to play without having to click the screen during the slide show.

Slide Show

24 Click the **Slide Show** button to start the slide show and view the new animation effect.

The title appears one letter at a time, accompanied by the camera shutter sound.

25 Click the screen to spin the subtitle, and then press [Esc] to end the slide show.

Next Slide

26 Click the **Next Slide** button two times to advance to Slide 3.

27 In the **Custom Animation** task pane, click the second animated item in the **Animation Order** list, click the down arrow, and then click **Effect Options**.

The **Fade** dialog box appears.

28 Click the **Text Animation** tab, click the **Group text** down arrow, and then click **By 1st level paragraphs**.

This option animates the first level paragraph lines separately.

29 Click **OK**.

The **Fade** dialog box closes, and the effect is demonstrated.

30 At the bottom of the **Custom Animation** task pane, click **Slide Show**.

The title and first bulleted item fade in.

31 Click the screen.

The next bulleted item and the indented item below it appear.

32 Click the screen to display the next bulleted item, and then press [Esc] to end the slide show.

Tip

To print a presentation that contains animated slides, select the **Include animations** check box in the **Print** dialog box to print each stage of animation in the slide on a separate page.

33 In the Slide pane, drag the scroll box to Slide 4.

34 Drag the mouse to draw a selection marquee around the three shapes and the connectors.

35 In the **Custom Animation** task pane, click **Add Effect**, point to **Entrance**, and then click **Diamond**.

The three objects and two connector lines are animated. The number 1 appears next to each of the five parts to show that they are all animated at the same time.

36 At the bottom of the **Custom Animation** task pane, click **Slide Show**, and then click the screen.

The three objects and connector lines appear all at once.

37 Press Esc to end the slide show.

Re-Order up arrow

38 In the **Animation Order** list, click **Elbow connector 5**, click the **Re-Order** up arrow at the bottom of the task pane two times, click the **Start** down arrow, and then click **After Previous**.

The Elbow connector 5 animation order changes from fourth to second.

39 In the **Animation Order** list, click **Elbow connector 6**, click the **Re-Order** up arrow once, click the **Start** down arrow, and then click **After Previous**.

The Elbow connector 6 animation order changes from fifth to fourth.

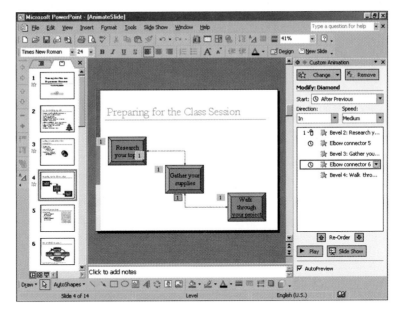

40 At the bottom of the **Custom Animation** task pane, click the **Slide Show** button, and then click the screen to view the entire slide content.

The objects and connector lines appear one after another from top to bottom.

41 Press Esc to end the slide show, and then in the **Custom Animation** task pane, click the **Close** button.

42 On the Standard toolbar, click the **Save** button to save the presentation.

Close Window

43 Click the **Close Window** button in the presentation window.

The AnimateSlide presentation closes.

Adding Transition Effects Between Slides

PP2002-4-3

Approved Courseware

Transition effects help your presentation make more of an impact by varying the way one slide replaces another. A slide transition is the visual effect of a slide as it moves on and off the screen during a slide show. Slide transitions include such effects as **Checkerboard Across**, **Cover Down**, **Cut**, and **Split Vertical Out**. You can set only one transition per slide. You can set a transition for one slide or a group of slides all at the same time by first selecting the slides in Slide Sorter view or in the Slide pane in Normal view and then applying the transition. You can also set the transition time between slides, the direction of the transition, and when the transition takes place. The **Slide Transition** task pane is the fastest and easiest way to apply a slide transition effect, set the transition speed and transition sound, and determine the settings for advancing a slide.

Tip

If you apply both a transition effect and an animation effect to a slide, the transition effect will occur first, followed by the animation effect.

AddTrans

In this exercise, you apply a slide transition effect to a single slide, apply a transition to multiple slides, and then change the transition speed.

1 On the Standard toolbar, click the **Open** button.

Open

The **Open** dialog box appears.

2 Navigate to the **SBS** folder on your hard disk, double-click the **PowerPoint** folder, double-click the **ShowingSlides** folder, and then double-click the **AddTrans** file.

The AddTrans presentation opens, displaying Slide 1 in Normal view.

Slide Sorter View

3 Click the **Slide Sorter View** button.

4 On the **Slide Show** menu, click **Slide Transition**.

The **Slide Transition** task pane appears with current slide transition options.

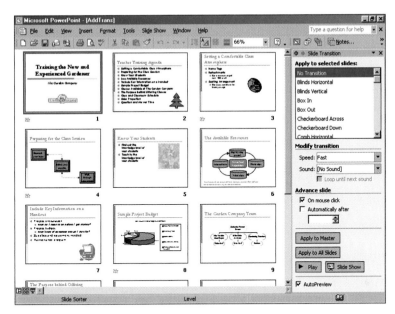

5 Under **Apply to selected slides**, scroll down, and then click **Dissolve**.

PowerPoint previews the transition effect on the slide miniature for Slide 1 in Slide Sorter view.

Tip

When there is already a transition or animation applied to a slide, PowerPoint places a transition symbol below the lower-left corner of the slide. The symbol indicates that PowerPoint has applied a slide transition effect to this slide.

6 Click the transition symbol below Slide 1.

PowerPoint demonstrates the Dissolve transition effect on Slide 1, followed by the animation effects.

Slide Show

7 Click the **Slide Show** button.

Slide Show view displays Slide 1 with the Dissolve transition effect, followed by the animation effect.

8 Click the screen to display the subtitle animation, and then press ⎋ to end the slide show.

9 On the **Edit** menu, click **Select All**.

All the slides in the presentation are selected.

10 Hold down ⌃, and then click Slide 1 to deselect it. Slide 1 already had a slide transition.

11 In the **Slide Transition** task pane, under **Apply to selected slides**, scroll down, and then click **Random Bars Horizontal.**

The preview box demonstrates the transition effect.

12 Under **Modify transition**, click the **Speed** down arrow, and then click **Medium**.

PowerPoint applies the transition effect to the selected slides. All the slides have a transition symbol below their left corners.

Slide Show

13 Click the **Slide Show** button.

Slide Show view displays Slide 2 with the Random Bars Horizontal effect.

14 Click the mouse several times to advance through the slides and watch the transition effect, and then press Esc to end the slide show.

PowerPoint returns you to Slide Sorter view.

15 In the **Slide Transition** task pane, click the **Close** button.

16 On the Standard toolbar, click the **Save** button to save the presentation.

Close Window

17 Click the **Close Window** button in the presentation window.

The AddTrans presentation closes.

Creating and Editing a Custom Show

If you plan to present a slide show to more than one audience, you don't have to create a separate presentation for each audience. Instead with PowerPoint, you can create a presentation within a presentation. Instead of creating multiple, nearly identical presentations for different audiences, you can group together various slides, name that group, and then display these slides during a presentation.

CustomShow

In this exercise, you create and edit a custom show and then save the presentation.

1 On the Standard toolbar, click the **Open** button.

Open

The **Open** dialog box appears.

2 Navigate to the **SBS** folder on your hard disk, double-click the **PowerPoint** folder, double-click the **ShowingSlides** folder, and then double-click the **CustomShow** file.

The CustomShow presentation opens, displaying Slide 1 in Normal view.

3 Click the **Slide Sorter View** button to switch to Slide Sorter view.

4 On the **Slide Show** menu, click **Custom Shows**.

The **Custom Shows** dialog box appears.

5   Click **New**.

The **Define Custom Show** dialog box appears. The default custom show name is selected in the **Slide show name** box.

6   In the **Slide show name** box, type **CustomShow**.

7   In the **Slides in presentation** box, click **Slide 1**, and then click **Add**.

Slide 1 appears in the **Slides in custom show** box on the right.

8   Select and add Slides 3, 4, 6, 8, 13, and 14 to the custom slide show.

9   Click **OK**.

The **Custom Shows** dialog box appears.

10   Click **Show** to start the slide show, and then click through all of the slides until Slide Sorter view appears, indicating that the slide show is complete.

11   In Slide Sorter view, on the **Slide Show** menu, click **Custom Shows**.

The **Custom Shows** dialog box appears.

12   In the **Custom shows** list, verify that **CustomShow** is selected, and then click **Edit**.

The **Define Custom Show** dialog box appears.

13   In the **Slides in custom show** box, click Slide 2 to select the item.

14   Click **Remove**.

PowerPoint removes Slide 2 from the custom show, but not from the presentation.

Tip

To change the order of the selected slide, click the up arrow or the down arrow.

15   Click **OK** to close the **Define Custom Show** dialog box.

16   Click **Show** to start the slide show, and then click through all of the slides until Slide Sorter view appears.

17   On the Standard toolbar, click the **Save** button to save the presentation.

Close Window

18 Click the **Close Window** button in the presentation window.

The CustomShow document closes.

Delivering a Slide Show

PP2002-7-1
PP2002-7-2

Approved Courseware

In addition to clicking the mouse to advance to the next slide in a slide show, PowerPoint provides you with several options for navigating through a slide show presentation. You can move from slide to slide by pressing keys on the keyboard or by using commands on the **Show Popup** menu in Slide Show view. With the **Slide Navigator**, you can jump to slides out of sequence. You can also start a slide show with any slide by selecting the slide in another view and then clicking the **Slide Show** button. To end a slide show at any time, you can click the **End Show** command on the **Show Popup** menu or press Esc.

During a slide show presentation, you can annotate slides by drawing freehand lines and shapes to emphasize a point. To do this, you choose the pen tool from the **Show Popup** menu and then begin drawing. You can change the pen color at any time during the presentation by choosing a new color from the **Show Popup** menu.

When delivering a show, you might want to customize a presentation for a specific audience, in which case all the slides in the current slide show might not be necessary. By using the **Hide Slide** command, you can hide the slides that you don't want to use during a slide show but still want to keep.

DeliverShow

In this exercise, you use the **Slide Navigator** on the **Show Popup** menu to navigate through a presentation in Slide Show view and to start or end a slide show with any slide. You also use the pen tool to underline the slide title during a slide show and change the pen color, and then you hide a slide in the current slide show.

Open

1 On the Standard toolbar, click the **Open** button.

The **Open** dialog box appears.

2 Navigate to the **SBS** folder on your hard disk, double-click the **PowerPoint** folder, double-click the **ShowingSlides** folder, and then double-click the **DeliverShow** file.

The DeliverShow presentation opens, displaying Slide 1 in Normal view.

Slide Show

3 Click the **Slide Show** button.

PowerPoint displays the first slide in the presentation.

4 Click anywhere on the screen, or press Space two times.

The slide show advances through the animation and to the next slide.

5 Press the ← key to display the previous slide, and then press the → key to display the next slide.

Show Popup
menu

6 Move the mouse to display the pointer.

The **Show Popup menu** button appears in the lower-left corner of the screen.

Tip

If the **Show Popup** menu doesn't appear, click **Options** on the **Tools** menu, click the **View** tab, select the **Show Popup menu** button check box, and then click **OK**.

7 Click the **Show Popup menu** button in the lower-right corner of the screen.

The **Show Popup** menu appears, showing the slide show navigation controls.

8 On the **Show Popup** menu, click **Next**.

The slide show advances to the first bulleted text line in Slide 3.

9 Right-click anywhere on the screen, and then click **Previous** on the **Show Popup** menu.

The first bulleted text line disappears in Slide Show view.

10 Right-click anywhere on the screen, point to **Go**, and then click **Slide Navigator**.

The **Slide Navigator** dialog box appears, showing a list of slides in the presentation, with the current slide selected.

11 In the list of slide names, click **Slide 9** to select the slide.

12 Click **Go To**.

Slide 9 appears in Slide Show view.

Tip

You can use the **By Title** command as an alternative to using the **Slide Navigator** dialog box.

13 Right-click anywhere on the screen, point to **Go**, point to **By Title**, and then click **Slide 14, The Garden Company**.

Slide 14 is the last slide in the presentation.

14 Click the screen to end the slide show, and then click the black screen, if necessary to display Slide 1.

Slide 1 appears in Normal view.

Tip

If a black screen appears at the end the slide show, click the screen to exit. To turn off this option, click **Options** on the **Tools** menu, click the **View** tab, clear the **End with black slide** check box, and then click **OK**.

15 In the Slide pane, scroll down to Slide 8.

Slide Show

16 Click the **Slide Show** button.

PowerPoint displays the current slide in slide show.

Pen Tool

17 Right-click anywhere on the screen, point to **Pointer Options**, and then click **Pen**.

The pointer changes to the pen tool. Now you are ready to draw on the slide.

Important

When the pen tool is active in Slide Show view, clicking the mouse does not advance the slide show to the next slide. You need to change the pen tool back to the pointer to advance using the mouse.

18 Draw a line under the word *Sample* in the title.

19 Right-click anywhere on the screen, point to **Screen**, and then click **Erase Pen** to erase the annotation.

20 Click the **Show Popup menu** button, point to **Pointer Options**, and then point to **Pen Color**.

The **Pen Color** submenu appears with a selection of different colors.

21 On the **Pen Color** submenu, click the Cyan color box.

Tip

If you advance to the next slide and then return to the slide that you annotated, your markings will be erased.

22 Draw a line under the text *$500* and *Fall/Winter* in the graph title.

23 Right-click anywhere on the screen, point to **Pointer Options**, and then click **Automatic**.

The pen tool changes back to the pointer, which allows you to click the mouse to advance to the next slide.

24 Press [Esc] to stop the slide show.

Slide 8 appears in Normal view.

Slide Sorter View

25 Click the **Slide Sorter View** button to display slides in Slide Sorter view.

26 Click Slide 10 to select the slide.

Hide Slide

27 On the Slide Sorter toolbar, click the **Hide Slide** button.

A hide symbol appears over the slide number to indicate that the slide will be hidden in a slide show.

28 In Slide Sorter view, click Slide 9 to select the slide.

Slide Show

29 Click the **Slide Show** button, and then click anywhere on the screen.

The slide show hides Slide 10 and displays Slide 11.

30 Press the [Esc] key to go back to Slide 9, the previous slide.

Tip

In slide show you can also press keys to perform operations. You can press [P] to go back to the previous slide, press [N] to go to the next slide, press [H] to show a hidden slide, press [E] to erase pen drawing, or press [A] to show the pointer arrow.

31 Right-click anywhere on the screen, point to **Go**, point to **By Title**, and then click **(10) The Purpose Behind Offering Classes** to show the hidden slide.

The hidden slide appears in Slide Show view.

32 Press [Esc] to end the slide show.

33 On the Standard toolbar, click the **Save** button to save the presentation.

Close Window

34 Click the **Close Window** button in the presentation window.

The DeliverShow presentation closes.

Using Presenter View with Multiple Monitors

If your computer is connected to two monitors, you can view a slide show on one monitor while you control it from another. This is useful when you want to control a slide show and run other programs that you don't want the audience to see. You can set up your presentation to use multiple monitors by choosing options in the **Multiple monitors** area in the **Set Up Show** dialog box. When you display your slide show on multiple monitors, you can present it using PowerPoint's new Presenter Tools in the Presenter view, which allows presenters to have their own view not visible to the audience. In addition to including details about what bullet or slide is coming next, this view also enables you to see your speaker notes and lets you jump directly to any slide. To use Presenter Tools in Presenter view, select the **Show Presenter View** check box in the **Set Up Show** dialog box. If you clear the **Show Presenter View** check box, the slide show runs as it would on a single monitor.

Before you can use multiple monitors, you need to install the proper hardware and software. Install the secondary monitor or project device according to the manufacturer's instructions, and install Microsoft Windows 98 or Microsoft Windows 2000 (for desktops only) software on your computer. The dual-monitor feature does not currently work with PC Card (PCMCIA) video adapters, so it will not work with all laptops. Check with your computer manufacturer to find out when integrated dual-monitor support will be available so that you can utilize the Presenter view.

To present a slide show on two monitors and to use Presenter view:

1   Open the PowerPoint presentation.

2   On the **Slide Show** menu, click **Set Up Show**.

The **Set Up Show** dialog box appears.

3   In the **Multiple monitors** options, click the **Display slide show on** down arrow.

4   Click the name of the monitor on which you want to project the slide show.

The slide show will run in full screen on the monitor that you choose but will appear in Normal view on the other monitor.

5   Select the **Show Presenter View** check box under the **Multiple monitors** options.

6   Click **OK** to present a slide show on two monitors.

Slide Show

7   Click **Slide Show** button to start the slide show.

8   In Presenter view, use the navigation tools to deliver the presentation on multiple monitors.

Taking Notes During a Slide Show

With PowerPoint's Meeting Minder feature, you can view the contents of your speaker notes pages, take meeting minutes, and enter action items during a slide show presentation. You can use the Meeting Minder to take notes unnoticed by the audience while you host an online broadcast. Because you are the host of the online broadcast, the **Meeting Minder** dialog box appears on your computer only.

The **Meeting Minder** dialog box contains two tabs: **Meeting Minutes** and **Action Items**. The **Meeting Minutes** tab displays a blank text box into which you enter text. The **Action Items** tab displays a **Description** field and an **Assigned To** field for you to fill in. You can access the **Meeting Minder** command on the **Tools** menu or on the **Show Popup** menu in Slide Show view.

TakeNotes

In this exercise, you enter notes and action items in the Meeting Minder.

1   On the Standard toolbar, click the **Open** button.

Open

The **Open** dialog box appears.

2   Navigate to the **SBS** folder on your hard disk, double-click the **PowerPoint** folder, double-click the **ShowingSlides** folder, and then double-click the **TakeNotes** file.

The TakeNotes presentation opens, displaying Slide 1 in Normal view.

Slide Sorter
View

3 Click the **Slide Sorter View** button to switch to Slide Sorter view.

4 Click the icon for Slide 11, and then click the **Slide Show** button.

5 Right-click anywhere on the screen, and then click **Meeting Minder** to display the **Meeting Minder** dialog box, showing the **Meeting Minutes** tab.

6 Click in the text box, if necessary, and then type Purchase 100 folding chairs and 10 tables.

7 Click the **Action Items** tab to display action item settings.

8 In the **Description** box, type Research cost of tables and chairs.

9 Press the [Tab] key, and then in the **Assigned To** box, type Kim Yoshida.

Meeting Minder	? X

Meeting Minutes | Action Items

Description: Research cost of tables and chairs

Assigned To: Kim Yoshida   Due Date: 2/24/03

Add

Edit

Delete

OK | Cancel | Schedule... | Export...

10 Click **Add**.

PowerPoint posts the action item in the Meeting Minder.

11 Click **OK** to return to slide show.

12 Click several times anywhere on the screen to advance to the last slide.

The last slide appears with a list of the action items that you created during the presentation.

13 Press [Esc] to end the slide show.

14 On the Standard toolbar, click the **Save** button to save the presentation.

Close Window

15 Click the **Close Window** button in the presentation window.

The TakeNotes presentation closes.

Chapter Wrap-Up

To finish the chapter:

Close

● On the **File** menu, click **Exit**, or click the **Close** button in the PowerPoint window.

PowerPoint closes.

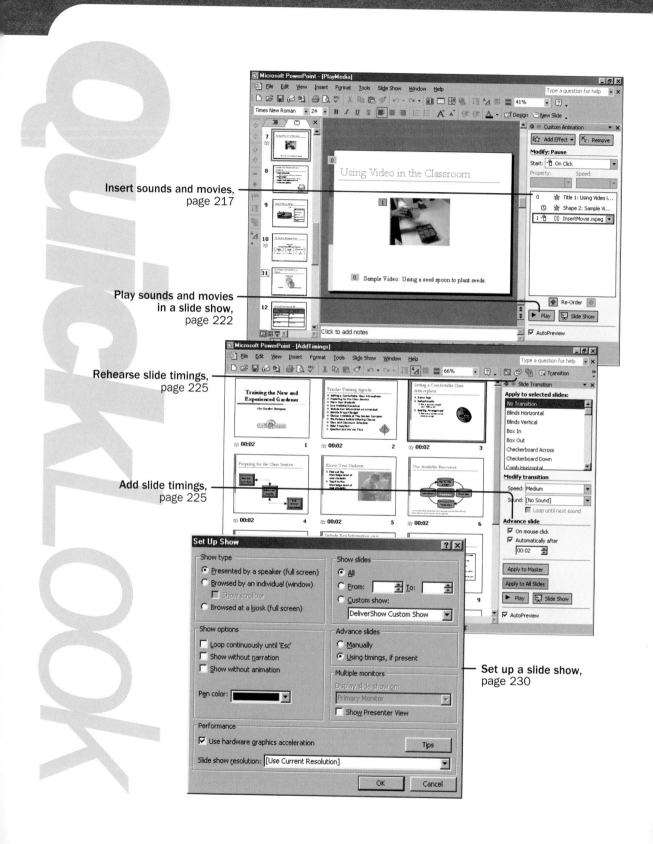

Insert sounds and movies, page 217

Play sounds and movies in a slide show, page 222

Rehearse slide timings, page 225

Add slide timings, page 225

Set up a slide show, page 230

Chapter 11
Creating a Multimedia Presentation

After completing this chapter, you will be able to:

✔ **Insert sounds and movies.**

✔ **Play sounds and movies in a slide show.**

✔ **Add slide timings.**

✔ **Record a narration in a slide show.**

✔ **Create a self-running presentation.**

With Microsoft PowerPoint, you can transform a slide show into a self-running multimedia presentation by adding sounds and movies, creating links to other slides, and setting slide timings. You can set PowerPoint to play the sounds and movies automatically, or you can play them manually.

The owner of The Garden Company has been working on a training presentation for gardening teachers. After adding transitions and animations, she decides to add sounds and movies to slides, add slide timings, and rehearse the presentation.

In this chapter, you'll insert sounds and a movie into a presentation, play sounds and movies in a slide show, add slide timings, rehearse slide timings, record narration, and set up a self-running presentation.

This chapter uses the practice files InsertMedia, InsertMovie, PlayMedia, AddTimings, RecNarration, and CreateShow that you installed from this book's CD-ROM. For details about installing the practice files, see "Using the Book's CD-ROM" at the beginning of this book.

Inserting Sounds and Movies

PP2002-6-2

Approved Courseware

With PowerPoint, you can make a presentation more interesting by adding sounds and movie clips to play during a presentation. You can insert sounds and movies from the Microsoft Clip Organizer or from a file by double-clicking a media placeholder or by clicking the **Movies and Sound** command on the **Insert** menu.

To play sounds, you need sound hardware (such as a sound card and speakers) installed on your computer. To play a sound, you double-click the sound icon in the Slide pane in Normal view or during the slide show. PowerPoint inserts sounds as objects, which you can then change and edit.

Movies can be digital videos produced with digitized video equipment, or they can be **animated pictures**, also known as animated GIFs (Graphics Interchange Format), such as cartoons. To play a movie, you double-click the movie object. After you start the movie, you can click the movie object to pause and restart it. PowerPoint inserts movies as objects, which you can then change and edit. After you insert a movie, you can change the way it plays by modifying custom animation effects and movie options. You can also change the action settings to play a movie or sound by moving the mouse over the object instead of clicking the object.

InsertMedia
InsertMovie

In this exercise, you add sound to a slide transition, insert a sound into a slide, insert and play a movie, and change the movie effect options and action settings.

1 Start PowerPoint, if necessary.

The PowerPoint program window opens.

Open

2 On the Standard toolbar, click the **Open** button.

The **Open** dialog box appears.

3 Navigate to the **SBS** folder on your hard disk, double-click the **PowerPoint** folder, double-click the **InsertingMedia** folder, and then double-click the **InsertMedia** file.

The InsertMedia presentation opens, displaying Slide 1 in Normal view.

4 On the **Slide Show** menu, click **Slide Transition**.

The **Slide Transition** task pane appears.

5 Click the **Sound** down arrow, and then click **Applause**.

PowerPoint applies the sound to the first slide.

Tip

For additional sound selections, click **Other Sound** at the end of the **Sound** list. In the **Add Sound** dialog box, navigate to the location of the sound file that you want to add, and then click **OK**.

Slide Show

6 Click the **Slide Show** button.

The sound plays during the animation to the first slide.

7 Press the Esc key to stop the slide show and return to Normal view.

8 In the Slide pane, drag the scroll box to Slide 10.

9 On the **Insert** menu, point to **Movies and Sounds**, and then click **Sound from Clip Organizer**.

The **Insert Clip Art** task pane appears with a selection of sounds.

10 In the **Insert Clip Art** task pane, scroll down the **Results** list, and then click **Tada**, or any other available sound.

A message box appears, asking if you want the sound to play automatically in the slide show.

11 Click **Yes**.

Sound icon

A small sound icon appears in the middle of the slide, as shown in the margin. The sound icon is small, but you can enlarge it for easier access by dragging a resize handle.

Tip

If you are connected to the Internet, you can click the **Clips Online** button in the **Insert Clip Art** task pane to open your browser and go to Microsoft's Design Gallery Live Web site to access hundreds of clip art images, photos, sounds, and movies.

12 Drag the sound icon to the lower-right corner of the slide, and then double-click the sound icon.

The sound plays.

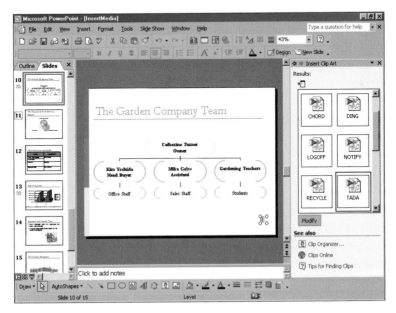

13 In the Slide pane, drag the scroll box to Slide 2.

14 On the **Insert** menu, point to **Movies and Sounds**, and then click **Movie from Clip Organizer**.

The **Insert Clip Art** task pane appears with a selection of movie clips.

Tip

Most of the movies in the **Clip Organizer** are actually animated pictures, also known as animated GIF files. Just like movies, animated GIF files add interest to your presentation, but you edit them more like an inserted picture than an inserted movie.

15 In the **Insert Clip Art** task pane, scroll down the **Results** list, and then click the **autumn tree with leaves** movie clip.

The movie clip is inserted into Slide 2. The automatic layout option changes the slide layout.

Automatic
Layout Options

16 In the Slide pane, click the **Automatic Layout Options** button, click **Undo Automatic Layout**, and then drag the movie clip to the blank area on the right side of the slide.

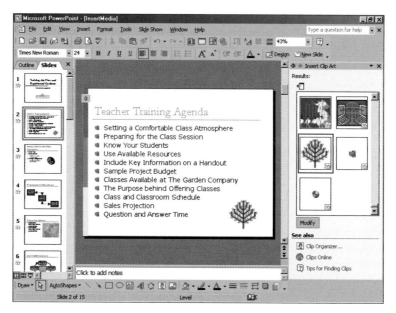

17 In the **Insert Clip Art** task pane, click the **Close** button.

Slide Show

18 Click the **Slide Show** button to view the movie clip on Slide 2.

Slide 2 appears, and the movie clip plays.

19 Press `Esc` to stop the slide show and return to Normal view.

20 In the Slide pane, drag the scroll box to Slide 7.

21 On the **Insert** menu, point to **Movies and Sound**, and then click **Movie from File**.

The **Insert Movie** dialog box appears.

22 Navigate to the **SBS** folder on your hard disk, double-click the **PowerPoint** folder, double-click the **InsertingMedia** folder, and then double-click the **InsertMovie** file.

A message box appears, asking if you want the movie to play automatically in the slide show.

23 Click **No**.

The movie clip is inserted into your slide.

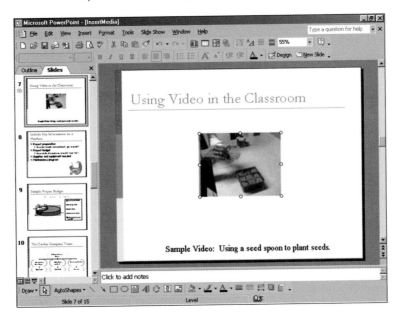

24 Double-click the movie object.

The movie object starts to play.

25 Click the movie object to pause the movie.

26 Click the movie object again to play the rest of the movie.

27 On the Standard toolbar, click the **Save** button to save the presentation.

Close Window

28 Click the **Close Window** button in the presentation window.

The InsertMedia presentation closes.

Playing Sounds and Movies in a Slide Show

After you insert a sound or movie object, you can change the way that it plays by modifying the animation or action settings. You can adjust the play settings so that PowerPoint plays the movie with the playback options that you set in the **Play Options** dialog box. You can also change the action settings to play a movie or sound by moving the mouse over the object instead of clicking the object. Additionally, you can change the animation order so that the movie plays either before PowerPoint animates the text or at the same time as PowerPoint animates the text. To find out the total playing time of the movie or to set play options, you right-click the movie object and then click **Edit Movie Object**.

PlayMedia

In this exercise, you modify the animation or action settings, adjust the play options, and change the animation order.

Open

1 On the Standard toolbar, click the **Open** button.

The **Open** dialog box appears.

2 Navigate to the **SBS** folder on your hard disk, double-click the **PowerPoint** folder, double-click the **InsertingMedia** folder, and then double-click the **PlayMedia** file.

The PlayMedia presentation opens, displaying Slide 1 in Normal view.

3 In the Slide pane, drag the scroll box to Slide 7.

4 Right-click the movie object, and then click **Edit Movie Object**.

The **Movie Options** dialog box appears, displaying movie play options and the total playing time of the movie.

5 Select the **Loop until stopped** check box.

Now when the movie object plays, the media clip continues to play until you stop it.

6 Click **OK** to close the **Movie Options** dialog box.

7 Double-click the movie object to play the movie until it plays more than once, and then click the movie object to stop the movie.

8 Right-click the movie object, and then click **Custom Animation** on the shortcut menu.

The **Custom Animation** task pane appears, displaying the media object in the **Animation Order** list.

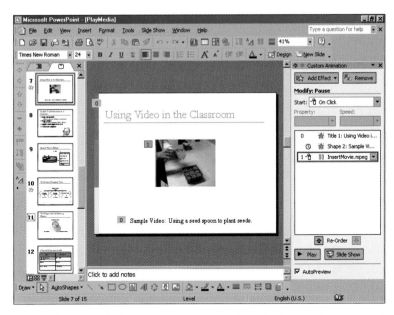

9 On the **Custom Animation** task pane, click the **InsertMovie** item in the **Animation Order** list (if necessary), click the **Start** down arrow, and then click **With Previous**.

The animation number is removed and will begin playing when the object right above it in the Animation Order list is displayed.

Tip

You can add and change custom animation settings for a specific media object by using the down arrow next to the media object. Click the media object down arrow in the Animation Order list, and then click **Effect Options** or **Show Advanced Timeline**.

Re-Order up
arrow

10 Click the **Re-Order** up arrow at the bottom of the **Custom Animation** task pane.

The animated movie now plays between the animated text during the slide show.

Tip

To remove a custom animation, click the media object down arrow in the **Animation Order** list, and then click **Remove**.

11 In the **Animation Order** list, click the **InsertMovie** down arrow, and then click **Show Advanced Timeline**.

A timeline appears at the bottom of the **Custom Animation** task pane.

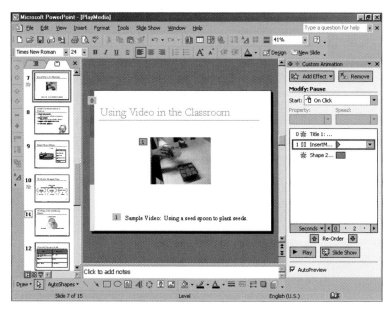

12 Click the **Play** button at the bottom of the **Custom Animation** task pane.

The slide appears in Normal view in the same way as in slide show, displaying the timeline indicator.

13 In the Slide pane, drag the scroll box to Slide 10.

14 Click the sound icon in the lower-right corner to select the object.

15 On the **Slide Show** menu, click **Action Settings**.

The **Action Settings** dialog box appears.

16 Click the **Mouse Over** tab, and then click the **Object action** option.

The **Play** option appears in the list.

Slide Show

17 Click **OK**, and then click the **Slide Show** button.

The sound plays once.

18 Move the mouse pointer over the sound icon to play the sound, and then click the mouse button to advance to the next slide.

19 Press Esc to stop the slide show.

20 On the Standard toolbar, click the **Save** button to save the presentation.

Close Window

21 Click the **Close Window** button in the presentation window.

The PlayMedia presentation closes.

Adding Slide Timings

PP2002-4-7

Approved Courseware

Slide timing refers to the length of time that a slide appears on the screen. As with transitions, you can set slide timings for one slide or a group of slides, depending on how many slides are selected when you apply the slide timing.

You advance the slide show in one of two ways: automatic advance, which you set with the timing feature; or manual advance, which you operate with the mouse. The automatic advance-timing feature moves slides through the slide show by itself, keeping each slide on the screen for the length of time that you designate. The mouse click-timing feature manually moves slides through the slide show.

Because you might want to spend more time talking about some slides than others, you can also set slide timings by using the **Rehearse Timings** button. If you are unsure of how fast to set the slide timings of a presentation, you can rehearse a slide show and adjust the timings appropriately for each slide during the rehearsal.

AddTimings

In this exercise, you apply slide timings in Slide Sorter view and then rehearse slide timings.

1 On the Standard toolbar, click the **Open** button.

Open

The **Open** dialog box appears.

2 Navigate to the **SBS** folder on your hard disk, double-click the **PowerPoint** folder, double-click the **InsertingMedia** folder, and then double-click the **AddTimings** file.

The AddTimings presentation opens, displaying Slide 1 in Normal view.

3 In the Slide pane, drag the scroll box to Slide 3.

Slide Sorter
View

🔳

4 Click the **Slide Sorter View** button.

The Slide Sorter View appears with Slide 3 selected.

Slide Transition

📑 T**r**ansition

5 On the Slide Sorter toolbar, click the **Slide Transition** button.

The **Slide Transition** task pane appears.

6 In the **Advance slide** area, select the **Automatically after** check box, and then click the up arrow twice to show **00:02**.

Because both check boxes in the **Advance slide** area are selected, the slides advance after two seconds or when you click the mouse.

Tip

In Slide Show view, a mouse click always advances a slide, even if the timing that is set in the **Slide Transition** task pane has not elapsed. Conversely, holding down the mouse button prevents a timed transition from occurring until you release the mouse button, even if the set timing has elapsed.

7 Click **Apply to All Slides**.

PowerPoint applies the current Slide Transition settings, including the new slide timing, to all of the slides and places the 00:02 timing under each slide in the Slide Sorter view.

Tip

It does not matter which slide is selected when you click **Apply to All Slides**.

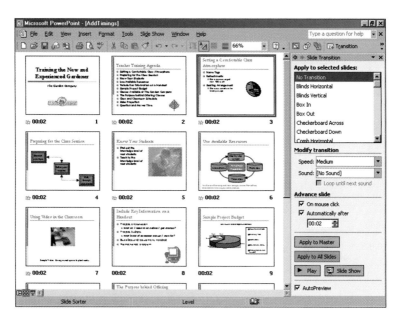

8 Scroll up (if necessary), and then click Slide 1 to select it.

Tip

Applying animations to multiple slides may affect how long the slide will stay on the screen during a slide show. Slide timings are divided equally among the animations for each slide, and you might need to adjust the slide timing to adequately show the animated items.

Slide Show

9 Click the **Slide Show** button.

PowerPoint runs the slide show in the presentation window, using the slide timing that you set in the **Slide Transition** task pane.

10 Press Esc to stop the slide show and return to Slide Sorter view.

Important

Before you begin this section, read all of the steps carefully so that you understand what happens when you click the **Rehearse Timings** button.

Rehearse
Timings

11 On the Slide Sorter toolbar, click the **Rehearse Timings** button.

The slide show begins. The **Rehearsal** dialog box is displayed in the upper-left corner of the screen.

Next button ——— Rehearsal ▾ ✕ ——— Repeat button
↦ ‖ 0:00:10 ↺ 0:00:10

The slide time begins running as soon as the first slide appears.

12 As soon as you feel that enough time has passed to adequately view or discuss the information on the slide, click the mouse or the **Next** button to select a new slide timing, or press the ↦ key to use the original timings for each slide in the presentation.

13 If the time is inadequate, click the **Repeat** button, and then rehearse the slide again. To stop the slide rehearsal at any time, click the **Close** button in the **Rehearsal** dialog box.

At the end of the slide rehearsal, a confirmation dialog box appears with the total time for the slide show.

14 Click **Yes** to save the new slide timings.

Slide Show

15 Click the **Slide Show** button.

Using the slide timings that you set during the slide show rehearsal, PowerPoint runs through the slide show in the presentation window.

When the slide show ends, you return to Slide Sorter view.

16 On the Standard toolbar, click the **Save** button to save the presentation.

Close Window

17 Click the **Close Window** button in the presentation window.

The AddTimings presentation closes.

Recording a Narration in a Slide Show

You can add voice narration or sound in a slide show when you are either creating a slide show for individuals who can't attend a presentation or archiving a meeting for presenters to review later and hear comments made during the presentation. To record a narration, your computer needs a sound card and a microphone. You can record a narration before you run a slide show, or you can record it during the presentation and include audience comments. As you record the narration, you can pause or stop the narration at any time. You can also delete a voice narration, as with any other PowerPoint object.

Important

You need to have a sound card or internal sound hardware, a microphone, and speakers installed on your computer to record and play a narration in a slide show. If you don't have sound recording and playing hardware installed on your computer, the **Record Sound** command on the **Movies and Sounds** submenu on the **Insert** menu and the **Record Narration** command on the **Slide Show** menu are dimmed. If these commands are dimmed on your computer, skip this section.

RecNarration

In this exercise, you record a sound or comment on a single slide, delete the sound or comment, and then record a voice narration during the presentation.

1 On the Standard toolbar, click the **Open** button.

Open

The **Open** dialog box appears.

2 Navigate to the **SBS** folder on your hard disk, double-click the **PowerPoint** folder, double-click the **InsertingMedia** folder, and then double-click the **RecNarration** file.

The RecNarration presentation opens, displaying Slide 1 in Normal view.

3 On the **Insert** menu, point to **Movies and Sounds**, and then click **Record Sound**.

The **Record Sound** dialog box appears.

Record Sound	? X
Name: Recorded Sound	OK
Total sound length: 0	Cancel
▶ ■ ●	

4 In the **Name** box, select the text, and then type **Welcome**.

Record

5 Click the **Record** button, and then say, "Welcome to The Garden Company teacher training day!"

Stop

6 Click the **Stop** button, click the **Play** button, and then click **OK**.

Your welcome plays back and a sound icon appears on the slide.

Sound icon

7 Click the sound icon, and then press [Del].

The sound recording on Slide 1 is deleted.

8 On the **Slide Show** menu, click **Record Narration**.

The **Record Narration** dialog box appears, showing the amount of free disk space and the number of minutes that you can record.

Record Narration	? X
Current recording quality	OK
Quality: [untitled]	Cancel
Disk use: 10 kb/second	
Free disk space: 2047 MB (on C:\)	Set Microphone Level...
Max record time: 3245 minutes	Change Quality...
Tip	
⚠ Adjust quality settings to achieve desired sound quality and disk usage. Higher recording quality uses more disk space. Large narrations should be linked for better performance.	
☐ Link narrations in: C:\...\PowerPoint\InsertingMedia\	Browse...

Important

You can insert narration into slides in one of two ways. Embedding the narration adds the sound objects to the presentation (increasing the size of the file), while linking the narration stores the sound objects in separate files. To insert the narration into slides as an embedded object and to begin recording, click **OK**. To insert the narration as a linked object, select the **Link narrations in** check box, and then click **OK** to begin recording. Notice that while you are recording, you won't hear the other sounds that you inserted into the slide show.

9 Click **OK**.

The first slide in the presentation animates and the recording begins.

10 Use the rehearsed slide timings, or click to advance through the slide show and add voice narration (your own explanation of the slides) as you go.

11 Right-click anywhere on the screen, and then click **Pause Narration**.

The voice narration recorder pauses.

12 Right-click anywhere on the screen, and then click **Resume Narration**.

The voice narration recorder resumes, and you can step through the rest of the slide show, adding narration. At the end of the slide show, a message appears, asking if you want to save the new slide timings along with the narration.

13 Click **Save**.

A sound icon appears in the lower-right corner of each slide that has narration.

Tip

To show a presentation with narration on a computer without sound hardware installed, click **Set Up Show** on the **Slide Show** menu, and then select the **Show without narration** check box to avoid problems running the presentation.

Slide Show

14 Click the **Slide Show** button.

The narration plays with the slide show.

15 On the Standard toolbar, click the **Save** button to save the presentation.

Close Window

16 Click the **Close Window** button in the presentation window.

The RecNarration presentation closes.

Creating a Self-Running Presentation

Self-running slide shows are a great way to communicate information without needing someone to run the show. You might want to set up a presentation to run unattended in a kiosk at a trade show or place it on your company's Intranet to run at the user's convenience. A self-navigating show turns off all navigation tools except action buttons and other action settings available to the user.

Normally, you open a presentation in PowerPoint and click the **Slide Show** button to start a slide show. You can skip a step by saving a presentation as a PowerPoint Show that will launch directly into a slide show when opened.

CreateShow

In this exercise, you set up a self-running slide show.

1 On the Standard toolbar, click the **Open** button.

Open

The **Open** dialog box appears.

2 Navigate to the **SBS** folder on your hard disk, double-click the **PowerPoint** folder, double-click the **InsertingMedia** folder, and then double-click the **CreateShow** file.

The CreateShow presentation opens, displaying Slide 1 in Normal view.

3 On the **Slide Show** menu, click **Set Up Show**.

The **Set Up Show** dialog box appears.

4 Click the **Browsed at a kiosk (full screen)** option.

When you click this option, the **Loop continuously until 'Esc'** check box turns on and dims. If you have recorded narration sound, it plays unless you choose to turn it off.

5 Click **OK**.

The slide show options are set and the **Set Up Show** dialog box closes.

Slide Sorter
View

6 Click the **Slide Sorter View** button to switch to Slide Sorter view.

7 In Slide Sorter view, click the slide icon for Slide 14, and then click the **Slide Show** button.

Slide Show

Slide Show runs the presentation continuously, using the slide times and transitions that were previously set.

8 Press [Esc] to stop the slide show, and then double-click Slide 1 to return to Normal view.

Save

9 On the Standard toolbar, click the **Save** button to save the presentation.

10 On the **File** menu, click **Save As**.

The **Save As** dialog box appears.

11 Navigate to the **InsertingMedia** folder.

12 Click the **Save as type** down arrow, and then click **PowerPoint Show**.

13 In the **File name** box, type **AutoShow**, and then click **Save**.

PowerPoint saves the presentation as a slide show.

Close

14 Click the **Close** button in the presentation window.

The AutoShow presentation closes. You now start the self-running slide show presentation using Windows Explorer.

15 Start Windows Explorer to open the Windows Explorer program window.

16 Navigate to the **SBS** folder on your hard disk, double-click the **PowerPoint** folder, double-click the **InsertingMedia** folder, and then double-click the **AutoShow** file.

The AutoShow presentation opens in slide show and begins to play.

17 Press [Esc] to stop the slide show and exit the presentation.

Chapter Wrap-Up

To finish the chapter:

Close

● On the **File** menu, click **Exit**, or click the **Close** button in the PowerPoint window.

PowerPoint closes.

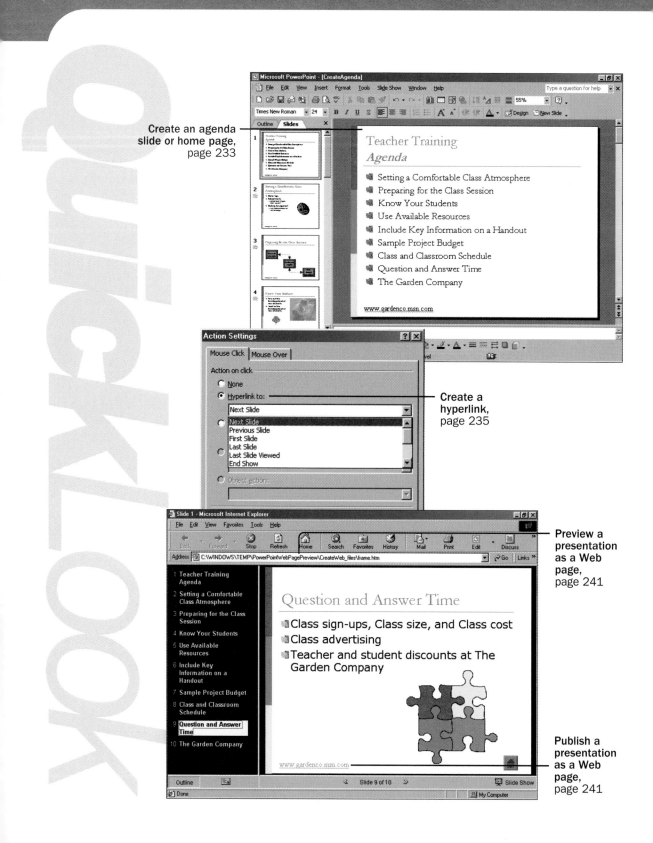

Create an agenda slide or home page, page 233

Create a hyperlink, page 235

Preview a presentation as a Web page, page 241

Publish a presentation as a Web page, page 241

Chapter 12
Creating a
Web Presentation

After completing this chapter, you will be able to:

✔ **Create an agenda slide or home page.**

✔ **Create a hyperlink.**

✔ **Preview and publish a presentation as a Web page.**

✔ **Add a digital signature.**

With Microsoft PowerPoint, you can publish a presentation on the World Wide Web by using online templates that help you design the presentation for Internet viewing. PowerPoint also features tools that help you save a presentation for the Internet, access the Internet, and create jumps, known as **hyperlinks**, to other slides and files.

The owner of The Garden Company has decided to publish her current presentation on the company Web site. She is also ready to modify the presentation for use on the Internet.

In this chapter, you'll create an agenda slide or home page, create a hyperlink to a slide, a Microsoft Excel chart, and the Web, create an action button, apply a digital signature for the Web, preview a presentation as a Web page, save and publish a presentation as a Web page for the Internet, and access the Internet from PowerPoint.

 This chapter uses the practice files CreateAgenda, CreateLink, GardenBudget, CreateWeb, and AddSignature that you installed from this book's CD-ROM. For details about installing the practice files, see "Using the Book's CD-ROM" at the beginning of this book.

Creating an Agenda Slide or Home Page

A summary slide is a bulleted list of titles from selected slides in your presentation. You can create a summary slide to use as an agenda slide or as the home page for an online presentation. With the agenda slide, you can link to a related slide in a presentation or return to the agenda slide from any slide in a presentation. To create an agenda or summary slide or home page, you select the slides that you want to include from Slide Sorter view, and then you click the **Summary Slide** button on the Slide Sorter toolbar. In front of the first selected slide, PowerPoint creates a new slide that has a bulleted list with titles from selected slides.

CreateAgenda

In this exercise, you create an agenda slide or home page.

1 Start PowerPoint, if necessary.

The PowerPoint program window opens.

Open

2 On the Standard toolbar, click the **Open** button.

The **Open** dialog box appears.

3 Navigate to the **SBS** folder on your hard disk, double-click the **PowerPoint** folder, double-click the **CreatingWeb** folder, and then double-click the **CreateAgenda** file.

The CreateAgenda presentation opens, displaying Slide 1 in Normal view.

Slide Sorter
View

4 Click the **Slide Sorter View** button.

Slide Sorter view appears with Slide 1 selected.

5 On the **Edit** menu, click **Select All** to select all of the slides in the presentation.

Summary Slide

6 On the Slide Sorter toolbar, click the **Summary Slide** button.

A new slide with bulleted titles from the selected slides appears in front of the first selected slide.

Normal View

7 Click the **Normal View** button to display Slide 1 in Normal view.

8 Select the title text *Summary Slide*.

9 Type **Teacher Training**, and then press the ⏎ Enter key.

The *Teacher Training* text moves up and becomes smaller to leave room for a second line of text within the title.

Font Size
36 ▾

10 On the Formatting toolbar, click the **Font Size** down arrow, and then click **36** to increase the font size.

Bold
B

11 On the Formatting toolbar, click the **Bold** button, and then click the **Italic** button to format the selected text.

12 Type **Agenda**.

13 Click a blank area to deselect the object.

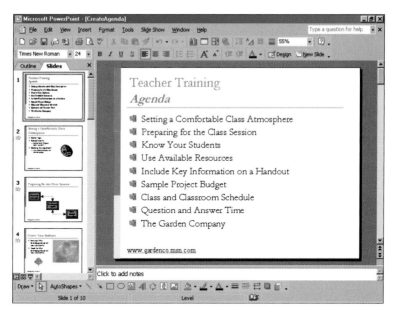

14 On the Standard toolbar, click the **Save** button to save the presentation.

Close Window

15 Click the **Close Window** button in the presentation window.

The CreateAgenda presentation closes.

Creating a Hyperlink

PP2002-4-10

Approved Courseware

The power of a Web presentation is its ability to link to different places: to another point in the presentation, to other slide shows or files on your computer or your company's intranet, or to Web site addresses (called Uniform Resource Locators, or URLs). During a PowerPoint slide show, you can use the **Action Settings** command to create a hyperlink that links to another slide, a different presentation, or a Web site.

You can add a hyperlink to any text or object, such as a shape, table, graph, or picture, to directly link it to another location when you click the object or hold the mouse pointer over it to start its action. If you have text within a shape, you can establish separate hyperlinks for both the shape and the text.

You can also create a hyperlink to a file from another program or another PowerPoint presentation during a slide show. For example, you can link to a Microsoft Excel chart to display additional detail on a topic. You can create a hyperlink from an object on a slide to a file, and you can edit or change that object without losing the hyperlink. However, if you delete all of the text or the entire object, you will lose the hyperlink.

PowerPoint provides a set of predefined navigation buttons, such as **Home**, **Help**, **Information**, **Back**, **Next**, **Beginning**, **End**, and **Return**. These are known as

action buttons, which help you navigate to a particular part of a presentation or a file. You create an action button by selecting a button from the **Action Buttons** submenu on the **Slide Show** menu and then dragging the pointer on the slide until the button appears.

CreateLink
GardenBudget

In this exercise, you create a hyperlink to a slide, create a hyperlink to a Microsoft Excel chart and to a Web site, create a home page button, link it to the home page, add a sound to the home page button, and return to the first slide or home page.

1 On the Standard toolbar, click the **Open** button.

Open

The **Open** dialog box appears.

2 Navigate to the **SBS** folder on your hard disk, double-click the **PowerPoint** folder, double-click the **CreatingWeb** folder, and then double-click the **CreateLink** file.

The CreateLink presentation opens, displaying Slide 1 in Normal view.

3 In the Slide pane, drag the scroll box to Slide 3.

4 Select the text *Walk through your project* in the bottom text box.

5 On the **Slide Show** menu, click **Action Settings**.

The **Action Settings** dialog box appears, displaying the **Mouse Click** tab.

6 Click the **Hyperlink to** option.

The **Hyperlink to** down list becomes available.

7 Click the **Hyperlink to** down arrow.

8 In the **Hyperlink to** list, scroll down, and then click **Slide**.

The **Hyperlink to Slide** dialog box appears.

9 In the **Slide title** list, click **5. Use Available Resources**.

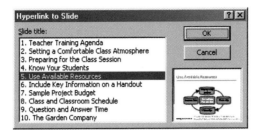

10 Click **OK**.

The **Action Settings** dialog box appears. The title of the slide that you selected appears in the text box below the **Hyperlink to** option.

11 Click **OK**, and then click a blank area of the slide.

The hyperlink text is underlined and in gold, which coordinates with the accent and hyperlink color in the slide color scheme.

Slide Show

12 Click the **Slide Show** button.

Slide 3 appears in Slide Show view, and the slide title animates.

Hand pointer

13 Click the mouse button to display the boxes and connectors, move the mouse to display the pointer, and then position the pointer (which changes to the hand pointer) over the text *Walk through your project*.

14 Click the underlined text in the bottom text box.

The slide show links to Slide 5, "Use Available Resources."

15 Press the Esc key to end the slide show.

16 In the Slide pane, drag the scroll box to Slide 7, and then click the chart object.

17 On the **Slide Show** menu, click **Action Settings**.

The **Action Settings** dialog box appears, displaying the **Mouse Click** tab.

18 Click the **Hyperlink to** option, click the **Hyperlink to** down arrow, and then click **Other File**.

The **Hyperlink to Other File** dialog box appears.

19 Navigate to the **SBS** folder on your hard disk, double-click the **PowerPoint** folder, double-click the **CreatingWeb** folder, and then double-click the **GardenBudget** file.

The **Action Settings** dialog box appears. The file name that you selected and its location appear in the text box below the **Hyperlink to** option.

Slide Show

20 Click **OK**, and then click the **Slide Show** button.

Slide 7 appears in Slide Show view, and the slide title animates.

Hand pointer

ᵕᣟᕋ

21 Move the mouse to display the pointer, position the pointer (which changes to the hand pointer) over the chart object, and then click the chart object.

Excel opens and displays a pie chart showing a Spring/Summer sample budget.

22 On the **File** menu in the Microsoft Excel window, click **Exit**, and then click **No**, if you are prompted to save any changes to the Excel file.

Excel quits and you return to the slide show.

23 Press [Esc] to end the slide show.

24 On the **View** menu, point to **Master**, and then click **Slide Master**.

The Slide Master appears.

25 Select the text *www.gardenco.msn.com*.

A slanted-line selection box appears around the highlighted text.

Insert Hyperlink

26 On the Standard toolbar, click the **Insert Hyperlink** button.

The **Insert Hyperlink** dialog box appears.

Important

The **Insert Hyperlink** dialog box appears with the blinking insertion point in the **Address** box. Now you are ready to type the URL to which you want to link. A Web site address consists of three parts: the prefix *http://*, which indicates an address on the Internet; a network identification, such as *www* for World Wide Web; and a Web site name, or domain name, such as *microsoft.com*.

27 In the **Address** box, type **http://www.gardenco.msn.com**.

As you type, the top URL in the list appears.

Edit Hyperlink		? X
Link to:	Text to display: www	ScreenTip...
Existing File or Web Page	Look in: CreatingWeb	Bookmark...
	Current Folder — AddSignature, CreateAgenda, CreateLink, CreateWeb, GardenBudget	
Place in This Document	Browsed Pages	
Create New Document	Recent Files	
	Address: http://www.gardenco.msn.com	Remove Link
E-mail Address		OK Cancel

28 Click **OK**.

The Web site address appears as a URL in the Slide Master.

Troubleshooting

If a red line appears under the URL (which means that the spell checker doesn't recognize it), right-click the URL, and then click **Ignore All**.

29 On the **Slide Show** menu, point to **Action Buttons**. The **Action Buttons** submenu appears.

Home

30 Click the **Home** button in the top row, second column.

The pointer changes to the cross-hair pointer.

31 Position the cross-hair pointer in the lower-right corner of the slide.

Cross-hair pointer

+

32 Drag the pointer to make the **Home** button appear, as shown in the following illustration:

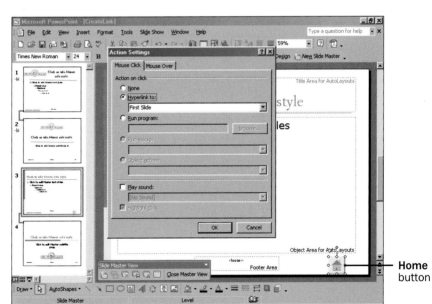

Home button

When you release the mouse, the **Action Settings** dialog box has the **Hyperlink to** option set to **First Slide** and the **Highlight click** check box at the lower-left of the dialog box selected.

33 Select the **Play sound** check box, click the **Play sound** down arrow, scroll down, click **Camera**, and then click **OK**.

The Camera sound is set to play when the **Home** button is used.

Fill Color

34 On the Drawing toolbar, click the **Fill Color** down arrow, and then click the Green color box.

The **Home** button now has a green background.

35 On the Slide Master View toolbar, click **Close Master View**.

Slide 7 appears in Normal view with the **Home** button in the lower-right corner.

Slide Show

36 Click the **Slide Show** button.

The slide entitled *Sample Project Budget* appears.

37 Click the **Home** button.

The slide show returns to the first slide or home page, and the camera sound plays.

38 Press Esc to end the slide show.

39 On the Standard toolbar, click the **Save** button to save the presentation.

Close Window

40 Click the **Close Window** button in the presentation window.

The CreateLink presentation closes.

Creating a Web Presentation with the AutoContent Wizard

You can use the AutoContent Wizard to create a presentation designed for Web viewing. When you create this type of presentation, PowerPoint places action buttons on the screen for the user to click to navigate through the slide show.

To create a Web presentation with the AutoContent Wizard:

1 On the Standard toolbar, click the **New** button, and then click the **From AutoContent Wizard** option in the **New Presentation** task pane.

The AutoContent Wizard opens.

2 After reading the introduction, click **Next**.

3 Select a presentation type, and then click **Next**.

4 Click the **Web presentation** option, and then click **Next**.

5 Type your presentation title, add information to the footer, if desired, and then click **Next**.

6 Click **Finish** to create a Web presentation.

Previewing and Publishing a Presentation as a Web Page

PP2002-7-5
PP2002-8-4

Approved Courseware

With PowerPoint, you can easily save a presentation as a Web page in HTML (Hypertext Markup Language) format with the extension .htm. HTML is a markup language of tags, which determine how text and graphics are displayed in a browser. The **Save as Web Page** command on the **File** menu creates a Web page from a presentation, giving the presentation a navigation frame down the left side of the page. You can also create a Web page from a presentation by using the **Save As** comand on the **File** menu. In the **Save As** dialog box, click the **Save as type** down arrow, and then click **Web Page** or **Web Archive**. The Web Page type produces the same results as the **Save as Web Page** command. PowerPoint creates a folder with the same name as the Web page presentation. In this folder is a set of files that PowerPoint uses to display the presentation as a Web page. If you move the Web page presentation to another location, you also need to move this folder. The Web Archive type saves all the elements of the presentation, including text and graphics, into a single file with the .mht extension. In your browser, you can open a PowerPoint presentation that you have saved in the Web Page or Web Archive format. To see what a presentation will look like as a Web page, you can preview it using the **Web Page Preview** command on the **File** menu.

Before you save a presentation as a Web page, you can choose to save the graphics in a presentation in PNG (Portable Networks Graphics) format. PNG graphic files are smaller, so you can save and download them faster. However, not all browsers support PNG format, which is recommended for Microsoft Internet Explorer 5.0 or later.

If you have access to the Internet or to an intranet through your corporate network, you can use the Web toolbar to browse through Internet presentations and other Microsoft Office documents on the World Wide Web. With the Web toolbar, you can access the Internet using common Microsoft Internet Explorer commands. You can also connect to the Microsoft Web site from PowerPoint. The Web site contains the latest PowerPoint tools and techniques, free downloads, product news, answers to frequently asked questions, and online support for Microsoft products.

CreateWeb

In this exercise, you preview a presentation as a Web page and save the graphics in PNG format, publish a presentation as a Web page and open the presentation in your browser, and use the Web toolbar to open an Internet presentation and connect to the Microsoft Web site.

Open

1 On the Standard toolbar, click the **Open** button.

The **Open** dialog box appears.

2 Navigate to the **SBS** folder on your hard disk, double-click the **PowerPoint** folder, double-click the **CreatingWeb** folder, and then double-click the **CreateWeb** file.

The CreateWeb presentation opens, displaying Slide 1 in Normal view.

3 On the **File** menu, click **Web Page Preview**, and then click the **Maximize** button, if necessary.

The message *Preparing for Web Page Preview* appears in the status bar, along with a status indicator, and then your browser opens, displaying your presentation as a Web page. In a frame on the left side of the window, PowerPoint lists all of the slide titles.

Tip

If you do not have Internet Explorer as your Web browser, click the necessary prompts to proceed in Netscape or another browser.

4 Scroll down the list of slide titles on the left, and then click **Question and Answer Time**.

The **Question and Answer Time** slide appears on the frame on the right.

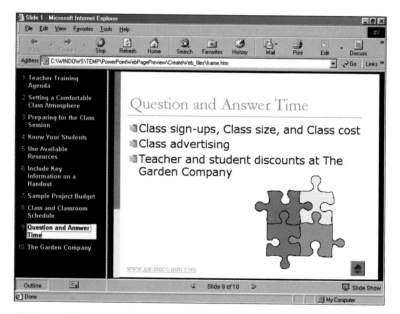

5 Click the **Home** button on the slide to link to the first slide.

6 On the **File** menu in the browser window, click **Close**.

Your browser closes and you return to PowerPoint.

7 On the **Tools** menu, click **Options**.

The **Options** dialog box appears.

8 Click the **General** tab, if necessary, and then click **Web Options**.

The **Web Options** dialog box appears.

9 Click the **Browsers** tab.

10 Select the **Allow PNG as a graphics format** check box, if necessary.

11 Click the **General** tab.

12 Select the **Add slide navigation controls** check box (if necessary), click the **Colors** down arrow, and then click **Presentation colors (accent color)**.

13 Select the **Show slide animation while browsing** check box.

14 Click **OK** to close the **Web Options** dialog box, and then click **OK** to close the **Options** dialog box.

The Web options are set and Normal view appears.

15 On the **File** menu, click **Save as Web Page**.

The **Save As** dialog box appears with **Web Page** in the **Save as type** list at the bottom of the dialog box.

16 Click in the **File name** box so that the insertion point follows the existing file name, and then type Page.

17 Navigate to the **CreatingWeb** folder, if necessary.

18 Click **Publish**.

The **Publish as Web Page** dialog box appears.

19 Click the **Complete presentation** option, if necessary, and then click the **All browsers listed above (creates larger files)** option.

This option makes the Web presentation compatible for all browsers.

20 Clear the **Open published Web page in browser** check box, if necessary, and then click **Publish**.

PowerPoint saves the presentation as a Web page.

Tip

You can also save a presentation to an FTP site. FTP (**File Transfer Protocol**) is a communications method that lets you quickly transfer and save files over the Internet. To save a presentation to an FTP site, click the **Save in** down arrow in the **Save As** dialog box, click **FTP Locations** in the list, double-click the site that you want, double-click the location where you want to save the presentation, type the presentation name, and then click **Save**.

21 On the Standard toolbar, click the **Save** button to save the presentation.

Close Window
☒

22 Click the **Close Window** button in the presentation window.

The CreateWeb presentation closes.

23 On the Standard toolbar, click the **Open** button.

The **Open** dialog box appears.

24 Navigate to the **CreatingWeb** folder.

Notice that there is a new folder at the top of the file list with the same name as the Web page file that you just saved.

25 In the folders and files list, click **CreateWebPage.htm**.

Tip

Depending on the computer's current Windows settings, the .htm extension might not appear in the file list.

26 Click the **Open** down arrow, and then click **Open in Browser**.

The presentation opens in your browser.

Tip

PowerPoint provides users with a variety of improved functionality when working with presentations in the browser. Improvements include displaying high quality images, printing multiple slides, saving presentations to FTP servers, playing sounds, and animating charts.

27 On the **File** menu in the browser window, click **Close**.

Your browser closes and you return to PowerPoint.

28 On the Standard toolbar, click the **Open** button.

The **Open** dialog box appears.

29 Navigate to the **CreatingWeb** folder, and then double-click **CreateWebPage.htm**

The Web presentation opens in PowerPoint.

Tip

If you know the Internet address or hard disk location that you want to access, you can click in the **Address** box on the Web toolbar and then type a file name or a Web site address. To open the Web toolbar, right-click any toolbar, and then click **Web**.

30 On the **Help** menu, click **Office on the Web**.

Your browser opens and displays the Office Update home page on the Microsoft Web site.

Troubleshooting

If you are not connected to the Internet, you will need to follow the instructions on your screen to establish a connection through your Internet Service Provider (ISP).

31 Click hyperlinks to navigate the Web site, and then on the browser's **File** menu, click **Close**.

Your browser closes and you return to PowerPoint.

32 On the Standard toolbar, click the **Save** button to save the presentation.

Close Window

33 Click the **Close Window** button in the presentation window, and then disconnect from the Internet, if necessary.

The CreateWeb presentation closes.

Adding a Digital Signature

Digital signature
new for
OfficeXP

Once you've finalized your Web document, you might consider adding a **digital signature**, an electronic, secure stamp of authentication on a document. When you apply your digital signature to a document, you verify the contents of the file and confirm that the file has not changed since you attached the signature. If someone modifies the file, the digital signature is removed.

When you add a digital signature to your file, you can sign either a file or a macro project. Sign a file when you are working with an unconverted PowerPoint presentation; sign a macro project when you are working with a presentation that has been converted to a Web page. To sign a file, you click **Options** on the **Tools** menu, click the **Security** tab, click **Digital Signatures**, click **Add**, click a certificate, and then click **OK** twice. To sign a macro project, you open the Visual Basic Editor using the **Macro** submenu on the **Tools** menu. The Visual Basic Editor window is probably unfamiliar to you. This window shows the programming needed to create a Web document. If you were a software developer, you would need to know the parts more closely. However, to apply a digital signature, you need only to confirm that you see the name of your file in the left pane of the window.

AddSignature

In this exercise, you open your Web page in PowerPoint and then assign a digital signature to your Web page using the macro project.

Important

Before you can start this exercise, you must install and run the Selfcert.exe file. This file enables you to create a digital signature that you will apply to your Web document in this exercise. The file is not installed during a normal Office installation. To install the file after you have already installed Office, insert your Office CD into your CD-ROM drive, run the Setup program, click the **Add or Remove Features** option, if necessary, click **Next**, click the **plus sign (+)** next to Office Shared Features to expand that option, click the **Digital Signatures for VBA Projects** down arrow, and then click **Update**. To run the Selfcert.exe file, start Windows Explorer using the **Start** button on the taskbar and then locate and double-click the **Selfcert.exe** file. The program is typically located in the Programs Files\Microsoft Office\Office folder. In the **Create Digital Certification** dialog box, type your name as instructed, and then click **OK**.

1 On the Standard toolbar, click the **Open** button.

Open

The **Open** dialog box appears.

2 Navigate to the **SBS** folder on your hard disk, double-click the **PowerPoint** folder, double-click the **CreatingWeb** folder, and then double-click the **AddSignature** file.

The **AddSignature** presentation opens, displaying Slide 1 in Normal view.

3 On the **Tools** menu, point to **Macro**, and then click **Visual Basic Editor**.

The **Microsoft Visual Basic** window opens.

4 Verify that the AddSignature file name is at the top of the page.

5 On the **Tools** menu in the Microsoft Visual Basic window, click **Digital Signature**.

The **Digital Signature** dialog box appears, indicating that no certificate is assigned to the document.

6   Click **Choose**.

The **Select Certificate** dialog box appears.

Select Certificate

Select a certificate you wish to use

Issued to	Issued by	Intended Pu...	Friendly name	Expiration D...
Catherine ...	Catherine T...	Code Signing	None	1/1/08

OK   Cancel   View Certificate...

7   Select a certificate in the list, and then click **View Certificate**.

The **Certificate** dialog box appears.

8   Click **OK** to close the **Certificate** dialog box.

The document contains a secure and authentic digital signature.

9   Click **OK** to close the **Select Certificate** dialog box, and then click **OK** to close the **Digital Signature** dialog box.

Close
☒

10   Click the **Close** button in the Microsoft Visual Basic window.

The Microsoft Visual Basic window closes, and the AddSignature presentation appears in PowerPoint.

11   On the Standard toolbar, click the **Save** button to save the presentation.

Close Window
☒

12   Click the **Close Window** button in the presentation window.

The AddSignature presentation closes.

Chapter Wrap-Up

To finish the chapter:

Close
☒

●   On the **File** menu, click **Exit**, or click the **Close** button in the PowerPoint window.

PowerPoint closes.

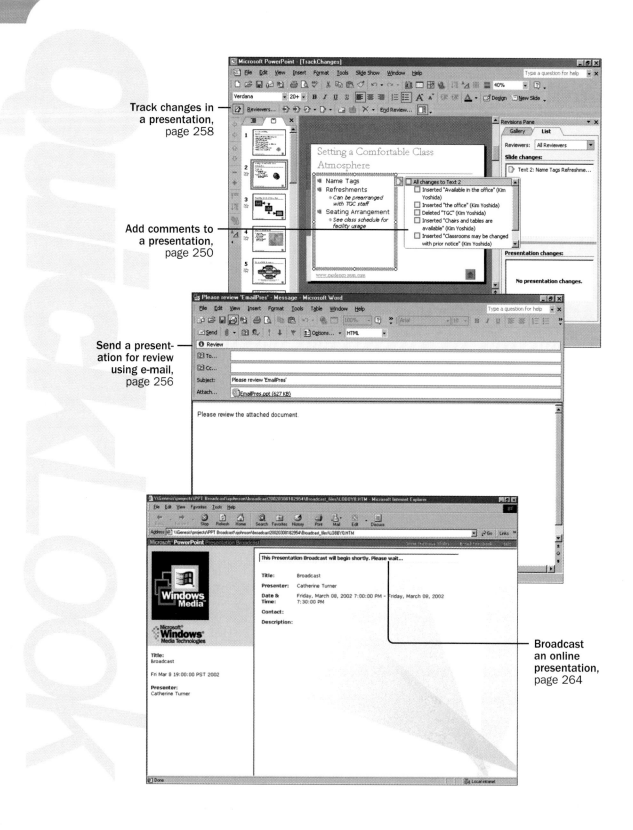

Track changes in a presentation, page 258

Add comments to a presentation, page 250

Send a presentation for review using e-mail, page 256

Broadcast an online presentation, page 264

Chapter 13
Reviewing and Sharing a Presentation

After completing this chapter, you will be able to:

✔ Add comments to a presentation.

✔ Add password protection to a presentation.

✔ Send a presentation for review using e-mail.

✔ Track changes in a presentation.

✔ Broadcast a presentation over a network.

✔ Collaborate in an online meeting.

✔ Deliver a presentation on the road.

After you create a draft of a presentation, you might want to distribute it to your coworkers for feedback. Collaborating with others can help you produce accurate and thorough presentations.

You can send a PowerPoint presentation to reviewers electronically so that they can read, revise, and comment on the presentation without having to print it. When reviewers return the edited presentations to you, you can track all of the revisions and comments, accept or reject them, and merge them into the original presentation.

In PowerPoint, you can track reviewer changes in two ways: by using the Reviewing toolbar, which contains buttons that let you accept and reject comments; and by using the **Revisions Pane**, which shows information related to the changes and comments in your presentation.

If your computer is on a network or if you have access to the Internet, you can give a slide show on any other computer on the network by using PowerPoint's online broadcasting feature. You can also allow other people to collaborate with you by using online collaboration, or by setting up and holding a Web discussion. Power-Point also includes features to help you deliver a presentation on the road.

The owner of The Garden Company has been working on a teacher training presentation. After completing it, she is ready to send the presentation to several co-workers for review and input. In particular, she is going to review the slide show over the company network with the head buyer, Kim Yoshida, before giving the presentation at the teacher training meeting.

In this chapter, you'll use comments in a presentation, add password protection to your presentation, send a presentation for review via e-mail, use Markup with a presentation, broadcast a presentation over a network, use online collaboration, hold a Web discussion, and use the PowerPoint Viewer and the Pack And Go Wizard to deliver a presentation on the road.

This chapter uses the practice files AddComments, AddPassword, EmailPres, Track-Changes, Merge, Broadcast, NetMeet, and RoadPres that you installed from this book's CD-ROM. For details about installing the practice files, see "Using the Book's CD-ROM" at the beginning of this book.

Adding Comments to a Presentation

PP2002-8-2

Approved Courseware

Asking others to review and comment on your presentation can assist you in perfecting the presentation before it is final. You or your reviewers can insert comments, which are notes about text or other parts of the presentation. Once comments are added to a presentation, you can edit or delete them, and you can choose to show or hide them.

You add a comment by clicking **Comment** on the **Insert** menu. To edit or delete a comment, you right-click the commented text and then click **Edit Comment** or **Delete Comment**. To hide or show a comment, you need to open the Reviewing toolbar and click the **Markup** button, which toggles on and off. You can also use the functions on the Reviewing toolbar to insert, delete, or edit comments.

Once you begin working with comments, you can open the **Revisions Pane** to view comments made for each slide. You can open the **Revisions Pane** by first right-clicking on any toolbar and then selecting **Revisions Pane** from the menu.

AddComments

In this exercise, you add and modify comments, open the Reviewing toolbar and the **Revisions Pane**, hide and show the comments in the presentation, and delete comments that you no longer need.

1 Start PowerPoint, if necessary.

The PowerPoint program window opens.

Open

2 On the Standard toolbar, click the **Open** button.

The **Open** dialog box appears.

3 Navigate to the **SBS** folder on your hard disk, double-click the **PowerPoint** folder, double-click the **Reviewing** folder, and then double-click the **AddComments** file.

The AddComments presentation opens, displaying Slide 1 in Normal view.

4 On the **Insert** menu, click **Comment**.

A comment box opens with your name, today's date, and a blinking cursor where you can begin typing your comment.

Tip

To change the name of the person making the comments, on the **Tools** menu, click **Options**, click the **General** tab, change the user information **Name** and **Initials**, and then click **OK**. All comments will have the new user information attached to them.

5 In the comment box, type **Does this cover everything?**

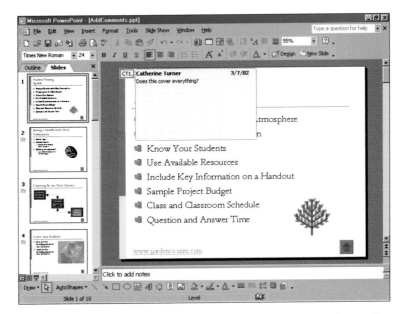

6 Click anywhere outside of the comment box, and then point to the small box to display the comment.

The comment box closes, and a small box with your initials and the number 1 appears in the upper-left corner.

7 In the Slide pane, drag the scroll box to Slide 3, and then select the first square object.

8 On the **Insert** menu, click **Comment**.

A comment box opens with your name, today's date, and a flashing cursor where you can begin typing your comment.

9 In the comment box, type **Any ideas for improving this slide?**

10 Click anywhere outside of the comment box.

The comment box closes, and a small box with your initials and the number 2 appear in the upper-left corner.

11 Double-click the small box.

The comment box reopens, allowing you to edit your comment.

12 Click after the word *slide* to place the insertion pointer, press [Space], type **visually**, and then click outside of the comment box to close it.

The edit is made, and the comment box closes.

13 On the **View** menu, point to **Toolbars**, and then click **Reviewing** to display the Reviewing toolbar.

Markup

14 On the Reviewing toolbar, click the **Markup** button.

The small comment box on Slide 3 disappears.

15 On the Reviewing toolbar, click the **Markup** button again.

The **Markup** button toggles on, and the comment box reappears.

Insert Comment

16 In the Slide pane, drag the scroll box to Slide 8, and then on the Reviewing toolbar, click the **Insert Comment** button.

A comment box opens with your name, today's date, and a flashing cursor where you can begin typing your comment.

17 In the comment box, type **Ask Kim to prepare a report on potential class sizes and class costs.**

18 Click anywhere outside of the comment box.

The comment box closes, and a small box with your initials and the number 3 appears in the upper-left corner.

19 Right-click on any toolbar, and then click **Revisions Pane**.

The **Revisions Pane** opens, showing comment number 3 in the **Slide changes** box.

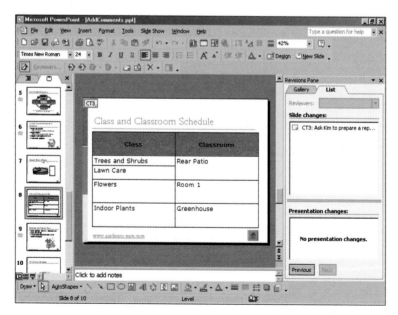

Tip

Resize pointer

+‖+

To change the size of the **Revisions Pane**, position the pointer (which changes to the resize pointer) on the left edge of the **Revisions Pane**, and then drag the edge.

20 Right-click anywhere on the comment box, and then click **Delete Comment**.

The comment is deleted from the slide and also from the **Revisions Pane**.

21 In the **Revisions Pane**, click **Previous** at the bottom of the pane.

Slide 2 appears with comment number 2 in the **Revisions Pane**.

22 In the **Revisions Pane**, click **Previous** at the bottom of the pane.

Slide 1 appears with comment number 1 in the **Revisions Pane**.

Delete
Comment

✕ ▾

23 On the Reviewing toolbar, click the **Delete Comment** button.

The comment is removed.

24 On the Standard toolbar, click the **Save** button to save the presentation.

Close Window

✕

25 Click the **Close Window** button in the presentation window.

The AddComments presentation closes.

Adding Password Protection to a Presentation

Password
protection
new for
OfficeXP

If you don't want reviewers to edit your work, you can protect a presentation so that others can only read it. For greater protection, you can assign a password so that only those who know the password can open the presentation. You can use the password and other security options in PowerPoint to protect the integrity of your presentation as it moves from person to person. At times, you will want the information to be used but not changed; at other times, you will want only specific people in your office to be able to view the presentation. To protect a presentation, you use the options on the **Security** tab in the **Options** dialog box on the **Tools** menu.

You can set a password that must be entered before someone can modify the presentation. If you want others to read or copy the file without making changes to the original, you can also set a password that must be entered before someone can open your presentation. Setting a presentation as read-only is useful when you want a presentation, such as a company-wide bulletin, to be distributed and read, but not changed. After you set a password in a presentation, close and open the presentation again, a password protection dialog box appears. You can enter a password or click **Read Only** to open an untitled version of the presentation so that you can view and make changes to the text without affecting the protected presentation.

Restricts opening the presentation.

Click to access advanced options for protection of the presentation.

Restricts modifying the presentation.

When you set a password, take a moment to write it down. PowerPoint doesn't keep a list of passwords. If you lose or forget the password for a protected presentation, you will not be able to open it. To open a protected presentation, you need to enter the password in the exact same way that it was set, which includes spaces, symbols, and uppercase and lowercase characters.

AddPassword

In this exercise, you set presentation password protection, open a presentation with password protection, change the password protection, and remove the protection so that reviewers can use it easily.

1   On the Standard toolbar, click the **Open** button.

Open

The **Open** dialog box appears.

2   Navigate to the **SBS** folder on your hard disk, double-click the **PowerPoint** folder, double-click the **Reviewing** folder, and then double-click the **AddPassword** file.

The AddPassword presentation opens, displaying Slide 1 in Normal view.

3   On the **Tools** menu, click **Options**.

The **Options** dialog box appears.

4   Click the **Security** tab to display security options.

5   In the **Password to modify** box, type **tulip**.

The password is set.

6   Click **OK** to close the **Options** dialog box.

The **Confirm Password** dialog box appears.

7   In the **Reenter password to modify** box, type **tulip**, and then click **OK**.

The password is set. Now, close the presentation and open it again to test the password protection.

8   On the Standard toolbar, click the **Save** button to save the presentation.

Close Window

9   Click the **Close Window** button to close the presentation window.

10   On the Standard toolbar, click the **Open** button.

The **Open** dialog box appears.

11   Navigate to the **Reviewing** folder, and then double-click the **AddPassword** file.

The **Password** dialog box appears. The presentation contains a password that protects it from modification.

12   In the **Password** box, type **roses**, and then click **OK**.

As you type the password, asterisks appear to keep your password confidential. An alert message appears, indicating an incorrect password.

Tip

To protect your presentations from being opened by unauthorized people, passwords should never be common words or phrases; the same password should never be used for multiple presentations.

13   Click **OK**, and then click **Read Only**.

An untitled version of the AddPassword presentation opens, displaying Slide 1 in Normal view.

14   Click the **Close Window** button to close the presentation window.

Now, you'll open the presentation and use the correct password.

15   On the Standard toolbar, click the **Open** button.

The **Open** dialog box appears.

16   Navigate to the **Reviewing** folder, and then double-click the **AddPassword** file.

The **Password** dialog box appears. The presentation contains a password that protects it from modification.

17   In the **Password** box, type **tulip**, and then click **OK**.

The AddPassword presentation opens, displaying Slide 1 in Normal view.

18   On the **Tools** menu, click **Options**, and then click the **Security** tab, if necessary.

The **Options** dialog box appears, displaying the **Security** tab.

19   Select the contents in the **Password to modify** box, and then press the Del key to remove the password protection.

20   Click **OK** to close the **Options** dialog box.

21   On the Standard toolbar, click the **Save** button to save the presentation.

22   Click the **Close Window** button to close the presentation window.

The AddPassword presentation closes.

Sending a Presentation for Review Using E-Mail

PP2002-8-1

Approved Courseware

After you finish making changes to a presentation, you can quickly send it to another person for review using e-mail. PowerPoint allows you to send presentations out for review using e-mail from within the program so that you do not have to open your e-mail program. To share your presentations with others, click the **File** menu and then point to **Send To**. The **Send To** menu includes the **Mail Recipient (for Review)** and **Mail Recipient (as Attachment)** commands. Click one of these commands to open an e-mail window in which the presentation is already listed as an attachment. If you use the **Mail Recipient (for Review)** command, the message also includes the text *Please review the attached document*. To send the presentation, enter the destination e-mail address and the Cc e-mail address for anyone who should receive a copy of the message and its attachments. The subject line of the e-mail will already contain the file name of the presentation that you are sending.

Important

To complete this exercise, you need to have an e-mail program installed on your computer and an e-mail account setup.

EmailPres

In this exercise, you send a presentation for review attached to an e-mail message.

1   On the Standard toolbar, click the **Open** button.

Open

The **Open** dialog box appears.

2   Navigate to the **SBS** folder on your hard disk, double-click the **PowerPoint** folder, double-click the **Reviewing** folder, and then double-click the **EmailPres** file.

The EmailPres presentation opens.

3   On the **File** menu, point to **Send To**, and then click **Mail Recipient (for Review)**.

The e-mail page opens, ready for you to type in the recipient's address.

Address for e-mail recipient
Attached file
Message pane

```
Please review 'EmailPres' - Message - Microsoft Word
File   Edit   View   Insert   Format   Tools   Table   Window   Help          Type a question for help

Send   Options...   HTML

Review
To...
Cc...
Subject:   Please review 'EmailPres'
Attach...   EmailPres.ppt (627 KB)

Please review the attached document.
```

Tip

E-mail (as
Attachment)

To send a copy of the current presentation as an attachment in an e-mail message, click the **E- mail (as Attachment)** button on the Standard toolbar.

4   Click in the **To:** box, if necessary, and then type **someone@microsoft.com**.

Tip

To select names from your address book or contacts list, click the **To:** button, click recipient names in the **Name** list, and then click **To**, **Cc**, or **Bcc**.

High:
Importance

5   On the Message toolbar, click the **High: Importance** button.

The message is set for delivery with high priority.

Message Flag

6   On the Message toolbar, click the **Message Flag** button.

The **Flag for Follow Up** dialog box appears.

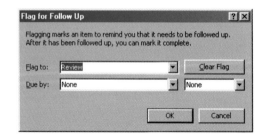

7 Click the **Due by** down arrow.

A calendar appears.

8 Click a date two days from the current date, and then click **OK.**

The review by date appears in a yellow message box above the **To:** box.

9 Click in the message area below the text *Please review the attached document*, and then type **Thank you for the quick turn around. CT.**

Send

10 On the Message toolbar, click the **Send** button.

The e-mail with the attached presentation is sent out for review, and you return to your PowerPoint presentation. The e-mail message is sent to an e-mail account at Microsoft, which automatically sends a response to the original author. You'll receive an e-mail response in your Inbox.

11 On the Standard toolbar, click the **Save** button to save the presentation.

Close Window

12 Click the **Close Window** button in the presentation window.

The EmailPres presentation closes.

Tracking Changes in a Presentation

PP2002-8-2

Approved Courseware

Once you send your presentation out for review, reviewers edit it using the markup feature so that you can see what they've changed.

After you receive the edited presentations back from reviewers, you have the ability to compare the various versions of the presentation and merge all of the revisions and comments into the original presentation.

Track changes
new for
OfficeXP

When you compare and merge presentations, PowerPoint shows the differences between them as markups. You can accept and reject one or all markups or revisions. The **Markup** command on the **View** menu allows you to track changes made to your presentation by using call-outs within the presentation. These call-outs show changes in detail without obscuring the presentation or affecting its layout. They also give you a more visible and comprehensive view of the changes that have been made.

Each change made in PowerPoint is marked with a call-out box that contains the reviewer's name/initials, the date, and the details of the actual comment or change.

PowerPoint uses a different color call-out box for each reviewer, so you can quickly identify who made the change.

You can use the Reviewing toolbar to track, accept, and reject revisions. The Reviewing toolbar gives you a variety of views and options when reviewing presentations. The following table lists the Reviewing toolbar buttons and a brief description of each.

Button Name	Icon	Description
Markup		Allows you to track changes made to your presentation by using call-outs within the presentation.
Reviewers	Reviewers...	Allows you to view changes by specific reviewers or all reviewers.
Previous Item		Allows you to move to the previous comment or tracked change.
Next Item		Allows you to move to the next comment or tracked change.
Apply		Allows you to apply a change in a presentation, all changes to a slide, or all changes to the presentation.
Unapply		Allows you to unapply a change in a presentation, all changes to a slide, or all changes to the presentation.
Insert Comment		Allows you to insert a comment into a presentation.
Edit Comment		Allows you to edit a comment within a presentation.
Delete Comment/ Marker		Allows you to delete a comment or marker within a presentation or to delete all comments or markers in a presentation.
Revisions Pane		Allows you to show or hide the Revisions Pane.

As you review the comments and changes, you can accept or reject them one at a time or all at once. When you accept a change, PowerPoint deletes the text or inserts it into the presentation, as appropriate. When you reject a change, PowerPoint restores the original text.

Revisions Pane
new for
OfficeXP

When you are comparing and merging changes, you can also open the **Revisions Pane** to easily identify the changes a reviewer has made to a presentation. You can see a list of the changes made by a given reviewer or get a graphical representation of the changes via the **Gallery** tab. A drop-down menu makes it simple to apply or unapply changes that the reviewer has made.

Tip

Use the scroll bar in the **Revisions Pane** to see all of the comments and changes in a presentation.

TrackChanges
Merge

In this exercise, you open your original presentation, compare and merge changes from another presentation, turn on **Markup** to track changes, accept and reject changes, and save the revised presentation.

1 On the Standard toolbar, click the **Open** button.

Open

The **Open** dialog box appears.

2 Navigate to the **SBS** folder on your hard disk, double-click the **PowerPoint** folder, double-click the **Reviewing** folder, and then double-click the **Track-Changes** file.

The TrackChanges presentation opens, displaying Slide 1 in Normal view.

3 On the **View** menu, point to **Toolbars**, and then click **Reviewing**, if necessary.

The Reviewing toolbar appears.

Tip

You can also display the Reviewing toolbar by right-clicking any visible toolbar and then clicking **Reviewing**.

4 On the **Tools** menu, click **Compare and Merge Presentations**.

The **Choose Files to Merge with Current Presentation** dialog box appears.

5 Navigate to the **Reviewing** folder, click the **Merge** file, and then click **Merge**.

A message box appears, indicating that the presentation that you selected was not sent by pointing to **Send To** on the **File** menu, and then clicking **Mail Recipient (for Review)**.

6 Click **Continue**.

The deletions and changes from both presentations appear on the screen in the current presentation. The color of each revision indicates a different reviewer.

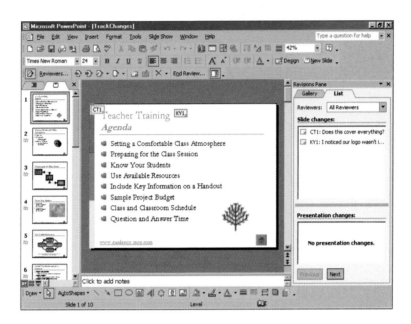

Markup

7 On the Reviewing toolbar, click the **Markup** button, if necessary, to display any comments and changes.

Any changes that you make or that have been made are now marked.

Tip

When **Markup** is turned on, the **Markup** button has a light gray background and is outlined; when **Markup** is turned off, the **Markup** button has a darker gray background.

Reviewers

Reviewers...

8 On the Reviewing toolbar, click the **Reviewers** button, click **Kim Yoshida** to clear the check box, and then click anywhere on the screen.

The revisions made by Kim Yoshida are hidden.

9 On the Reviewing toolbar, click the **Reviewers** button, click **All Reviewers** to select all of the reviewer check boxes, and then click anywhere on the screen.

The revisions made by all reviewers appear. There are two comments on Slide 1, one from Catherine Turner (CT1) and another from Kim Yoshida (KY1).

Tip

When you point to a comment or change on the screen, the name that appears in the ScreenTip is the user name entered when the operating system was installed. If no name was entered, the ScreenTip shows "end user" as the name. You can change the name in the **Options** dialog box. On the **Tools** menu, click **Options**, click the **General** tab, type a user name in the **Name** box and user initials in the **Initials** box, and then click **OK**.

10 In the **Revisions Pane** in the **List** tab, click **KY1** under **Slide Changes** to display the comment by Kim Yoshida.

11 In the **Revisions Pane**, click the **Gallery** tab.

The **Gallery** tab appears, indicating that no other changes have been made to the slide.

12 In the **Revisions Pane**, click the **List** tab to display slide changes by reviewer.

Delete Comment

13 On the Reviewing toolbar, click the **Delete Comment** down arrow, and then click **Delete All Markers on the Current Slide**.

Both comments are deleted.

Next Item

14 On the Reviewing toolbar, click the **Next Item** button.

PowerPoint takes you to Slide 2 where there is a marker displaying all of the changes made by Kim Yoshida.

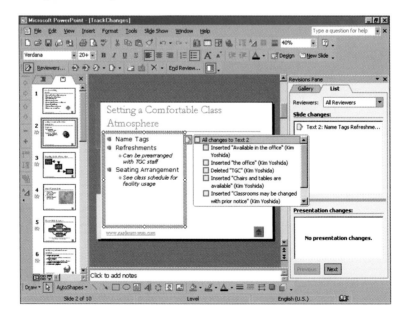

Troubleshooting

If the marker is not open, click **Text 2: Name Tags ...** on the **List** tab in the **Revisions Pane** to display all of the changes made by Kim Yoshida.

15 In the **Track Changes** box, select the **Inserted "Available in the office" (Kim Yoshida)** check box.

The change appears in the bulleted text box.

16 Click in a blank area of the slide to close the **Track Changes** box.

Apply

17 On the Reviewing toolbar, click the **Apply** button.

All of the changes proposed by Kim Yoshida are applied to the slide.

Track Changes
Marker

18 In the Slide pane, click the **Track Changes Marker**.

The **Track Changes Marker** is selected.

Delete Marker

19 On the Reviewing toolbar, click the **Delete Marker** button.

The marker is deleted.

Tip

To delete a marker, you can also right-click the marker and then click **Delete Marker**.

20 At the bottom of the **Revisions Pane**, click the **Next** button.

PowerPoint takes you to Slide 3 where there are two revision markers.

Tip

Revisions
Pane

If your **Revisions Pane** is not showing, click the **Revisions Pane** button on the Reviewing toolbar, or right-click any toolbar, and then click **Revisions Pane**.

21 In the **Revisions Pane**, click the **Gallery** tab.

The **Gallery** tab appears, showing the changes that Kim made to the slide.

22 On the Reviewing toolbar, click the **Apply** down arrow, and then click **Apply All Changes to the Current Slide**.

The fill colors for two of the objects change. You can now delete the markers and move on.

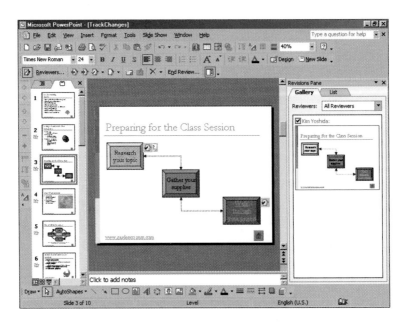

Delete
Comment

23 On the Reviewing toolbar, click the **Delete Comment** down arrow, and then click **Delete All Markers on the Current Slide**.

Both markers are deleted.

24 In the **Revisions Pane**, click the **List** tab to display no other changes in the presentation.

25 On the Standard toolbar, click the **Save** button to save the presentation.

Close Window

26 Click the **Close Window** button in the presentation window.

The TrackChanges presentation closes.

Broadcasting a Presentation over a Network

PP2002-8-3

Approved Courseware

With online broadcasting, you can give or view a slide show over a computer network or on the Internet. You can also save the presentation on a Web server for someone to view later. To use online broadcasting, you need Netscape Navigator 4 or Microsoft Internet Explorer 4.0 or later installed on your computer. If you are going to broadcast to an audience of 16 or more people, you need a Windows Media server.

When you set up an online broadcast, PowerPoint creates a lobby page. This page appears on the server before the broadcast starts. It contains audience information about the broadcast, such as the person giving the presentation and the date and time of the presentation.

As the presenter, you can view speaker notes, take meeting minutes, preview slides, and control the presentation slide sequence. As a member of the slide show audience, you can watch the slide show on your computer screen just as you would a slide show that you created.

To participate in an online broadcast as the audience, you need to open the URL where the broadcast is stored.

Broadcast

In this exercise, you schedule and deliver an online broadcast, host an online broadcast, and then participate in an online broadcast as an audience member.

1 On the Standard toolbar, click the **Open** button.

Open

The **Open** dialog box appears.

2 Navigate to the **SBS** folder on your hard disk, double-click the **PowerPoint** folder, double-click the **Reviewing** folder, and then double-click the **Broadcast** file.

The Network presentation opens, displaying Slide 1 in Normal view.

3 On the **Slide Show** menu, point to **Online Broadcast**, and then click **Schedule a Live Broadcast**.

Troubleshooting

If a message box appears indicating that the broadcasting feature is not installed, click **Yes** to install the feature. If necessary, insert the Microsoft Office XP Professional CD-ROM.

The **Schedule Presentation Broadcast** dialog box appears. The name in the **Speaker** box is the registered PowerPoint user.

Schedule Presentation Broadcast	? X
Please enter presentation information here. This information will appear on the lobby page.	

Title: Broadcast

Description:

Microsoft Windows Media Technologies

You can use PowerPoint to broadcast a live presentation to other users on your network. You can send slides, audio and video. A Web browser is used to view the broadcast.

Speaker: Catherine Turner

Copyright:

Keywords: Broadcast;Catherine Turner

Email: catherinet

Tips for Broadcast...

Settings...   Schedule...   Cancel

4 Click **Settings**.

The **Broadcast Settings** dialog box appears.

Important

You need to specify the directory on your network in which you want to store the presentation. For this exercise, you select the path to a shared network folder. For example, a typical path might be N:\Broadcast (where *N* refers to the network disk drive and *Broadcast* is the shared folder). If you are connecting to the Internet, type the Internet address of the folder name, such as *http://www.gardenco.msn.com/ Broadcast/*, in the text box.

5 Click **Browse**, navigate to a shared folder on a network server, and then click **Select**.

The network server name appears in the **Save broadcast file in** box.

Your network location will be different.

Tip

As you give an online broadcast, you can record the presentation on a hard drive or network drive for later a re-broadcast. After you complete an online broadcast, PowerPoint allows you to re-record all or part of an archived broadcast and add rich media (audio and video) to your online broadcast.

6 Click **OK** to close the **Broadcast Settings** dialog box.

The **Schedule Presentation Broadcast** dialog box appears.

7 Click in the **Description** box, and then type **You will be watching a presentation that will be used at a training session for those who will teach the gardening classes offered by The Gardening Company.**

8 Click **Schedule**.

The **Broadcast Meeting** window opens, displaying online meeting information.

Your e-mail program opens.

Your meeting information will be different.

9 If you use Microsoft Outlook, arrange an online meeting. If you use another e-mail program, the URL for the broadcast is embedded in the body of your message. Specify the e-mail addresses of the people whom you would like to participate in the meeting.

10 On the Message toolbar, click **Send**, and then when the successfully scheduled message appears, click **Yes** to continue.

11 On the **Slide Show** menu, point to **Online Broadcast**, and then click **Start Live Broadcast Now**.

The **Live Presentation Broadcast** dialog box appears.

12 In the **Select event to broadcast live** list, click the schedule broadcast, if necessary.

13 Click **Broadcast** to display the **Broadcast Presentation** dialog box, and then click **Audience Message**.

The **Audience Message** dialog box appears. You can send a message to your audience to be posted on the lobby page.

14 Type **Be ready to discuss which parts of the teacher training you feel comfortable handling. Be prepared to run the PowerPoint presentation as well.**

15 Click **Update** to close the **Audience Message** dialog box.

The **Broadcast Presentation** dialog box appears.

16 Click **Preview Lobby Page**.

Your browser starts, and the lobby page appears in the window.

17 On the **File** menu in the browser window, click **Close** to close the browser.

The **Broadcast Presentation** dialog box appears.

18 Click **Start**, and then click **Yes** to start, if necessary.

Once PowerPoint establishes the connections, it broadcasts the presentation to the participant's computers.

Tip

To stop an online broadcast at any time during the broadcast, press Esc, and then click **Yes**.

19 If you have Outlook, open the e-mail message that invited you to the broadcast, and then click the URL in the message. If necessary, click the **Open This File** option, and then click **OK**.

If you join a scheduled broadcast early, you see a lobby page where you can read information about the broadcast and see how much time is left before the broadcast begins.

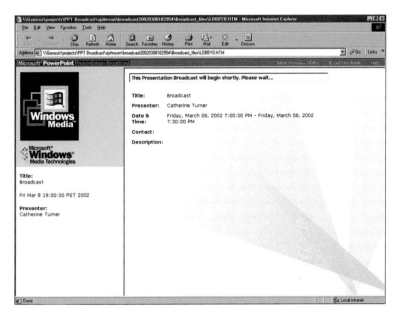

Once the presenter connects to the network and starts the broadcast slide show, the presenter's slide presentation fills your computer screen, and the slide show begins.

20 Click the slides in the slide show to complete the presentation broadcast.

Slide 1 appears in Normal view.

21 On the Standard toolbar, click the **Save** button to save the presentation.

Close Window

22 Click the **Close Window** button in the presentation window.

The Broadcast presentation closes.

Collaborating in an Online Meeting

When you operate an online meeting from PowerPoint, Microsoft NetMeeting runs in the background, allowing you to share the contents of your file with your colleagues.

You can schedule a meeting ahead of time, or you can start an impromptu meeting. When you start an online meeting, by default, participants can edit your presentation. To prevent participants from making changes to the presentation, you need to turn off the collaboration option by clicking the **Allow others to edit** button on the Online Meeting toolbar.

Important

This section is written for Microsoft NetMeeting 3.0. The steps may vary for later versions of the product.

When the meeting is scheduled to start, a **Microsoft Outlook Reminder** dialog box appears. Only the host of the online meeting needs to have PowerPoint installed on the host computer. Participants need to have Microsoft NetMeeting 3.0 or later installed on their computers to collaborate in the online meeting. During the meeting, participants can communicate with each other by using the Chat window in NetMeeting. Everyone also has access to the Whiteboard, in which participants can type text and draw objects by using commands on the Drawing toolbar.

NetMeet

In this exercise, you schedule an online meeting, host and participate in an online meeting, send messages during an online meeting, work on the Whiteboard, and end an online meeting.

1 On the Standard toolbar, click the **Open** button.

Open

The **Open** dialog box appears.

2 Navigate to the **SBS** folder on your hard disk, double-click the **PowerPoint** folder, double-click the **Reviewing** folder, and then double-click the **NetMeet** file.

The NetMeet presentation opens, displaying Slide 1 in Normal view.

3 On the **Tools** menu, point to **Online Collaboration**, and then click **Schedule Meeting**.

If this is the first time that you have used NetMeeting, a **NetMeeting** dialog box appears. Fill in the requested user information, and then click **OK**. Microsoft Outlook starts, and the **Appointment** tab appears to request a meeting.

NetMeeting

My Information

Enter the information others can use to find you in the directory, or see while in a meeting with you.

First name:

Last name:

Email name:

Location:

Directory

Enter the name of the directory others can use to find you.

Server name:

OK   Cancel

4   Click **To**.

The **Select Attendees And Resources** dialog box opens.

5   Click the recipient names in the **Name** list, and then click **Required** or **Optional**.

6   When you are finished inviting people, click **OK**.

The **Appointment** tab in Outlook appears with invitees in the **To** box.

7   Click in the **Subject** box, and then type Online meeting to discuss general presentation.

8   Click the **Start Time** down arrow next to the date, and then select today as the start date.

PowerPoint sets the end time for one half-hour later than the start time.

Send

9   On the Message toolbar, click the **Send** button.

PowerPoint sends the message to the people whom you selected. You should receive an Outlook Reminder message in your e-mail.

Tip

If you don't get an **Outlook Reminder** message dialog box, you can use the **Meet Now** command. On the **Tools** menu, point to **Online Collaboration**, click **Meet Now**, select participant names, and then click the **Call** button.

10 If you are hosting the meeting, verify that the presentation is open, and then click the **Start NetMeeting** button in the **Outlook Reminder** message dialog box to start the meeting.

The meeting presentation appears along with the Online Meeting toolbar.

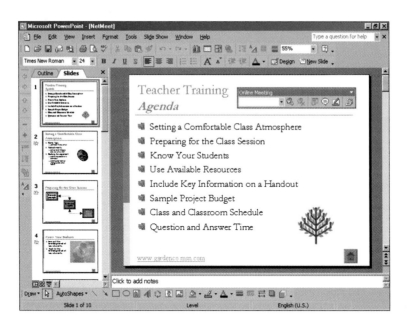

Tip

To start an impromptu meeting, on the **Tools** menu, point to **Online Collaboration**, and then click **Meet Now**. In the **Place A Call** dialog box, select the names of the people whom you want to invite, and then click the **Call** button. When they receive the invitation, they can click the **Accept** or **Ignore** button in the **Join Meeting** dialog box that appears. NetMeeting must be running on their computers for them to receive the invitation.

11 If you are an invited participant in the meeting, click **Join NetMeeting** in the Outlook message dialog box.

All of the participants see the current presentation on their screens. By default, collaboration is turned off.

Allow others to edit

12 If you want other participants to be able to edit the presentation, on the **Online Meeting** toolbar, click the **Allow others to edit** button.

Collaboration is turned on. When collaboration is turned on, only one person can have control of the presentation at a time. Click anywhere on the presentation screen to take control.

13 To turn off collaboration, on the **Online Meeting** toolbar, click the **Allow others to edit** button.

If the host does not have control of the presentation, the host can press Esc to turn off collaboration.

Display Chat
Window

14 On the **Online Meeting** toolbar, click the **Display Chat Window** button.

The **Chat** window appears.

15 In the message box, type the following:

Welcome to the meeting. Feel free to jump in at any time with your ideas.

16 Press the ⌷Enter⌷ key.

All of the meeting participants see your message and can respond to it.

17 Click the **Close** button in the upper-right corner of the Chat window, and then click **No** to save changes, if necessary.

Display
Whiteboard

18 On the **Online Meeting** toolbar, click the **Display Whiteboard** button.

The Whiteboard window appears. With collaboration turned off, all participants can draw on the Whiteboard.

Text

A

19 Click the **Text** button on the left side of the window.

20 Click anywhere in the Whiteboard window.

A box with a blinking insertion point appears.

21 Type **If you have any ideas for interesting graphics, draw them here.**

The meeting participants can see your note and add their own notes.

End Meeting

22 Click the **Close** button, click **No** to save the Whiteboard contents (if necessary), and then on the **Online Meeting** toolbar, click the **End Meeting** button.

If you are a participant, PowerPoint disconnects you from the meeting. If you are the host, the meeting ends for the entire group, and PowerPoint disconnects all of the participants from each other.

23 On the Standard toolbar, click the **Save** button to save the presentation.

Close Window

✕

24 Click the **Close Window** button in the presentation window.

The NetMeet presentation closes.

Holding a Web Discussion

In addition to online broadcasts and online meetings, you can set up online Web discussions. A Web discussion allows you to attach comments to presentations that can be opened in a browser. The comments are attached to the presentation but are stored on a Web server. To hold a Web discussion, you need to have access to a Windows NT-based Web server with Microsoft Office Server Extensions. Users reviewing your presentation can use the Web Discussions toolbar to view and reply to any discussion. You can then review discussions and incorporate changes to your presentation based on the feedback you receive.

To set up and hold a Web discussion about a presentation:

1   On the **Tools** menu, point to **Online Collaboration**, and then click **Web Discussions**.

The Discussions toolbar opens.

Insert Discussion about the Presentation

2   On the Discussions toolbar, click **Insert Discussion about the Presentation** button.

The **Discussions** dialog box opens.

3   If prompted to specify a discussion server in order to use the Discussions feature, click **Yes**, click the **Add** button in the **Discussion Options** dialog box. When the **Add or Edit Discussion Servers** dialog box comes up, type the name of a discussion server, and then type your name. Click **OK**, and then click **OK** again.

4   In the **Discussion Subject** box, type a subject for the discussion.

5   In the **Discussion Text** box, start typing your discussion.

6   Click **OK**.

The Discussion Pane opens, showing the discussion text.

7   On the Discussion toolbar, click the **Close** button to close the Web discussion.

Delivering a Presentation on the Road

PP2002-7-4
PP2002-7-6

Approved Courseware

If you need to transport your presentation to another computer, you can use the **Pack and Go Wizard** to compress and save the presentation to a floppy disk, other removable media, or a hard drive. With the **Pack and Go Wizard**, you can include linked files and fonts that are used in the presentation to which the remote computer might not have access. The **Pack and Go Wizard** includes linked files by default. When you select the **Embed TrueType Fonts** option, the wizard stores TrueType fonts in the presentation. It is especially important to select this option if you are using fonts in a presentation that are not typically installed by Windows. Then when you open or show a presentation on another computer that doesn't have these TrueType fonts, the presentation looks the same as it did on your computer. Be aware that including embedded fonts in a presentation increases the file size.

You can also embed fonts when you save a presentation. In the **Save As** dialog box, click **Tools**, click **Save Options**, select the **Embed TrueType Fonts** check box, and then click **Embed characters in use only (best for reducing file size)** option to embed only those characters used in the presentation or click **Embed all characters (best for editing by others)** option to embed all the characters in the font set.

PowerPoint comes with a special program called the **PowerPoint Viewer**, which allows you to show a slide show on a computer that does not have PowerPoint installed. You can easily install the PowerPoint Viewer program on any compatible system. When you run the **Pack and Go Wizard**, you have the option to include the PowerPoint Viewer with the packed presentation.

When you complete the **Pack and Go Wizard** process, PowerPoint creates two files, a Pngsetup and Pres0.ppz. Pngsetup is a setup file that unpackages and delivers your presentation and Pres0.ppz is a compressed version of your presentation. To unpack and deliver your presentation, double-click the Pngsetup file and follow the instructions. The Pngsetup and Pres0.ppz files need to be in the same folder for the slide show delivery to be successful.

RoadPres

In this exercise, you start the **Pack and Go Wizard**, embed fonts in a presentation, close the presentation and show a presentation using the PowerPoint Viewer.

1   On the Standard toolbar, click the **Open** button.

Open

The **Open** dialog box appears.

2   Navigate to the **SBS** folder on your hard disk, double-click the **PowerPoint** folder, double-click the **Reviewing** folder, and then double-click the **RoadPres** file.

The RoadPres presentation opens.

3   On the **File** menu, click **Pack and Go**.

The Pack and Go Wizard displays an introduction dialog box.

4   Read the introduction, and then click **Next**.

The Pack and Go Wizard asks you which presentation you would like to package. The current (active) presentation is selected by default, though you can select any presentation.

5   Click **Next**.

The Pack and Go Wizard asks you in which drive you want to store the presentation, such as your hard disk or a network drive. Drive A appears by default.

6 Click the **Choose destination** option, click **Browse**, navigate to the **Reviewing** folder, click **Select**, and then click **Next**.

The Pack and Go Wizard asks you if you would like to include linked files and fonts used in your presentation.

7 Clear the **Include linked files** check box to not include linked files in the presentation.

8 Select the **Embed TrueType fonts** check box, and then click **Next**.

The Pack and Go Wizard asks if you want to include the PowerPoint Viewer. The Pack and Go Wizard does not include the PowerPoint Viewer by default.

Troubleshooting

If the **Viewer for Microsoft Windows** option is dimmed, you need to install the PowerPoint Viewer to your hard disk to use it with the Pack and Go Wizard. To download the PowerPoint Viewer from within the Pack and Go Wizard, click **Download the Viewer** to access a Microsoft Web site where you can download the program to your hard disk, and then double-click the setup program to install it.

9 Click the **Viewer for Microsoft Windows** option, click **Next**, and then click **Finish**.

You are now ready to take your presentation on the road.

10 On the Standard toolbar, click the **Save** button to save the presentation.

Close Window

11 Click the **Close Window** button in the presentation window.

The RoadPres presentation closes.

12 On the taskbar, click **Start**, point to **Programs**, and then click **Microsoft PowerPoint Viewer**.

The Microsoft PowerPoint Viewer appears.

13 Navigate to the **SBS** folder on your hard disk, double-click the **PowerPoint** folder, and then double-click the **Reviewing** folder.

14 In the list of file and folder names, click the **RoadPres** file.

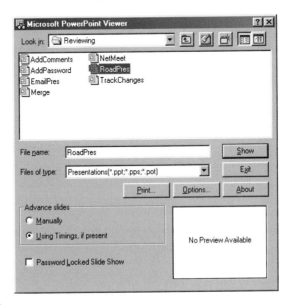

15 Click **Show**.

The PowerPoint Viewer shows the presentation as a slide show.

16 Click the mouse to advance through the presentation slides.

When the slide show ends, the **PowerPoint Viewer** dialog box reappears.

17 Click **Exit**.

The Microsoft PowerPoint Viewer closes.

Chapter Wrap-Up

To finish the chapter:

Close

● On the **File** menu, click **Exit**, or click the **Close** button in the PowerPoint window.

PowerPoint closes.

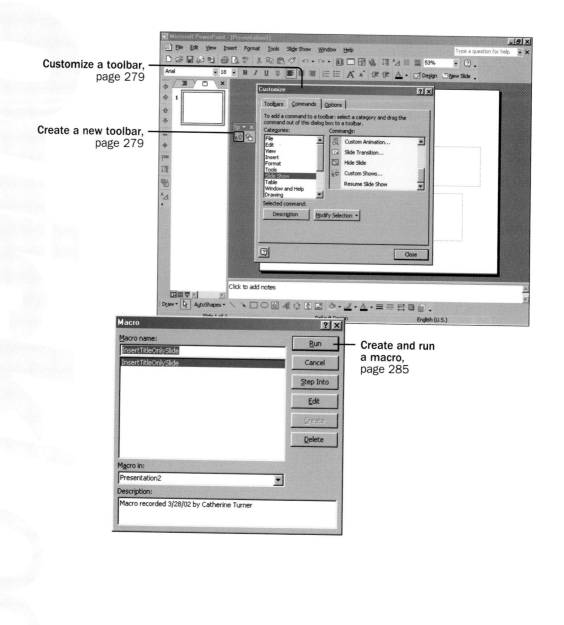

Chapter 14
Customizing PowerPoint

After completing this chapter, you will be able to:

✔ Customize the way you perform commands.

✔ Customize the way you create objects.

✔ Simplify tasks with macros.

Microsoft PowerPoint has many optional settings that can affect either the screen display or the operation of certain functions. You can change PowerPoint's optional settings to customize the way you work and perform tasks. For example, you can change toolbars so that the tools that you use most often are easy to find. Or, you can change the initial font type and style of text that appears in text boxes. If you frequently perform a repetitive task in PowerPoint, you can also record the sequence of steps as a macro to automate the task and save you time.

In this chapter, you'll customize the PowerPoint screen display to meet your needs. You'll also change toolbars so that the tools that you use most often are easy to find. In addition, you will find out how to customize default drawing attributes. Finally, you'll create macros to help you automate a repetitive task.

 You will not need any practice file for this chapter. Instead, you will create all of the files that you need during the course of the chapter.

Customizing the Way You Perform Commands

PowerPoint has several preset toolbars with buttons that can save you time and effort. The toolbars that appear depend on which view is active. In Normal view, for example, you see three default toolbars: Standard, Formatting, and Drawing.

The Standard and Formatting toolbars are on the same row below the menu bar. If you like, you can customize the toolbars so that each is displayed on its own row. If you leave the Standard and Formatting toolbars on one row, they are self-adjusting. That is, commands that you use more often stay on the toolbars, and commands that you use less often are replaced with more frequently used commands. Both the Standard and Formatting toolbars have additional buttons that you can add to the toolbar itself or to the **Add or Remove Buttons** list under **Toolbar Options**. Toolbars are also movable; you can drag entire toolbars to new locations on the screen.

You can also create new toolbars that contain only the buttons that you need or use most frequently. You can customize the arrangement of buttons on a new or existing toolbar, or you can move buttons from one toolbar to another.

In this exercise, you reposition the Formatting toolbar, put the Standard and Formatting toolbars back on the same row, reset the toolbar buttons to display the default PowerPoint settings, and add and remove a toolbar button. You also create a toolbar and add and arrange buttons.

1   Start PowerPoint, if necessary.

PowerPoint displays a blank presentation with the default Title Slide layout in Normal view.

2   Position the pointer over the gray, vertical bar at the left edge of the Formatting toolbar.

Four-headed
arrow pointer

The pointer changes to the four-headed arrow pointer.

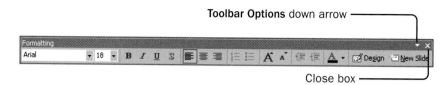

3   Drag the title bar to the middle of the screen.

The floating toolbar now has a title bar, a **Toolbar Options** down arrow, and a **Close** box.

Toolbar Options down arrow ———

Close box ———

4   On the **Tools** menu, click **Customize**.

The **Customize** dialog box appears.

5   Click the **Options** tab, if necessary.

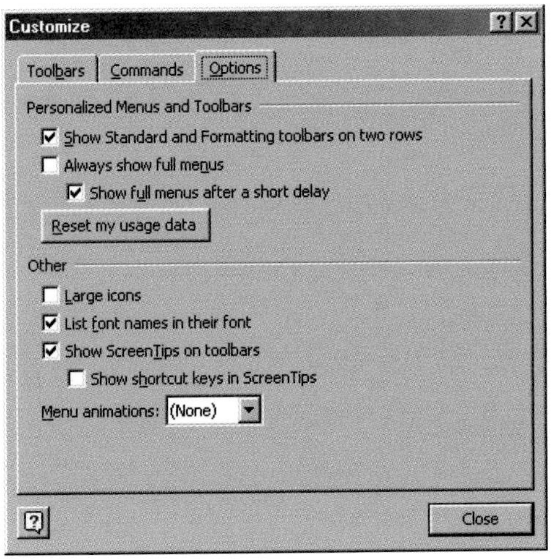

6   Clear the **Show Standard and Formatting toolbars on two rows** check box to display the toolbar on one row.

7   Click **Reset my usage data**, and then click **Yes** in the alert box.

8   Click **Close**.

The toolbars appear on one row again.

Toolbar Options

9   On either toolbar, click the **Toolbar Options** down arrow.

10   Click **Add or Remove Buttons**, and then click **Formatting**.

A list opens with buttons that you can add to or delete from the Formatting toolbar.

11   Point to the down arrow at the end of the list, if necessary.

The list scrolls to the end. The buttons with a check mark next to them appear on the Formatting Toolbar or on the **Toolbar Options** list.

12   Click the **Layout** button in the list.

A check mark appears next to it, and the button appears on the Formatting toolbar just to the left of the **Toolbar Options** down arrow.

13   Click the **Layout** button again.

The button is removed from the toolbar.

14   Click anywhere in the presentation window to close the list.

15   On the **Tools** menu, click **Customize**.

The **Customize** dialog box appears.

16 Click the **Toolbars** tab.

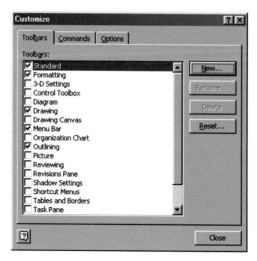

17 Click **New**.

The **New Toolbar** dialog box appears.

18 In the **Toolbar name** box, type **Special**, and then click **OK**.

Special is added to the toolbar list with a check mark next to it, and a small, empty toolbar appears in the presentation window. You might need to drag the dialog box out of the way to see the new toolbar.

19 Click the **Commands** tab to display a list of available commands in PowerPoint.

Tip

To display a description of what each button in the **Commands** list does, click the command, and then click the **Description** button.

20 In the **Categories** list, click **Slide Show** to display a list of commands related to the slide show.

21 In the **Commands** list, scroll down, and then drag the **Action Settings** button to the Special toolbar that you created.

A black insertion bar appears as you drag the button onto the Special toolbar to indicate the new location of the button. The **Action Settings** button appears on the Special toolbar.

22 In the **Commands** list, scroll to the end of the list, and then drag the **Custom Shows** button to the Special toolbar.

The **Custom Shows** button appears on the Special toolbar. You can move a toolbar button to another location on a different toolbar by dragging the button.

23 Drag the **Custom Shows** button to the other side of the **Action Settings** button.

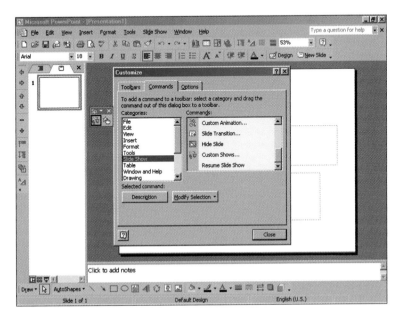

Tip

If you add the wrong button, you can remove it by dragging the button off of the toolbar to a blank area of the window.

24 Drag the **Custom Shows** button off the toolbar.

The button is removed.

25 In the **Customize** dialog box, click the **Toolbars** tab to display a list of current toolbars.

26 In the **Toolbars** list, click **Special**, click **Delete**, and then in the alert box, click **OK**.

The toolbar is deleted.

27 Click **Close** to close the **Customize** dialog box.

Close Window

❌

28 Click the **Close Window** button in the presentation window, and then click **No** if you are prompted to save changes to the presentation.

Customizing the Way You Create Objects

When you create a text box, PowerPoint applies a set of default text attributes. Some examples of PowerPoint's font default settings include font style, size, and formatting options, such as bold, italic, and underline. To find out the current font default settings for your presentation, you can create a text object and check the object's attributes. When you draw an object, PowerPoint applies a set of default object attributes. Examples of object default settings include fill color, shadow, and line style. To find out the current default settings for your presentation, you can draw an object or create a text object and check the object's attributes.

In this exercise, you change font defaults and object attribute defaults.

1 On the **View** menu, click **Task Pane**, if necessary, to display the **New Presentation** task pane.

New

2 On the Standard toolbar, click the **New** button.

PowerPoint displays a blank presentation with the default Title Slide layout in Normal view.

Text Box

3 On the Drawing toolbar, click the **Text Box** button.

4 Click a blank area of the Slide pane to create a text box.

5 Type **Current default font**, and then select the text box.

6 On the **Format** menu, click **Font**.

The **Font** dialog box appears with the current default font and size.

7 In the **Font** list, click **Book Antiqua** to change the default font to Book Antiqua.

8 In the **Size** list, click **20** to change the default font size to 20 points.

9 Select the **Default for new objects** check box, and then click **OK**.

The Book Antiqua font and the 20 point font size are applied to the text as defaults.

10 On the Drawing toolbar, click the **Text Box** button, and then click a blank area of the Slide pane to create a text box.

11 Type **Book Antiqua, size 20, is now the default font**.

The text appears in the default font, Book Antiqua font and 20 point font size are applied to the text defaults.

Oval

12 On the Drawing toolbar, click the **Oval** button.

13 In the Slide pane, drag to draw an oval.

The oval appears with the current default fill color, shadow, and line style settings.

Fill Color

14 On the Drawing toolbar, click the **Fill Color** down arrow, and then click a new fill color.

Tip

You can make additional changes, such as font type, font style, shadow style, line color and style, to the object to set as default.

15 On the Drawing toolbar, click **Draw**, and then click **Set AutoShapes Default** to set the new default.

Oval

16 On the Drawing toolbar, click the **Oval** button, and then drag it in the Slide pane to draw an oval.

Both oval objects have the new attributes that you just selected.

17 Click the original oval object, and then press ⌨ to delete the object.

Tip

Another way to change the default attributes of an object is to first modify the object to look the way that you want it to. Then, with the object still selected, click the **Draw** button on the Drawing toolbar, and then click **Set AutoShape Defaults.**

18 Click the **Close Window** button in the presentation window, and then click **No** if you are prompted to save changes to the presentation.

Simplifying Tasks with Macros

If you perform a task often, you can record a macro that automates the task. A macro is a series of commands and functions—stored in a Visual Basic module—that you can run with one step whenever you need to perform a task. You can record a macro in PowerPoint to combine multiple commands into one, speed up routine editing and formatting tasks, or make a dialog box option more accessible.

Before you record or write a macro, you need to plan the steps and commands that you want the macro to perform. If you make a mistake while recording, you can record a correction instead of rerecording.

With the **Macro** dialog box, you can run a macro completely. You can also create, edit, or delete a macro.

In this exercise, you record a macro, open and view a macro, and run a macro.

1 On the **View** menu, click **Task Pane**, if necessary, to display the **New Presentation** task pane.

New

2 On the Standard toolbar, click the **New** button.

PowerPoint displays a blank presentation with the default Title Slide layout in Normal view.

3 On the **Tools** menu, point to **Macro**, and then click **Record New Macro**.

The **Record Macro** dialog box appears. The default macro name appears selected in the **Macro name** box.

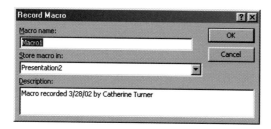

4 In the **Macro name** box, type **InsertTitleOnlySlide**.

Tip

Macro names cannot contain spaces.

5 Click **OK**.

The Stop Recording toolbar appears with a **Stop Recording** button.

New Slide

6 On the Standard toolbar, click the **New Slide** button.

The **Slide Layout** task pane appears.

7 In the **Slide Layout** task pane under **Text Layouts**, click the **Title Only** layout to change the layout of the new slide.

Stop Recording

8 On the Stop Recording toolbar, click the **Stop Recording** button.

The macro is recorded, and the Stop Recording toolbar closes.

9 On the **Tools** menu, point to **Macro**, and then click **Macros**.

The **Macro** dialog box appears.

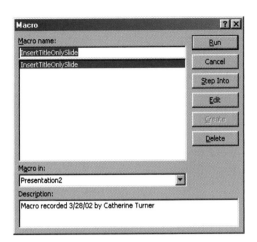

10 In the **Macro name** area, click **InsertTitleOnlySlide**, if necessary, to select the macro.

11 Click **Run**.

The **Macro** dialog box closes and executes the macro.

Tip

You can create more advanced macros by entering Visual Basic commands in the Visual Basic Editor. To open the Visual Basic Editor, point to **Macro** on the **Tools** menu, and then click **Visual Basic Editor**. You can click the **Help** button to learn how to use the program.

Close Window

12 Click the **Close Window** button in the presentation window, and then click **No** if you are prompted to save changes to the presentation.

Adding Functionality to PowerPoint with Add-Ins

Add-ins are supplemental programs that extend the capabilities of PowerPoint by adding custom commands and specialized features. You can write your own add-ins using the PowerPoint Visual Basic Editor, or you can obtain add-ins from independent software vendors. You can also find PowerPoint add-ins on the Office XP CD-ROM or on the Microsoft Web site at *http://www.microsoft.com*. To use an add-in, you must first install it on your computer and then load it into PowerPoint. PowerPoint add-ins have the filename extension .ppa. To conserve memory and maintain PowerPoint's running speed, it's a good idea to unload add-in programs that you don't use often. When you unload an add-in, its features and commands are removed from Power-Point. However, the program itself remains on your computer for easy reloading.

(continued)

To view, install, and unload an add-in program:

1 On the **Tools** menu, click **Add-Ins**.

   The **Add-Ins** dialog box appears.

2 Click **Add New**.

   The **Add New PowerPoint Add-In** dialog box appears.

3 Click the **Look in** down arrow, and then click the folder where you stored your PowerPoint add-in programs.

4 In the list of file and folder names, click a PowerPoint add-in program.

5 Click **OK**.

   The add-in program is loaded.

6 In the **Available add-ins** list, click the add-in that you want to load, and then click **Load**.

   The add-in program is registered and appears in the list of available add-ins.

7 Click **Close**.

   The **Add-Ins** dialog box closes, and the add-in program is available for use in PowerPoint.

8 On the **Tools** menu, click **Add-Ins**.

   The **Add-Ins** dialog box appears.

9 Click the add-in that you want to unload.

10 Click **Unload** to remove the add-in from memory but keep its name in the list, or click **Remove** to remove the add-in from the list and from the registry file.

11 Click **Close** to close the **Add-Ins** dialog box.

Chapter Wrap-Up

To finish the chapter:

Close

● On the **File** menu, click **Exit**, or click the **Close** button in the PowerPoint window.

   PowerPoint closes.

Quick Reference

20 **To get help using the Ask A Question box**

1 On the right side of the menu bar, click in the Ask A Question box.

2 Type a question or keyword, and press `Enter`.

20 **To get help using the Office Assistant**

1 On the **Help** menu, click **Show the Office Assistant**.

2 Click the **Office Assistant**, type a question or keyword in the box, and then click **Search**.

3 Click the topic in which you want help, and then click the **Close** button.

4 Right-click the **Office Assistant**, and then click **Hide**.

Chapter 2 **Working with a Presentation**

Page 26 **To create a new presentation with a design template**

1 In the **New Presentation** task pane, click **From Design Template**.

2 Click a **design template** in the Slide Design task pane.

29 **To enter text in the Slide pane**

1 In the Slide pane, click the text placeholder *Click to add title* or click the text placeholder *Click to add subtitle*.

2 Type your text.

31 **To create a new slide**

New Slide

[New Slide button]

1 On the Standard toolbar, click the **New Slide** button.

2 In the **Slide Layout** task pane, select a slide layout.

34 **To insert slides from other presentations**

1 On the **Insert** menu, click **Slides from Files**.

2 Click the **Find Presentation** tab, and then click **Browse**.

3 Navigate to the location of the presentation that you want to insert, click the presentation, and then click **Open**.

4 Click the slides that you want to insert, click **Insert**, and the click **Close**.

36 **To rearrange slides in Slide Sorter view**

Slide Sorter
View

[Slide Sorter View button]

1 Click the **Slide Sorter View** button.

2 Drag the slide to a new position.

37 **To enter text in the Notes pane**

● In Normal view, click in the **Notes** pane, and then type your text.

37 **To enter speaker notes in Notes Page view**

1 On the **View** menu, click **Notes Page**.

2 Click the Notes placeholder *Click to add text*, and then type your text.

40 **To create a folder to store a presentation**

1 On the **File** menu, click **Save As.**

Create New
Folder

2 Click the **Create New Folder** button.

3 In the **New Folder** dialog box, type the name of the folder, and then click **OK**.

4 In the **File name** box, type the new name to rename the file, and then click **Save**.

Chapter 3 Printing a Presentation

Page 46 **To open an existing presentation**

Open

1 On the Standard toolbar, click the **Open** button.

2 Navigate to the location of the presentation that you want to open, click the presentation, and then click **Open**.

49 **To add a header and a footer to a presentation**

1 On the **View** menu, click **Header and Footer**.

2 Click the **Slides** or **Notes and Handouts** tab.

3 Select date and time, slide number, or footer options.

4 Click **Apply to All**.

53 **To preview your presentation**

Print Preview

1 On the Standard toolbar, click the **Print Preview** button.

2 On the Print Preview toolbar, click the **Print what** down arrow, and then click an option in the list.

53 **To preview slides in pure black and white or grayscale**

Color/
Grayscale

1 On the Standard toolbar, click the **Color/Grayscale** button or if in Print Preview, click the **Options** down arrow, and point to **Color/Grayscale**.

2 On the menu, click **Pure Black and White** or **Grayscale**.

56 **To print presentation slides, audience handouts, or speaker notes**

1 On the **File** menu, click **Print**.

2 Click the **Print what** down arrow, and then click **Slides**, **Handouts Pages**, or **Notes Pages**.

3 Type a range to choose the slides to print, and then click **OK**.

Chapter 4 **Outlining Your Ideas**

Page 64 **To create a blank presentation**

New

● On the Standard toolbar, click the **New** button or in the **New Presentation** task pane, click **Blank Presentation** under **New**.

65 **To view and enter text in Outline view**

1 In the **Outline/Slides** pane, click the **Outline tab**.

2 Click to place the insertion point, type your text, and then press [Enter].

3 Press the [Tab] key, if necessary, and then type your text.

69 **To insert an outline developed in another program into a presentation**

1 In the **Outline** tab, click a blank area to place the insertion point where you want to insert the outline.

2 On the **Insert** menu, click **Slides from Outline**.

3 Navigate to the location of the outline that you want to insert, click an outline, and then click **Insert**.

71 **To delete an entire slide or paragraph**

Four-headed
arrow pointer

1 Position the I-beam pointer (which changes to the four-headed arrow) over the icon for a slide or the bullet next to a paragraph, and then click the icon to select the slide.

2 Press the [Del] key.

71 **To rearrange a slide or paragraphs**

Four-headed
arrow pointer

1 Position the four-headed arrow over a slide icon or the bullet of your text line.

2 Drag the slide icon or bullet where you want the selected slide or paragraph to appear.

1 Select the text in which you want to change text style.

2 On the Formatting toolbar, click a formatting button (such as **Font**, **Font Size**, **Bold**, **Italic**, **Underline**, **Shadow**, and **Font Color**).

1 On the **File** menu, point to **Send To**, and then click **Microsoft Word**.

2 Click a send option, and then click **OK**.

1 On the **File** menu, click **Save As**.

2 Navigate to the location in which you want to save the outline file.

3 In the **File name** box, type the file name.

4 Click the **Save as type** down arrow, and then click **Outline/RTF**.

5 Click **Save**.

Chapter 5 Adding and Modifying Slide Text

● Click in the text object to place the insertion point, and then type the text.

1 Select the text object.

2 Drag the edge of the selection box to place the text object where you want it.

Text Box

1 On the Drawing toolbar, click the **Text Box** button.

2 Click where you want the text label to appear, and then type the text.

Text Box

1 On the Drawing toolbar, click the **Text Box** button.

2 Position the pointer on the slide, drag the pointer to create a box the length you want, and then type the text.

86 **To change text alignment**

1 Select the text box.

2 On the Formatting toolbar, click an alignment button (**Align Left**, **Center**, or **Align Right**).

86 **To adjust line spacing**

1 Select the text object with the dotted selection box.

2 On the **Format** menu, click **Line Spacing**.

3 Click the **Before paragraph** or **After paragraph** arrow to select a setting, and then click **OK**.

90 **To replace text**

1 On the **Edit** menu, click **Replace**.

2 Click the **Find what** box, and then type the text you want to replace.

3 Click in the **Replace with** box, and then type the replacement text.

4 Click **Find Next**, and then click **Replace**.

5 Click **OK**, and then click **Close** to close the **Replace** dialog box.

92 **To add an AutoCorrect entry**

1 On the **Tools** menu, click **AutoCorrect Options**, and then click the **AutoCorrect** tab, if necessary.

2 Click in the **Replace** box, and then type a misspelled word.

3 Press Tab, and then type the correctly spelled word.

4 Click **Add**, and then click **OK**.

92 **To use AutoCorrect to fix a misspelled word**

1 Click to position the insertion point where you want to type text.

2 Type the misspelled word, and then press Space.

95 **To mark a word as a foreign language word**

1 Select the foreign word or phrase that you want to mark.

2 On the **Tools** menu, click **Language**.

3 Click the foreign language, and then click **OK**.

95 **To select and correct a misspelled word**

● Right-click a misspelled word, and then click the correct spelling on the shortcut menu.

95 To check the spelling in a presentation

Spelling

1 On the Standard toolbar, click the **Spelling** button.

2 When the spelling checker stops because it fails to recognize a proper name, click **Add** to add the proper name to its dictionary, or click **Ignore All**.

3 When the spelling checker stops at a misspelled word, and shows possible correct spellings, click the accurate spelling from the suggestions, and then click **Change** to correct the spelling.

4 Click **OK** when prompted that the spelling check is complete.

95 To set style options

1 On the **Tools** menu, click **Options**, and then click the **Spelling and Style** tab.

2 Select the **Check style** check box, and then click **Style Options**.

3 Select the style options that you want to set, and then click **OK** twice.

95 To check the style of a presentation

Spelling

1 Click the light bulb or on the Standard toolbar, click the **Spelling** button.

2 Click the option that you want from the list, or click **OK** to ignore.

3 On the **Help** menu, click **Hide the Office Assistant**.

Chapter 6 Applying and Modifying Design Templates

Page 102 To apply a template

Slide Design

4 On the Formatting toolbar, click **Slide Design.**

5 In the **Slide Design** task pane, click **Design Templates**, and then click **Browse**.

6 Navigate to the folder that contains the template that you want to apply, click a template, and then click **Apply**.

104 To view the Title Master and the Slide Master

1 On the **View** menu, point to **Master**, and then click **Slide Master**.

2 Click the slide miniature of the Title Master or Slide Master.

104 To insert another slide or title master

● On the **Slide Master View** toolbar, click the **Insert New Slide Master** button.

● On the **Slide Master View** toolbar, click the **Insert New Title Master** button.

137 **To copy multiple objects using the Office Clipboard task pane**

Copy

1 Select multiple objects.

2 On the Standard toolbar, click the **Copy** button.

3 In the **Clipboard** task pane, click an item to paste it on the slide.

141 **To format an object**

1 Select an object.

2 On the Drawing toolbar, click a formatting button (such as **Fill Color**, **Line Color**, **Font Color**, **Line Style**, **Dash Style**, **Arrow Style**, **Shadow Style**, and **3-D Style**).

147 **To align an object**

1 Select the objects you want to align.

2 On the Drawing toolbar, click **Draw**, point to **Align or Distribute**, and then click an alignment.

147 **To turn on the visible grid and guides to align objects**

1 On the **View** menu, click **Grid and Guides**.

2 Select the **Display grid on screen** check box, select the **Display drawing guides on screen** check box, and then click **OK** to close the **Grid and Guides** dialog box.

150 **To connect two objects**

AutoShapes

AutoShapes ▾

1 On the Drawing toolbar, click **AutoShapes**, point to **Connectors**, and then click a connector.

2 Position the pointer over an object handle, and then click the object to select a connection point.

3 Position the pointer over the object handle on another object, and then click the object to select another connection point.

153 **To change object stacking order**

1 Select an object.

2 On the Drawing toolbar, click **Draw**, point to **Order**, and then click a stacking order option.

155 **To rotate or flip an object**

1 Select an object.

2 On the Drawing toolbar, click **Draw**, point to **Rotate or Flip**, and then click a rotate or flip option.

156 **To draw an arc**

Arc

1 On the Drawing toolbar, click **AutoShapes**, point to **Basic Shapes**, and then click the **Arc** button.

2 Drag an arc.

160 **To group or ungroup objects**

1 Select the objects or object you want to group or ungroup.

2 On the Drawing toolbar, click **Draw**, and then click **Group** or **Ungroup**

160 **To regroup objects**

1 Select one of the objects in the set of previously grouped objects.

2 On the Drawing toolbar, click **Draw**, and then click **Regroup**.

Chapter   9 **Inserting Information into PowerPoint**

Page   164 **To apply a different layout to a slide**

1 Display the slide to which you want to apply a different slide layout.

2 On the **Format** menu, click **Slide Layout** to display the **Slide Layout** task pane, and then click a new slide layout.

166 **To insert a clip art image using an AutoLayout with the content placeholder**

1 In the content placeholder, click the **Insert Clip Art** icon.

2 In the **Select Picture** dialog box, in the **Search text** box, type what you want to search for, and then click **Search**.

3 Click a clip art image.

166 **To insert a clip art image using the Insert Clip Art task pane**

Insert Clip Art

1 On the **Insert** menu, point to **Picture**, and then click **Clip Art**.

2 In the **Insert Clip Art** task pane, in the **Search text box,** type what you want to search for, and then click **Search**.

3 Click a clip art image.

171   **To scale an object**

Format Picture

1   Select the clip art image.

2   On the **Picture** toolbar, click the **Format Picture** button.

3   Click the **Size** tab, type a number in the **Height** box in the **Scale** area, and then click **OK**.

172   **To recolor an image**

Recolor Picture

1   Select a clip art object.

2   On the **Picture** toolbar, click the **Recolor Picture** button.

3   Under **New**, click the down arrow next to a color.

4   Click a color box or click an option to select a color, and then click **OK**.

174   **To insert a table**

1   On the **Insert** menu, click **Table**, or in the content placeholder, click the **Insert Table** icon, or double-click the table placeholder on a slide.

2   Click the **Number of rows** and **Number of columns** arrows to select the number of rows and columns you want, and then click **OK**.

3   Type text in the table, using ⌨Tab to move from cell to cell.

174   **To format a table**

1   Select the cells in the table in which you want to format.

2   On the **Tables and Borders** or Formatting toolbars, click a formatting button.

177   **To insert a Word table**

1   On the **Insert** menu, click **Object**, and then click **Create New**.

2   In the **Object type** box, click **Microsoft Word Document**, and then click **OK**.

3   Use the commands on the **Table** menu to create the table that you want.

4   Click outside of the table to return to Microsoft PowerPoint.

177   **To insert an Excel chart object in a slide**

1   On the **Insert** menu, click **Object**.

2   Click the **Create from File** option, click **Browse**, and then navigate to the location of the Excel file that you want to insert.

3   Click the Excel file that you want to insert, click **OK** to close the **Browse** dialog box, and then click **OK**.

179 **To insert a Microsoft Graph chart**

● On the **Insert** menu, click **Chart,** or in the Content placeholder, click the **Insert Chart** icon, or double-click the chart placeholder on a slide.

179 **To import data into chart**

1 Double-click the Microsoft Graph chart, and then click the cell(s) where you want to import the data.

2 On the Graph Standard toolbar, click the **Import File** button.

3 Navigate to the location of the file that you want to insert, and then double-click the file.

4 Click **OK** to overwrite the current data in the datasheet.

179 **To format a Microsoft Graph chart**

1 Double-click the Graph chart.

2 On the **Chart** menu, click **Chart Type**, and then click a chart type tab.

3 Click a chart type, click a chart sub-type, and then click **OK**.

4 Use the options on the Graph Standard toolbar, Graph Formatting toolbar, and **Chart Options** on the **Chart** menu to format the chart.

185 **To insert and create an Organization Chart**

1 On the **Insert** menu, click **Diagram**, or in the content placeholder, click the **Insert Diagram or Organization Chart** icon, or double-click the org chart placeholder on a slide.

2 Select **Organization Chart**, and then click **OK**.

3 Click the chart box, and then type new text.

4 On the Organization Chart toolbar, click the **Insert Shape** down arrow, and then click an option to insert a chart box, if necessary.

5 Click a blank area of the presentation window to quit Organization Chart.

188 **To insert and create a diagram**

Insert Diagram or Organization Chart

1 On the Drawing toolbar, click the **Insert Diagram or Organization Chart** button.

2 Select a diagram, and then click **OK**.

3 Click a text box, select the current text, and then type new text.

4 Click a blank area of the presentation window to quit Diagram.

190 **To insert a picture**

1 On the **Insert** menu, point to **Picture**, and then click **From File**.

2 Navigate to the location where you want to insert a picture.

3 Click the picture you want to insert, and then click **Insert**.

192 **To resize a picture**

● Select the picture, hold down Shift, and then drag the corner resize handles on the picture to enlarge the picture on the slide.

192 **To crop a picture**

1 Select the picture.

Crop

2 On the **Picture** toolbar, click the **Crop** button.

3 Position the center of the cropping tool over a resize handle and drag to crop the picture.

4 On the **Picture** toolbar, click the **Crop** button or click a blank area of the slide.

192 **To compress a picture**

1 Select the picture.

Compress
Pictures

2 On the **Picture** toolbar, click the **Compress Pictures** button.

3 Click the compression options that you want.

4 Click **OK**, and then click **Apply**.

195 **To insert WordArt in a slide**

Insert WordArt

1 On the Drawing toolbar, click the **Insert WordArt** button.

2 Click a style, and then click **OK**.

3 In the **Text** box, type text, and then click **OK**.

4 Click a blank area of the presentation window to quit WordArt.

Chapter 10 **Setting Up and Delivering a Slide Show**

Page **200** **To apply an animation scheme to a slide**

Slide Sorter
View

1 Click the **Slide Sorter View** button, and then click a slide.

2 On the **Slide Show** menu, click **Animation Schemes**.

3 In the **Slide Design** task pane, under **Apply to selected slides**, click an animation.

200   **To animate the text in a slide**

1   In Normal view select a slide.

2   On the **Slide Show** menu, click **Custom Animation**.

3   Click the text you would like to animate, and then click **Add Effect** in the **Custom Animation** task pane.

4   Point to an effect category, and then click an effect.

206   **To apply a slide transition effect**

Slide Sorter
View

1   Click the **Slide Sorter View** button, and then select a slide.

2   On the **Slide Show** menu, click **Slide Transition** to open the **Slide Transition** task pane.

3   Under **Apply to selected slides**, click a transition effect.

4   Click the transition symbol below the slide to preview the effect.

208   **To create a custom show**

Slide Sorter
View

1   On the **Slide Show** menu, click **Custom Shows**.

2   Click **New**.

3   In the **Slide show name** box, type the slide show name.

4   In the **Slides in presentation** box, click a slide, and then click **Add**.

5   Select and add more slides to the custom slide show.

6   Click **OK**, and then click **Close** or **Show**.

210   **To start a slide show on any slide**

1   Select a slide.

Slide Show

2   Click the **Slide Show** button.

3   Click the screen, press [Space], or press the [→] to advance to the next slide, or press the [←] to return to the previous slide.

210   **To end a slide show on any slide**

●   Right-click anywhere on the screen, and then click **End Show** or press [Esc].

210   **To draw an annotation in slide show using the pen tool**

1   Click the **Slide Show** button.

2   Right-click the screen, point to **Pointer Options**, and then click **Pen**.

3   Draw an annotation, and then press [P] to erase annotations.

210   To hide a slide during a slide show

1   Click the **Slide Sorter View** button.

2   Select the slide that you want to hide.

Hide Slide

3   On the Slide Sorter toolbar, click the **Hide Slide** button.

214   To enter notes and action items in the Meeting Minder

Slide Show

1   In Slide Show, right-click the screen, and then click **Meeting Minder**.

2   In the **Meeting Minder** tab, click the text box, and then type your text.

3   Click the **Action Items** tab, type description text, and then type the recipient name(s).

4   Click **Add**, and then click **OK**.

Chapter 11   Creating a Multimedia Presentation

Page   217   To insert a sound

1   On the **Insert** menu, point to **Movies and Sounds**, and then click **Sound from Clip Organizer**.

2   Click a movie, and then click **Yes** or **No** to play automatically in slide show.

217   To insert a movie

1   On the **Insert** menu, point to **Movies and Sounds**, and then click **Movie from Clip Organizer**.

2   Click a sound, and then click **Yes** or **No** to play automatically in slide show.

222   To play a movie or sound

●   Double-click the movie or sound object.

222   To change the play settings

1   Right-click the movie object, and then click **Custom Animation**.

2   In the **Custom Animation** task pane, click the **movie object** item, click the **Start** down arrow, and then click an option.

225   To apply slide timings

1   Click the **Slide Sorter View** button.

Slide Transition
Transition

2   On the Slide Sorter toolbar, click the **Slide Transition** button.

3   Select the **Automatically after** check box, and then type a value.

304

4   Click **Apply** or **Apply to All Slides**.

225   **To rehearse slide timings**

Rehearse
Timings

1   In Slide Sorter view, on the Slide Sorter toolbar, click the **Rehearse Timings** button.

2   As soon as you feel enough time has passed to adequately view the slide, click the mouse or **Next** to select a new slide timing, or press ➡ to use the original timings for each slide in the presentation.

3   If the time is inadequate, click the **Repeat** button to rehearse the slide again. You can stop the slide rehearsal at any time by clicking the **Close** button in the **Rehearsal** dialog box.

4   Click **Yes** to save the new slide timings.

228   **To record a voice narration during a presentation**

1   On the **Slide Show** menu, click **Record Narration**.

2   Click **OK**, and then use the rehearsed slide timings, or click to advance through the slide show and add narration as you go.

3   Click **Yes** or **No** to review the slide timings in the Slide Sorter view.

230   **To set up a self-running slide show**

1   On the **Slide Show** menu, click **Set Up Show**.

2   Click the **Browsed At A Kiosk (Full Screen)** option, and then click **OK**.

Chapter 12   **Creating a Web Presentation**

Page   234   **To create a summary slide**

1   Click the **Slide Sorter View** button.

2   On the **Edit** menu, click **Select All**.

Summary Slide

3   On the Slide Sorter toolbar, click the **Summary Slide** button.

235   **To create a hyperlink to a slide or external file**

1   Select the text you want as a hyperlink.

2   On the **Slide Show** menu, click **Action Settings**.

3   Click the **Hyperlink to** option.

4   Click the **Hyperlink to** down arrow, and then click **Slide** or **Other File**.

5   Click a slide or double-click the file you want to link to, and then click **OK** twice.

235 **To create a hyperlink to a Web site**

 1 Select the text of a Web site address.

Insert
Hyperlink

 2 On the Standard toolbar, click the **Insert Hyperlink** button.

 3 Type the Web page address, and then click **OK**.

241 **To preview a presentation as a Web page**

 1 On the **File** menu, click **Web Page Preview**.

 2 Scroll down the list of slide titles on the left, and then click a title.

 3 On the **File** menu in your browser, click **Close**.

241 **To save and publish a presentation as a Web page**

 1 On the **File** menu, click **Save as Web Page**.

 2 In the **File name** box, type the Web page name.

 3 Navigate to the location where you want to publish the presentation, and then click **Publish**.

 4 Click Web page options, and then click **Publish**.

Chapter 13 **Reviewing and Sharing a Presentation**

Page **250** **To add comments to a presentation**

 1 On the **Insert** menu, click **Comment**

 2 In the comment box, type the comment.

 3 Click anywhere outside of the comment box.

253 **To add password protection to a presentation**

 1 On the **Tools** menu, click **Options**, and then click the **Security** tab.

 2 In the **Password to modify** box or the **Password to open** box, type a password, and then click **OK**.

256 **To send a presentation via e-mail**

 1 On the **File** menu, point to **Send To**, and then click **Mail Recipient (for Review)**.

 2 Click **To**, click the recipient names, and then click **To**, **Cc**, or **Bcc**.

 3 Click **OK**, and then click the **Send** button on the toolbar.

258   To compare and merge presentations and track the changes

1   On the **Tools** menu, click **Compare and Merge Presentations**.

2   Navigate to the location of the presentation that you want to compare and merge with the currently opened presentation.

3   Click a presentation file, click **Merge**, and then click **Continue**.

Markup

4   On the Reviewing toolbar, click the **Markup** button.

5   In the **Revisions Pane**, accept or reject changes, and then click the **Close** button in the **Revision Pane**.

264   To set up an online broadcast

1   On the **Slide Show** menu, point to **Online Broadcast**, and then click **Schedule a Live Broadcast**.

2   Click **Settings**, click **Browse**, navigate to a shared folder on a network server, and then click **Select**, and then click **OK**.

3   Click **Schedule**, and then arrange an Outlook online meeting. If you use another e-mail program, the URL for the broadcast is embedded in the body of your message. Specify the people whom you would like to participate in the e-mail message.

4   Click **Send**, and then click **Yes** to continue.

5   Click **Broadcast**, click **Start**, and then click **Yes** to start.

270   To set up an online meeting

1   On the **Tools** menu, point to **Online Collaboration**, and then click **Schedule Meeting**.

2   Click **To**, click the recipient names in the Name list, click the **Required** or **Optional** button, and then click **OK**.

3   Click in the **Subject** box, and then type the subject of the online meeting.

4   Click the **Start time** down arrow next to the date, select a start date, and then click **Send**.

274   To start the Pack and Go Wizard

1   On the **File** menu, click **Pack and Go**.

2   Read the introduction, click **Next**, and then click **Next** again.

3   Select the drive where you want to store the file, and then click **Next**.

4   Select the **Embed TrueType Fonts** check box.

5 Click **Next**, click the **Viewer for Microsoft Windows** option, if necessary (download and install the viewer), click **Next**, and then click **Finish**.

274 **To show a presentation with the PowerPoint Viewer**

Start

Start

1 On the Windows taskbar, click **Start**, point to **Programs**, and then click **Microsoft PowerPoint Viewer**.

2 Navigate to the location of the presentation that you want to open, and then click the file.

3 Click **Show**, click the mouse to advance through the presentation slides, and then click **Exit**.

Chapter 14 **Customizing PowerPoint**

Page 279 **To customize a toolbar**

1 On the **Tools** menu, click **Customize**.

2 Click the **Toolbars** tab, click **New**, type a toolbar name, and then click **OK**.

3 Click the **Commands** tab, click a category, and then click a command.

4 Drag the command to a toolbar to add it to the toolbar or drag a button off the toolbar to remove it from the toolbar, and then click **OK**.

284 **To customize the way you create text objects**

1 Create a text box, and then on the Format menu, click Font.

2 Change the font options, select the **Default for new objects** check box, and then click **OK**.

284 **To customize the way you create shape objects**

1 Create a shape, and then change the shape attributes.

2 On the Drawing toolbar, click **Draw**, and then click **Set AutoShapes Default**.

285 **To record and run a macro**

1 On the **Tools** menu, point to **Macro**, and then click **Record New Macro**.

2 Type a macro name, and then click **OK**.

3 Perform a set of steps, and then click the **Stop Recording** button.

4 On the **Tools** menu, point to **Macro**, and then click **Macros**.

5 Select a macro, and then click **Run**.

Glossary

action buttons   Predefined navigation buttons, such as Home, Help, Back, Next, and End, that help you navigate to a particular part of a presentation or a file.

active cell   A selected cell.

Active Directory   A network service that stores information about resources, such as computers and printers.

adjustable objects   Objects with an adjustment handle (which looks like a small yellow diamond) that allow you to alter the appearance of the object without changing its size.

animated pictures   GIF (Graphics Interchange Format) or digital video files that you can insert into a slide presentation as a movie.

animation scheme   A set of professionally designed animations divided into three categories: Subtle, Moderate, and Exciting.

arc   A curved line whose angle you can change by dragging an adjustment handle.

AutoContent Wizard   A wizard that takes you through a step-by-step process to create a presentation, prompting you for presentation information as you go.

automatic layout behavior   A feature that recognizes when you insert an object onto a slide and changes the layout to fit the objects on the slide.

background   The underlying colors, shading, texture, and style of the color scheme.

bullet text   A list of items in which each item is preceded by a symbol.

cell   The intersection of a row and a column.

color menu   The color palette associated with Drawing toolbar buttons, such as Fill Color, Line Color, or Font Color.

color scheme   The basic set of eight colors provided for any slide. The color scheme consists of a background color, a color for lines and text, and six additional colors balanced to provide a professional look to a presentation.

connection pointer   A small box pointer that allows you to drag a connection line between two connection sites.

connection sites   Small blue handles on each side of an object that allow you to add a connection line between two objects.

control boxes   Headings in a datasheet that correspond to the different data series.

datasheet   A numerical representation of chart data that form rows and columns.

data series   A group of related data points.

data series marker   A graphical representation of the information in the data series.

design template   A presentation with a designed format and color scheme.

digital signature   An electronic, secure stamp of authentication on a document.

dotted selection box   The border of a selected object that indicates that you can manipulate the entire object.

embedded object   An object created with another program but stored in Power-Point. You can update an embedded object in PowerPoint.

export   The process of converting and saving a file format to be used in another program.

grayscale   A black and white image that displays shades of gray.

hanging indent   Paragraph formatting adjusted by small triangles on the ruler where the second and subsequent lines of text are indented more than the first.

hyperlinks   "Hot spots" or "jumps" to a location in the same file, another file, or an HTML page, represented by colored and underlined text or by a graphic.

import   The process of converting a file format created in another program.

indent markers   Markers on the ruler that control the indent levels of a text object.

insertion point   A blinking bar that indicates where text will be entered or edited as you type.

landscape   Horizontal orientation (10 x 7.5 inches) of an image on the output media.

legend   A list that identifies each data series in the datasheet.

linked object   An object created in another program that maintains a connection to its source. A linked object is stored in its source document, where it was created. You update a linked object within its source program.

lobby page   A page that appears on the server before the broadcast starts and contains information about the broadcast.

margin markers   Small squares on the ruler that move both the upper and lower indent markers.

masters   Special slides that control the properties of slides in a presentation.

menu   A list of commands or options available in a program.

more colors   Additional colors that you can add to each color menu.

Normal view   View that contains all three panes: Outline/Slides, Slide, and Notes.

Notes Page view   View where you can add speaker notes and related graphics.

Notes pane   Area in Normal view where you can add speaker notes.

object   Any entity in PowerPoint that you can manipulate.

Office Assistant   A help system that answers questions, offers tips, and provides help for Microsoft Office XP program features.

Office Clipboard   A storage area shared by all Office programs where multiple pieces of information from several different sources are stored.

offset   The direction and distance in which a shadow falls from an object.

Outline/Slides pane   Area in Normal view where you can organize and develop presentation content in text or slide miniature form.

paragraph   Text that begins and end when you press Enter.

places bar   A bar on the left side of the Save As and Open dialog boxes that provides quick access to commonly used locations in which to store and open files.

portrait   Vertical orientation (7.5 x 10 inches) of an image on the output media.

PowerPoint Viewer   A program that allows you to show a slide show on a computer that does not have PowerPoint installed.

presentation window   The electronic canvas on which you type text, draw shapes, create graphs, add color, and insert objects.

program window   An area of the screen used to display the PowerPoint program and the presentation window.

pure black and white   A black and white image that displays only black and white without any shades of gray.

resize handle   A white circle on each corner and side of an object that you can drag to change the objects size.

RGB   The visible spectrum represented by mixing red, green, and blue colors.

Rich Text Format (RTF)   A common text format that many programs can open.

scaling   Resizing an entire object by a set percentage.

ScreenTip   A yellow box that tells you the name of or more information about a button, icon, or other item on the screen when you place the pointer over the item.

selection box   A gray slanted line or dotted outline around an object.

slanted-line selection box   The border of a selected object that indicates that you can edit the object's content.

Slide Master   A master slide that controls the characteristics (background color, text color, font, and font size) of a presentation.

Slide pane   Area in Normal view where you can view a slide and add text, graphics, and other items to the slide.

Slide Show view   View where you can preview slides as an electronic presentation.

Slide Sorter view   View where you can see all slides in a presentation in miniature.

slide timing   The length of time that a slide appears on the screen.

Smart Tag   A button that helps you control the result of certain actions, such as automatic text correction, automatic layout behavior, or copy and paste.

source document   The original document created in the source program.

source program   The program that created a document that is a linked object.

status bar   The bar at the bottom of the presentation window that displays messages about the current state of PowerPoint.

subfolder   A folder within a folder.

task pane   A pane that allows you to quickly access commands related to a specific task without having to use menus and toolbars.

template   A presentation whose format and color scheme you apply to another presentation.

text animation slide   A slide with text that you set to appear incrementally.

text label   A text object used primarily for short phrases or notes.

text object   A box that contains text in a slide.

text placeholder   A dotted-lined box that you can click to add text.

tick-mark labels   Labels that identify the data plotted in a chart.

Title Master   A master slide that contains placeholders that are similar to those of the Slide Master but that affect the title slide only.

title slide   The first slide in a presentation.

title text   Text that identifies the name or purpose of a slide.

toolbar   A graphical bar in the presentation window with buttons that perform some of the common commands in PowerPoint.

window   An area of the screen used to display a PowerPoint program or presentation window.

word processing box   A text object used primarily for longer text.

word wrap   A feature that automatically moves the insertion point to the next line within an object as you type.

Index

Numerics

3-D effects, adding to objects, 152–153
3-D views, in Graph charts, 182

A

accent color, 120
action buttons, 235–236, 309
  adding sounds to, 240
  creating, 236, 239–240
action items, entering during slide shows, 214–215, 304
action settings, for playing sounds or movies, 222, 224
actions, undoing/redoing, 12–13, 14–15
active cell, 180, 309
Active Directory network service, 61, 309
add-in programs, 287–288
adjustable objects, 134, 309
adjusting objects, 136–137, 297
adjustment handles, 134, 150, 309
agenda slides, creating, 234–235
aligning objects, 147–149, 298
aligning text, 86–87, 89, 294
alignment buttons (Formatting toolbar), 86
animated pictures, 218, 309
  See also movies
animating slides, 200–205, 226
  objects, 200, 201, 204–205
  text, 200, 201–204, 303
animation effects
  applying, 200, 201–205, 302
  schemes, 200, 309
  transition effects, 206
animation order, 204–205
  changing, 205
  inserting movies in, 222–224
animation schemes (designs), 200, 309
animation slides. *See* text animation slides

animation symbol, 201
animations
  custom animations, 200, 202–205, 223
  effects. *See* animation effects
  order of appearance. *See* animation order
  playing sounds during, 203
  printing slides with, 204
  slide timings, 226
annotating slides during slide shows, 210, 212, 303
  erasing annotations, 213, 303
Answer Wizard, 21
applications
  inserting outlines from other applications, 69–70, 292
  See also add-in programs
arcs, 309
  connecting to shapes, 157
  copying, 159
  drawing, 156–157, 299
  editing, 156, 157–159
art. *See* clip art; graphics; pictures
asking questions
  Ask A Question box, 2, 20–21, 290
  Office Assistant, 22, 290
attached files, sending, 257
attributes. *See* object attributes
audience handouts, printing, 57, 292
AutoContent Wizard, 309
  creating presentations with, 6–9, 240–241, 289
  starting, 7
AutoCorrect
  adding entries to, 97, 294
  correcting spelling errors, 92, 93–94, 294
  options, 92, 94, 164, 169
AutoFit, 92, 94–95
automatic advance timing (slides), 225, 304
automatic layout behavior, 164, 169, 175, 309
Automatic Word Selection, 73

AutoRecover option, 9
AutoShapes
  displaying more, 166, 169
  drawing, 134–135, 297
axes (of charts), 180
  data labels, 183

B

background color, 120
background objects. *See* master objects
background printing, 60
backgrounds. *See* slide backgrounds
black and white
  previewing slides in, 53–54, 291
  printing slides in, 58
blank presentations, creating, 6, 26, 64–65, 292
blue boxes under first letters of words, 92
blue handles (connection sites), 150
bold typeface
  formatting text in, 75, 146
  as used in this book, xvi
bringing objects forward/to front, 153–154
Broadcast Meeting window, 266–267
broadcasting. *See* online broadcasts
browsers
  opening presentations, 242, 244–245
build slides. *See* text animation slides; animations
bullet points, (Outline tab), 65
bullet text (paragraph text), 12, 309
  editing, 13–16
  entering, 32–34, 65–67
  formatting, 109
  indenting, 32, 67, 109, 113–115

Microsoft PowerPoint. *See* PowerPoint (Microsoft)

Microsoft Web site, connecting to, 245

Microsoft Word. *See* Word (Microsoft)

miniatures. *See* **slide miniatures**

mistakes. *See* **correcting mistakes**

monitors
running slide shows on a second monitor, 213–214

more colors, 126, 127, 310

MOS program, xix
certification, xxii
levels, xix–xx
certification exams, xx–xxi
tips for taking, xxi–xxii
objectives, xx
coverage in this book, xvii–xviii

mouse
action settings for playing sounds or movies, 222, 224
advancing slides in slide shows, 19, 210, 212, 213, 225
See also mouse pointers

mouse pointers
adjustment pointer, 136
connection pointer, 150, 309
constrain pointer, 193
copy pointer, 139
cropping tool, 193
cross-hair pointer, 135
drag pointer, 36
Format Painter pointer, 146
Free Rotate pointer, 155
hand pointer, 237
magnifying glass, 55
pen tool, 210, 212
selection pointer, 82, 83
two-headed arrows, 73, 74, 136
upside-down-T pointer, 85
See also four-headed arrow; I-beam pointer

movies, 218, 220
accessing, 219
inserting, 217, 220–221, 222–224, 304
pausing, 221
playing, 218, 220, 221, 304
in slide shows, 221, 222–224, 304
playing time, determining, 222
resuming, 221

moving
from cell to cell, 174, 175
datasheet data, 182
objects, 83, 139, 293, 297
single objects in groups, 160
from slide to slide
in the Slide pane, 10, 289
in slide shows, 210–211, 213
slides between presentations, 37
toolbars, 280
See also rearranging

multimedia presentations, 217–231
See also movies; narrations (in slide shows); sounds

multiple masters, 104, 106

multiple objects
copying, 137, 140–141, 298
selecting/deselecting, 139–140

multiple paragraphs, selecting, 72–73

multiple slide transitions, applying, 207–208

multiple slides, animating, 201, 226

N

names
changing commenters'/reviewers' names, 251, 262

naming presentations, 6, 8

narrations (in slide shows)
recording, 228–230, 305
showing presentations without, 230

navigating through slide shows, 210–211, 213

NetMeeting (Microsoft), 270–271

networks
showing presentations on, 249, 264–269
storing presentations on, 266

New Folder dialog box, 41

New Presentation task pane, 4
starting presentations from, 5–6

New Slide command (Insert menu), 31

Normal view, 4, 17, 18, 310
applying animation effects, 200
panes and tabs, 3–4

See also Notes pane (Normal view); Outline/Slides pane (Normal view); Slide pane (Normal view)

notes
entering speaker notes, 17, 37–40
taking notes during slide shows, 214–215, 304
See also notes pages

Notes Master, 105, 108

Notes Page view, 17, 39, 310
entering text, 17, 37–38, 39–40, 291
scaling, 39
switching to, 17

notes pages, 37
entering text on, 17, 37–40, 291
printing, 57, 60, 292
sending to Word, 77–79, 293
See also Notes Page view

Notes pane (Normal view), 3, 4, 311
entering text, 17, 37, 38, 291

Number Area placeholder, 106

O

object attributes, 141
changing defaults, 284–285, 308
modifying, 134, 135, 141–147

objects, 81–82, 134, 311
3-D effects, 152–153
adjustable, 134, 309
adjusting, 136–137, 297
aligning, 147–149, 298
animating, 200, 201, 204–205
attributes. *See* object attributes
background. *See* master objects
bringing forward/to front, 153–154
changing the shape of, 142
coloring, 152
connecting, 150–152, 298
copying, 83, 84, 137–138, 139, 297
multiple, 137, 140–141, 298
deleting, 134
deselecting, 82, 134
multiple, 139–140
drawing (creating), 134–135, 297
arcs, 156–157, 299
connector lines, 150–152
customizing, 284–285, 308
freehand lines, 210, 212

Get a **Free**
e-mail newsletter, updates,
special offers, links to related books,
and more when you
register on line!

Register your Microsoft Press® title on our Web site and you'll get a FREE subscription to our e-mail newsletter, *Microsoft Press Book Connections.* You'll find out about newly released and upcoming books and learning tools, online events, software downloads, special offers and coupons for Microsoft Press customers, and information about major Microsoft® product releases. You can also read useful additional information about all the titles we publish, such as detailed book descriptions, tables of contents and indexes, sample chapters, links to related books and book series, author biographies, and reviews by other customers.

Registration is easy. Just visit this Web page and fill in your information:

http://mspress.microsoft.com/register

Microsoft®

- -

Proof of Purchase

Use this page as proof of purchase if participating in a promotion or rebate offer on this title. Proof of purchase must be used in conjunction with other proof(s) of payment such as your dated sales receipt—see offer details.

Microsoft® PowerPoint® Version 2002 Step by Step
0-7356-1297-8

CUSTOMER NAME

Microsoft Press, PO Box 97017, Redmond, WA 98073-9830

MICROSOFT LICENSE AGREEMENT
Book Companion CD

IMPORTANT—READ CAREFULLY: This Microsoft End-User License Agreement ("EULA") is a legal agreement between you (either an individual or an entity) and Microsoft Corporation for the Microsoft product identified above, which includes computer software and may include associated media, printed materials, and "online" or electronic documentation ("SOFTWARE PRODUCT"). Any component included within the SOFTWARE PRODUCT that is accompanied by a separate End-User License Agreement shall be governed by such agreement and not the terms set forth below. By installing, copying, or otherwise using the SOFTWARE PRODUCT, you agree to be bound by the terms of this EULA. If you do not agree to the terms of this EULA, you are not authorized to install, copy, or otherwise use the SOFTWARE PRODUCT; you may, however, return the SOFTWARE PRODUCT, along with all printed materials and other items that form a part of the Microsoft product that includes the SOFTWARE PRODUCT, to the place you obtained them for a full refund.

SOFTWARE PRODUCT LICENSE

The SOFTWARE PRODUCT is protected by United States copyright laws and international copyright treaties, as well as other intellectual property laws and treaties. The SOFTWARE PRODUCT is licensed, not sold.

1. **GRANT OF LICENSE.** This EULA grants you the following rights:

    a. **Software Product.** You may install and use one copy of the SOFTWARE PRODUCT on a single computer. The primary user of the computer on which the SOFTWARE PRODUCT is installed may make a second copy for his or her exclusive use on a portable computer.

    b. **Storage/Network Use.** You may also store or install a copy of the SOFTWARE PRODUCT on a storage device, such as a network server, used only to install or run the SOFTWARE PRODUCT on your other computers over an internal network; however, you must acquire and dedicate a license for each separate computer on which the SOFTWARE PRODUCT is installed or run from the storage device. A license for the SOFTWARE PRODUCT may not be shared or used concurrently on different computers.

    c. **License Pak.** If you have acquired this EULA in a Microsoft License Pak, you may make the number of additional copies of the computer software portion of the SOFTWARE PRODUCT authorized on the printed copy of this EULA, and you may use each copy in the manner specified above. You are also entitled to make a corresponding number of secondary copies for portable computer use as specified above.

    d. **Sample Code.** Solely with respect to portions, if any, of the SOFTWARE PRODUCT that are identified within the SOFTWARE PRODUCT as sample code (the "SAMPLE CODE"):

    i. **Use and Modification.** Microsoft grants you the right to use and modify the source code version of the SAMPLE CODE, *provided* you comply with subsection (d)(iii) below. You may not distribute the SAMPLE CODE, or any modified version of the SAMPLE CODE, in source code form.

    ii. **Redistributable Files.** Provided you comply with subsection (d)(iii) below, Microsoft grants you a nonexclusive, royalty-free right to reproduce and distribute the object code version of the SAMPLE CODE and of any modified SAMPLE CODE, other than SAMPLE CODE, or any modified version thereof, designated as not redistributable in the Readme file that forms a part of the SOFTWARE PRODUCT (the "Non-Redistributable Sample Code"). All SAMPLE CODE other than the Non-Redistributable Sample Code is collectively referred to as the "REDISTRIBUTABLES."

    iii. **Redistribution Requirements.** If you redistribute the REDISTRIBUTABLES, you agree to: (i) distribute the REDISTRIBUTABLES in object code form only in conjunction with and as a part of your software application product; (ii) not use Microsoft's name, logo, or trademarks to market your software application product; (iii) include a valid copyright notice on your software application product; (iv) indemnify, hold harmless, and defend Microsoft from and against any claims or lawsuits, including attorney's fees, that arise or result from the use or distribution of your software application product; and (v) not permit further distribution of the REDISTRIBUTABLES by your end user. Contact Microsoft for the applicable royalties due and other licensing terms for all other uses and/or distribution of the REDISTRIBUTABLES.

2. **DESCRIPTION OF OTHER RIGHTS AND LIMITATIONS.**

    - **Limitations on Reverse Engineering, Decompilation, and Disassembly.** You may not reverse engineer, decompile, or disassemble the SOFTWARE PRODUCT, except and only to the extent that such activity is expressly permitted by applicable law notwithstanding this limitation.

    - **Separation of Components.** The SOFTWARE PRODUCT is licensed as a single product. Its component parts may not be separated for use on more than one computer.

    - **Rental.** You may not rent, lease, or lend the SOFTWARE PRODUCT.

    - **Support Services.** Microsoft may, but is not obligated to, provide you with support services related to the SOFTWARE PRODUCT ("Support Services"). Use of Support Services is governed by the Microsoft policies and programs described in the user manual, in "online" documentation, and/or in other Microsoft-provided materials. Any supplemental software code provided to you as part of the Support Services shall be considered part of the SOFTWARE PRODUCT and subject to the terms and conditions of this EULA. With respect to technical information you provide to Microsoft as part of the Support Services, Microsoft may use such information for its business purposes, including for product support and development. Microsoft will not utilize such technical information in a form that personally identifies you.

- **Software Transfer.** You may permanently transfer all of your rights under this EULA, provided you retain no copies, you transfer all of the SOFTWARE PRODUCT (including all component parts, the media and printed materials, any upgrades, this EULA, and, if applicable, the Certificate of Authenticity), **and** the recipient agrees to the terms of this EULA.

- **Termination.** Without prejudice to any other rights, Microsoft may terminate this EULA if you fail to comply with the terms and conditions of this EULA. In such event, you must destroy all copies of the SOFTWARE PRODUCT and all of its component parts.

3. **COPYRIGHT.** All title and copyrights in and to the SOFTWARE PRODUCT (including but not limited to any images, photographs, animations, video, audio, music, text, SAMPLE CODE, REDISTRIBUTABLES, and "applets" incorporated into the SOFTWARE PRODUCT) and any copies of the SOFTWARE PRODUCT are owned by Microsoft or its suppliers. The SOFTWARE PRODUCT is protected by copyright laws and international treaty provisions. Therefore, you must treat the SOFTWARE PRODUCT like any other copyrighted material **except** that you may install the SOFTWARE PRODUCT on a single computer provided you keep the original solely for backup or archival purposes. You may not copy the printed materials accompanying the SOFTWARE PRODUCT.

4. **U.S. GOVERNMENT RESTRICTED RIGHTS.** The SOFTWARE PRODUCT and documentation are provided with RESTRICTED RIGHTS. Use, duplication, or disclosure by the Government is subject to restrictions as set forth in subparagraph (c)(1)(ii) of the Rights in Technical Data and Computer Software clause at DFARS 252.227-7013 or subparagraphs (c)(1) and (2) of the Commercial Computer Software—Restricted Rights at 48 CFR 52.227-19, as applicable. Manufacturer is Microsoft Corporation/One Microsoft Way/Redmond, WA 98052-6399.

5. **EXPORT RESTRICTIONS.** You agree that you will not export or re-export the SOFTWARE PRODUCT, any part thereof, or any process or service that is the direct product of the SOFTWARE PRODUCT (the foregoing collectively referred to as the "Restricted Components"), to any country, person, entity, or end user subject to U.S. export restrictions. You specifically agree not to export or re-export any of the Restricted Components (i) to any country to which the U.S. has embargoed or restricted the export of goods or services, which currently include, but are not necessarily limited to, Cuba, Iran, Iraq, Libya, North Korea, Sudan, and Syria, or to any national of any such country, wherever located, who intends to transmit or transport the Restricted Components back to such country; (ii) to any end user who you know or have reason to know will utilize the Restricted Components in the design, development, or production of nuclear, chemical, or biological weapons; or (iii) to any end user who has been prohibited from participating in U.S. export transactions by any federal agency of the U.S. government. You warrant and represent that neither the BXA nor any other U.S. federal agency has suspended, revoked, or denied your export privileges.

DISCLAIMER OF WARRANTY

NO WARRANTIES OR CONDITIONS. MICROSOFT EXPRESSLY DISCLAIMS ANY WARRANTY OR CONDITION FOR THE SOFTWARE PRODUCT. THE SOFTWARE PRODUCT AND ANY RELATED DOCUMENTATION ARE PROVIDED "AS IS" WITHOUT WARRANTY OR CONDITION OF ANY KIND, EITHER EXPRESS OR IMPLIED, INCLUDING, WITHOUT LIMITATION, THE IMPLIED WARRANTIES OF MERCHANTABILITY, FITNESS FOR A PARTICULAR PURPOSE, OR NONINFRINGEMENT. THE ENTIRE RISK ARISING OUT OF USE OR PERFORMANCE OF THE SOFTWARE PRODUCT REMAINS WITH YOU.

LIMITATION OF LIABILITY. TO THE MAXIMUM EXTENT PERMITTED BY APPLICABLE LAW, IN NO EVENT SHALL MICROSOFT OR ITS SUPPLIERS BE LIABLE FOR ANY SPECIAL, INCIDENTAL, INDIRECT, OR CONSEQUENTIAL DAMAGES WHATSOEVER (INCLUDING, WITHOUT LIMITATION, DAMAGES FOR LOSS OF BUSINESS PROFITS, BUSINESS INTERRUPTION, LOSS OF BUSINESS INFORMATION, OR ANY OTHER PECUNIARY LOSS) ARISING OUT OF THE USE OF OR INABILITY TO USE THE SOFTWARE PRODUCT OR THE PROVISION OF OR FAILURE TO PROVIDE SUPPORT SERVICES, EVEN IF MICROSOFT HAS BEEN ADVISED OF THE POSSIBILITY OF SUCH DAMAGES. IN ANY CASE, MICROSOFT'S ENTIRE LIABILITY UNDER ANY PROVISION OF THIS EULA SHALL BE LIMITED TO THE GREATER OF THE AMOUNT ACTUALLY PAID BY YOU FOR THE SOFTWARE PRODUCT OR US$5.00; PROVIDED, HOWEVER, IF YOU HAVE ENTERED INTO A MICROSOFT SUPPORT SERVICES AGREEMENT, MICROSOFT'S ENTIRE LIABILITY REGARDING SUPPORT SERVICES SHALL BE GOVERNED BY THE TERMS OF THAT AGREEMENT. BECAUSE SOME STATES AND JURISDICTIONS DO NOT ALLOW THE EXCLUSION OR LIMITATION OF LIABILITY, THE ABOVE LIMITATION MAY NOT APPLY TO YOU.

MISCELLANEOUS

This EULA is governed by the laws of the State of Washington USA, except and only to the extent that applicable law mandates governing law of a different jurisdiction.

Should you have any questions concerning this EULA, or if you desire to contact Microsoft for any reason, please contact the Microsoft subsidiary serving your country, or write: Microsoft Sales Information Center/One Microsoft Way/Redmond, WA 98052-6399.

New Features in PowerPoint 2002

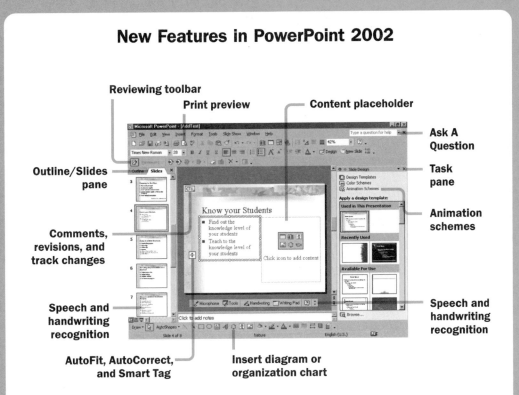

Reviewing toolbar

Print preview

Content placeholder

Ask A Question

Outline/Slides pane

Task pane

Animation schemes

Comments, revisions, and track changes

Speech and handwriting recognition

Speech and handwriting recognition

AutoFit, AutoCorrect, and Smart Tag

Insert diagram or organization chart

Common Keyboard Shortcuts

Shortcut	Description
Ctrl + N	Create a new presentation
Ctrl + M	Create a new slide
Ctrl + C	Copy the selected text or object
Ctrl + X	Cut the selected text or object
Ctrl + V	Paste text or an object
Ctrl + Z	Undo the last action
Ctrl + Y	Redo the last action
Ctrl + T	Change formatting of characters
Shift + F9	Show or hide the grid
Alt + F9	Show or hide the guide
F7	Check spelling
F5	Run a presentation slide show
Esc	Cancel a menu or dialog box action, or stop a slide show

To create a presentation using suggested content

1. In the **New Presentation** task pane, click **From AutoContent Wizard**.
2. Click **Next**, click **All**, click a presentation, and then click **Next**.
3. Click a presentation style, and then click **Next**.
4. Click the **Presentation title** box, type a presentation title, press ⎆, and then type footer text.
5. Click **Next**, and then click **Finish**.

To create a new slide

1. On the Standard toolbar, click the **New Slide** button.
2. In the **Slide Layout** task pane, select a slide layout.
3. In the Slide pane, click the text placeholder *Click to add title* or click the text placeholder *Click to add subtitle*.
4. Type in text.

To change or add text

1. Position the pointer (which changes to the I-beam) over the text, and then select the text to change or click the text where you want to add.
2. Type in text.

To select and correct a misspelled word

- Right-click a misspelled word, and then click the correct spelling on the shortcut menu.

To format bullets with a different symbol or picture

1. Click the bulleted line of text that you want to format.
2. On the Format menu, click **Bullets and Numbering**.
3. Click **Customize** or **Picture**, click a bullet, and then click **OK**. Click **OK** again, if necessary.

To draw an shape

1. On the Drawing toolbar, click the **AutoShapes** button.
2. Point to a category, and then click a shape button.
3. In the Slide pane, drag to draw a shape.

To insert a clip art image using the Insert Clip Art task pane

1. On the **Insert** menu, point to **Picture**, and then click **Clip Art**.
2. In the **Insert Clip Art** task pane, in the **Search text** box, type what you want to search for, and then click **Search**.
3. Click a clip art image.

To rearrange slides

1. Click the **Slide Sorter View** button.
2. Drag the slide to a new position.

To apply a template

1. On the Formatting toolbar, click **Slide Design**.
2. In the **Slide Design** task pane, click **Design Templates**, and then click a design template.

To apply an animation scheme to a slide

1. Click the **Slide Sorter View** button, and then click a slide.
2. On the **Slide Show** menu, click **Animation Schemes**.
3. Under **Apply to selected slides**, click an animation.

To apply a slide transition effect

1. Click the **Slide Sorter View** button, and then select a slide.
2. On the **Slide Show** menu, click **Slide Transition** to open the **Slide Transition** task pane.
3. Under **Apply to selected slides**, click a transition effect.

To start and end a slide show on any slide

1. On the **Slide Show** menu, click **Slide Transition** to open the **Slide Transition** task pane.
2. Click the **Slide Show** button.
3. Click the screen or press the → to advance to the next slide, or press the ← to return to the previous slide.
4. Press ⎋ to stop the slide show.

To print presentation slides, audience handouts, or speaker notes

1. On the **File** menu, click **Print**.
2. Click the **Print what** down arrow, and then click **Slides**, **Handouts Pages**, or **Notes Pages**.
3. Click **OK**.

To save a new presentation

1. On the Standard toolbar, click the **Save** button.
2. In the **File name** box, type a file name.
3. In the **Save in** box, navigate to the location in which you want to save the presentation, and then click **Save**.